Gesture Drawing

A Story-Based Approach

Gesture Drawing
A Story-Based Approach

April Connors

CRC Press
Taylor & Francis Group
Boca Raton London New York

CRC Press is an imprint of the
Taylor & Francis Group, an **informa** business
A FOCAL PRESS BOOK

CRC Press
Taylor & Francis Group
6000 Broken Sound Parkway NW, Suite 300
Boca Raton, FL 33487-2742

International Standard Book Number-13: 978-1-4987-9927-0 (Paperback)
978-1-138-10629-1 (Hardback)

Library of Congress Cataloging-in-Publication Data

Names: Connors, April, author.
Title: Gesture drawing : a story-based approach / April Connors.
Description: Boca Raton, FL : CRC Press, Taylor & Francis Group, 2018. |
Includes bibliographical references.
Identifiers: LCCN 2017016807| ISBN 9781498799270 (pbk. : alk. paper) | ISBN
9781138106291 (hardback : alk. paper)
Subjects: LCSH: Drawing--Technique.
Classification: LCC NC715 .C66 2018 | DDC 741.2--dc23
LC record available at https://lccn.loc.gov/2017016807

Visit the Taylor & Francis Web site at
http://www.taylorandfrancis.com

and the CRC Press Web site at
http://www.crcpress.com

Dedication

Dedicated to all of my past, present, and future drawing students.

Contents

Preface

Readers will find this book to be particularly useful if they are able to execute the suggested drills and exercises found within each chapter, ideally from life reference. In the event that the reader has limited access to life-drawing resources, such as studio facilities or live models, it is recommended that the reader find alternative resources, such as friends and family; uninstructed workshops or classes; or photo references, from magazines, books, the Internet, etc. Each chapter will cover an individual Key Topic and include study questions the reader may use when practicing observational drawing, as well as drills and/or exercise ideas to practice these concepts, including exploratory exercise ideas meant to combine creativity with observational studies centered around gesture drawing and storytelling. One may also use this book to supplement current studies, whether in uninstructed workshops or instructed classes. It is recommended to execute observational studies on a daily basis, whether as part of a warm-up set before working or only to sharpen the battle-axe, so to speak. The suggested drills and exercises serve to inspire the reader to develop problem-solving skills as they relate to his or her own learning; for example, if the reader finds himself or herself lacking confidence in any particular facet or element of drawing, he or she must analyze *what* that facet is, and *how* that facet may be improved. In doing so, the reader will begin to develop the autodidactism necessary for the continued discovery, comprehension, and development of the craft of drawing. The drills and exercises can be manipulated and tailored by the reader so as to address the particular problems being faced at any given time. They may be reinvented, combined, recombined, and mixed with other methodologies to produce a curriculum that is individually tailored to any particular reader. The ideas in this book are meant to be played with and expounded upon by other artists, and the reader is invited to use as much or as little imagination and creativity with the lessons as he or she wishes. In this way, the reader may continuously be challenged by observational drawing, and gesture drawing in particular, in addition to the endless possibilities that arise when approaching life and gesture drawing from a place of story.

This study guide may further be complemented by any courses in perspective, visual communication, and analytical figure drawing, as these particular foundation studies help provide the basis for solid drawing, which is a critical and necessary component of successful visual communication and storytelling. It is therefore recommended to any novice artists and undergraduate art students to concurrently practice the studies of gesture/figure drawing, perspective, and visual communication in order to see the interrelation of these particular studies. Perspective and visual communication will help the artist achieve an understanding of three-dimensional (3D) space, and the subsequent translation of 3D space to the 2D picture plane, and aid in the further comprehension of how to communicate ideas successfully, achieving visual clarity.

I would like to note that this Breakdown and procedural approach to figure drawing is by no means employed by only myself; many artists use different incarnations, and this particular iteration has been developed over the course of many years, being kept fluid enough to allow for influence and inspiration from instructors, peers and colleagues, or other artists whose work I admire. It is presented here (and utilized in my drawing classes) as a means of remembering the different *tools* that the craft of drawing presents to the artist. One may think of it as a checklist, with the freedom of using as much or as little from that list as is necessary in any order to solve the infinite variety of problems that observational drawing presents. The reader will see influence from such instructors as Steve Huston, Bob Kato, Kevin Chen, Miguel Angel Reyes, Andrea Adams, and Raul Aguirre, Jr. (whose introduction to traditional animation has changed the way I approach a drawing immensely), to name a few, and every term I recommend my own students to study with them if and whenever possible, even if only in the form of master copies. No matter what stage one is at in their individual artistic career, one must always keep an open and inquisitive mind so as to be inspired by other artists.

Additionally, this study guide has been formatted as follows: The first portion of each chapter serves as Lecture and Demo regarding the Key Topic presented; the second portion delves into how that Key Topic has been approached for different results relating to the development and practice of story ideas and elements; and the concluding portion of each chapter presents the reader with drills and exercises they are invited to experiment with. Additionally, there will be photo references throughout the guide the reader may use to learn each drill/exercise before executing during their regular drawing sessions.

April Connors
Los Angeles

Acknowledgments

I would like to thank the wonderful model Ashli Gonzales-Griffin for providing her likeness throughout this guide, and for continuing to provide inspiration to countless visual artists.

This study guide would not have been possible without the amazing artists' models of Los Angeles. They provide thousands of artists of all calibers and insights into the human form through their skills. The following people have provided their valuable insights, inspiration, and knowledge throughout my journey: Peter Kim, Miguel Angel-Reyes, Daniella Traub, Bob Kato, and Andrea Adams.

Shout out to James Morioka for his generosity with equipment.

Many, many thanks to all of the students who have participated in all of the exercises mentioned throughout this book and for providing critical feedback and ideas.

Author

April Connors is an illustrator and instructor in Los Angeles, California. She has been teaching figure and gesture drawing throughout Los Angeles and abroad, and her illustrations have been exhibited both locally and internationally. April has taught at Otis College of Art and Design, Gnomon School of Visual Effects, Walt Disney Animation Studio, 3Kicks Art Studio, and her own private studio.

Introduction to Gesture

Drills and Study Questions   References

What is gesture drawing? In its common definition, it is the spontaneous capture of a moment in time, usually drawn from life or an alternate means of direct observation. One may choose to develop a gesture drawing from a live model in a life-drawing class, draw from animals at the zoo, develop a still life, or sit at a coffee shop or other public space and study the constant movement of forms and shapes. One may also choose to utilize gesture drawing as a way of warming up the eye, mind, and arm before work or use it for understanding characters and how we act and react to each other as living creatures. The *lay-in* of a finished work may also be described as a gesture drawing, in this case acting as the life force of the architecture that will become the finished work. Indeed, the uses and applications of gesture drawing are numerous, and potentially endless. We can use gesture drawings in the following ways: as studies of the mechanics of motion of volumetric forms in space (see Figure 1.1); as studies of acting and expressions; to develop the characterization of character archetypes; to develop a thesaurus of body types and styles of motion; and as a lay-in for a more finished work (see Figure 1.2). Depending on the nature or goal of the intended use of the gesture drawing, we can further decide what *kind* of gesture drawing: a quick sketch that explicitly explores specific concepts or a slightly longer drawing that captures more finite ideas for ease of communication in a finished work. Gesture drawings are typically spontaneous in nature and relatively short in duration (depending upon the nature of the application or development).

Whatever the method of study, whatever the location, and regardless of the application, gesture drawing is simply the study of capturing the essence of life and imbuing the artist's own work with that energy. This life energy is critical

Figure 1.1

A quick-sketch/short-pose gesture drawing.

Figure 1.2

A simple quick sketch. A lay-in of a longer drawing may also resemble this.

1. Introduction to Gesture

in the development of storytelling; without it, our stories are unappealing and unrelatable. In visual storytelling, the goal of the artist is to efficiently communicate either a simple or an abstract concept as universally as possible and to guide the eye in such a way that the audience not only comprehends what they're being shown but will also feel the emotional resonance of the story being told. It is this emotional resonance that we study and attempt to capture when drawing from life; that resonance is what causes us as the audience to connect with what we're looking at and feel the life force of an artist's work. The goal of this book is to provide the artist—whether a student or a professional—with a study guide that can be used to explore the fundamentals of gesture drawing and develop work full of story, life, vivacity, and passion. One may choose to utilize this book in conjunction with a life-drawing or gesture-drawing class, use the exercises contained within to supplement the reader's workflow, or simply use the drills for warm-ups. This book is in no way meant to be self-contained, and the readers are encouraged to add to, subtract from, or otherwise manipulate both the breakdown described herein and the drills and exercises included to their liking or skill level. The readers are also encouraged to develop an inquisitive, autodidactic mindset. The craft of drawing and the study of visual storytelling are lifelong endeavors, and as such the readers should not feel overwhelmed by such an intensive study; rather they are encouraged to practice patience, carefully observe the world and its inhabitants, and find inspiration in the life around them.

Before we begin, we must define the common terms usually associated with life drawing and—more specifically—gesture drawing. The terms most commonly used in classes are the following:

- Line of action
- Rhythm
- Harmony
- Flow
- Axes and shoulder line/hip line; center front and center back
- S curves, C curves, straight lines
- Exaggeration
- Action and acting

Additionally, we will define the term *microgestures*, as it is one we will see throughout this study guide. It is a concept that I have not yet heard outside of my own classes but describes a very specific idea. The reader may or may not already be aware of such an idea as it exists under a different name.

Microgestures: Smaller lines of action that describe the inherent flow of energy of shapes and forms. For example, a microgesture might be a finger or part of a finger that, while not ultimately important when compared to larger ideas, might contain a particular beauty or other quality that the artist deems as necessary to incorporate into a drawing (see Figure 1.3). These microgestures can also be found in the face, where we see a plethora of different form and shape configurations, which further contort when activated for expression. Being aware of the relationships between these so-called microgestures and the larger overlying rhythms of the whole figure aids the artist in creating harmony between larger ideas and smaller ideas. We can think of gesture almost as a fractal of sorts—albeit with variation to keep our drawings dynamic and visually interesting: we see the overlying rhythm in the silhouette, and from there can continue to

Figure 1.3

Bounce is created within this drawing by paying attention to the "microgestures" repeated down and through the figure.

break down smaller and smaller rhythms until we've created a song with multiple voices, each gesture being an individual voice that must harmonize with the rest of the choir of gestures in order to produce a powerful impact. Alternately, we can use this same idea to intentionally create discord if desired.

We will also be using the concepts of:

- Tone (we will be using its definition from writing and literature)
- Mood

While most of these terms have commonly accepted definitions and are used by countless artists, we will define them for the scope of this book.

Line of action: Typically, it refers to the directional force an object tends to follow, or the flow of energy and movement present in a living body. One may interpret this visually as the longest uninterrupted line they see in the body of any particular object moving in space; or one may interpret it as the flow of energy moving through any particular body (see Figure 1.4).

Within the scope of this book, we will be using the common definition: finding the directional force or flow of energy in any particular body moving in space. Taking this concept one step further, we will be using more than one line of action: in addition to looking for a strong primary line of action—a thesis

Figure 1.4

Primary line of action.

statement, if you will—we will also be aware of the supporting lines of action that define the individual parts of the body, so that we may work from big to small, simple to complex, relating the whole to the pieces. I will often refer to them as *secondary*, *tertiary*, or simply *supporting lines of action*, referring to the strongest major force present as the *primary line of action* (see Figure 1.5). In this way, we will be constructing a visual story with a hierarchy of information that includes a thesis statement and supporting ideas in order to achieve visual clarity with consistency. When referring to the singularly strongest line of action, we will be using both the terms *primary line of action* and *dominant directional force line* (depending on context), as well as denoting major and minor ideas.

Rhythm may be defined in a variety of ways, but we will be using it here to provide a musical quality in our work. One may define it as *tempo*, or the underlying bounce we see in a drawing, picture, or painting (see Figure 1.6).

We may further define rhythm as the repetition of a particular sound (such as in music) or movement (such as in dance or other kinesthetic activities). We can apply this definition to our work, albeit with a visual interpretation. Using rhythm in the construction of a drawing accentuates and embellishes the life force we are attempting to capture and conveys information in a way that is visually interesting. Furthermore, it allows us to find microgestures and to develop any idiosyncrasies of the models we draw. By using cross-disciplinary and

Figure 1.5

Primary line of action in blue, supporting lines of action in olive green and red.

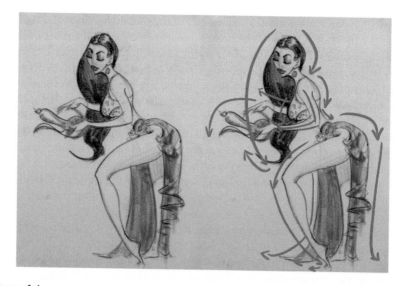

Figure 1.6

The rhythms of the figure are further complemented by those found and embellished in props and costume.

1. Introduction to Gesture

multisensory concepts in our work, we can attain a more sophisticated level of emotional resonance. The concept of rhythm is often associated with the ideas of S and C curves.

Harmony often refers to the flow in which disparate parts move together to create a unified whole (see Figure 1.7). We hear the term commonly used in relation to color theory: color harmony. We also use the term in music when parts of a song or composition work together to communicate a singular concept or theme, or any other intended idea, whether literal or abstract, whether it be so much or so little as a general mood or tone.

Flow: This term may be used to describe the rhythms present within the line(s) of action, the directional force present within the figure, or the way anatomy interconnects in a living body, depending on the context or the person defining it. In this case, we will be using it in conjunction with the concepts of rhythm and harmony to describe how we see the essence of life move through any particular body (including the action and anatomy of any particular figure) in space. We can associate it with the concept of energy, and it would be appropriate to think of the physical properties of water in this case. We will also be associating flow with the concepts of S and C curves.

Axes: These are first introduced to most of us in mathematics, and they are indeed regularly utilized in geometry, algebra, and calculus. They help us to visualize and comprehend complex and often abstract ideas, and to understand the three-dimensional (3D) space in which we inhabit. Within the scope of this book, we will use the mathematical concept of x-, y-coordinate systems as well as x-, y-, z-coordinate systems to help us in the translation of 3D space to a 2D picture plane. While it is not necessary to think in these terms, they help associate geometric forms as seen in Visual Communication classes to the organic living figure. We may practically define x-axis as the *horizontal axis* and y-axis as the *vertical axis* of a shape or form. When measuring or figuring proportions, it is common to utilize the x- and y-axes; when figuring foreshortening, we may introduce the z-axis by

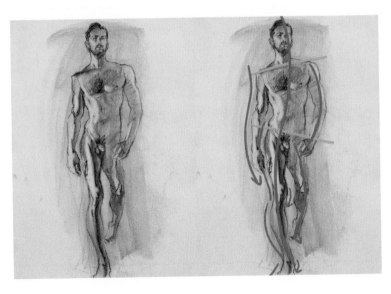

Figure 1.7

Shoulder and hip axes in blue; "S" and "C" curves are in red.

way of a 3D form, such as a cylinder, box, cone, sphere, or any combination of these forms, to convey the illusion of 3D space on a two-dimensional (2D) picture plane while retaining accurate measurements. In drawing classes with sculpting and 3D students, the inclusion of an x-, y-, z-coordinate system comes in handy, as some artists are more comfortable with thinking in terms of 3D, mathematics, and/or geometry, while others prefer to think in 2D. We may also associate the x-axis with the *shoulder and hip lines* in the human figure, as these are commonly the strongest horizontals we see in the human body, particularly in the standing or classically contrapposto figure. When using an x-axis in this manner, the shoulder and hip lines are not horizontal; rather the horizontal x-axis is laid in to better gauge the angle of the shoulder and hip lines. It is also helpful to use the concepts of the *center front* line and *center back* line from fashion to aid in the construction of a figure, particularly if orientation is still an issue the reader deals with while drawing. We can associate the y-axis with the center front and center back lines to provide consistency in the placement or general geography of features, or any other pertinent information or details. The shoulder/hip lines and center front and back lines will also aid us greatly when constructing clothed or costumed figures (see Figure 1.8).

S and C curves and straight lines: One of the most universal concepts introduced early on when learning figure drawing is the idea of using *S and C curves* and *straight lines* to aid in the analyzation and simple breakdown of movement. We commonly associate the concepts of harmony and rhythm with the use of S and C curves, and use straight lines to further accentuate or heighten the effects of those curves, much like adding salt to food. We may also utilize S and C curves in defining the particular flow of a body or part(s) of a body when analyzing the movement of energy within.

Exaggeration: Typically it refers to pushing the limits of whatever concept the artist is attempting to capture. In gesture drawing, it usually refers to over-emphasizing an action (see Figure 1.9) or any other particular quality we see as being essential to the story we are telling. It may not necessarily be an action

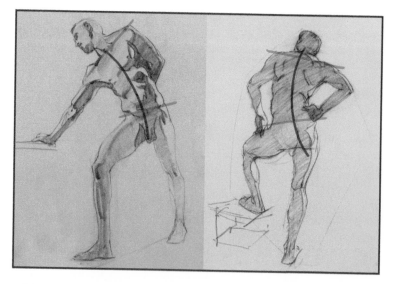

Figure 1.8

The center front and back lines. They help one define orientation, plane changes, and movement in the torso.

1. Introduction to Gesture

Figure 1.9

An exaggerated gesture study.

we exaggerate; we may exaggerate abstract concepts as well, such as body language, or facial/hand/feet expressions; we may also exaggerate subtleties or delicate ideas. In this case, we use exaggeration to clearly communicate an idea. We may also exaggerate any particular facet or concept of a drawing, whether it is the line of action, the flow of energy, or the literal body language of a particular model we are drawing, etc. We typically see exaggeration applied successfully in animation, with key poses being the drawings most commonly exaggerated. The concept of exaggeration is not limited to only action or movement; we may exaggerate subtlety as well, such as in the delicate microgesture of the flick of a hand, or the tiniest crick of a finger, if the story we are telling needs such ideas to be communicated to the audience to enrich their experience (see Figure 1.10).

Action: Typically it refers to the particular deed being performed by a subject, or the *what* the subject is doing. In life drawing, we can see the actual pose being taken by the model to be the *action*.

Acting: It refers to the characterization or expression—the *how*—present in the execution of an action. Acting is the *why, how*—and sometimes *where* and *when* depending on the context we are creating—that either the model or we as artists incorporate into the action (see Figure 1.11). Because one cannot have a

Figure 1.10

A short-pose drawing focused more on subtlety.

Figure 1.11

Quick-sketch studies are an excellent opportunity to study acting.

story with the *what* alone, we must also think in terms of the *why* and *how* when creating the first marks that will begin our drawing. The actions one takes derive from the choices one makes, and the acting present in both the subject matter and the ultimate visual representation of that subject provides both context and subtext to our drawing. This is one facet of storytelling.

Tone [1] (as we will apply it): Tone is generally regarded in literature as being the writer's attitude toward his or her subject matter and/or the audience (see Figure 1.12). It is usually conveyed in literature through language choices, such as diction and syntax. We use tone to communicate visually as well, utilizing a *visual language* to do so—effectively, the elements of drawing and visual communication create a visual language to be used as the grammar of a drawing or painting. This means that all of the choices we make while drawing ultimately impact the tone of our drawing, and thus the story that we are telling. Visual tone can be affected by such things as the shapes we choose to use to describe

Figure 1.12

Drawing approached from a fashion sensibility and mindset, which is ultimately seen in the style used in execution.

our subject, the types of marks we physically make, what media we choose to utilize, or even what lines we think are the most important or central to our story. How we choose to utilize the different elements of design and visual communication ultimately impacts the tone of our work. It should be noted that we are not using the word *tone* to define the visual concept of *value* (black, white, gray scale). Although the word *tone* can indeed mean value, and many drawing instructors and artists do refer to it as such, for the sake and scope of this specific study guide, we will be referring to *tone* with its writing/literature definition, as this definition is the most precise with regard to what it is we are defining: the creator's attitude toward his or her subject and audience.

Mood [2] is most typically defined as the atmosphere of a story. We tend to think of not only the language the creator has used to tell us a story but the setting of the story as well. In the case of visual storytelling and picture-making, we can utilize contextual clues to create mood or atmosphere. We use mood to affect the audience's emotions regarding what they are looking at. Again, mood is created through the choices we make while telling a visual story, and it may be influenced by not only the elements of design and visual communication but also the actual media used to complete the work (see Figure 1.13). Visually speaking, tone and mood are created and interpreted very similarly, although we can

Figure 1.13

Mixed media can be utilized to begin the exploration of mood which may later be developed in longer studies or finished works.

1. Introduction to Gesture

see *tone* represented as the sum of an artist's style, taste, approach, and esthetics, and *mood* as the choices made regarding composition, placement of camera, lighting, color, etc., all components of staging. We can usually see this application of *mood* used successfully in commercial works—most notably in animation and advertising. Works such as these ask the audience to *feel* something when experiencing them. Our goal within the scope of this study guide is to develop the foundations of mood as much as possible while working from life, since it is easier to develop emotional resonance when working with live models as they provide acting (context and subtext) for us to work with, which in turn allows us to combine their information with our emotional life experiences, which helps us think of our audience, and how best to potentially develop atmosphere within a picture. Incorporating as much mindfulness of tone and mood as possible while drawing will allow us to practice for eventual world building, picture-making, and/or illustration or other finished works. The more we can practice this type of thinking while in an academic or controlled environment, the easier it will be for us to develop these concepts within our own work. This particular concept is not always suited to short pose or quick-sketch-style gesture drawings; therefore, the level of refinement that we can develop within the mood of a piece varies from situation to situation. Nevertheless, it is worth the effort to make conscientious decisions regarding its development as much or as often as possible.

Measuring: During quick sketching, it is common practice to either disregard the absolute accuracy of our proportions or take quick, simple measurements if we find our proportions lacking too greatly in general accuracy. Typically, I will advise gesture-drawing students to worry about any measuring if they find their proportions so inaccurate that it ultimately affects the intended statement of the drawing, and if the pose durations are 3 minutes or longer; any shorter and it is quite stressful to take measurements while also being concerned with capturing any kind of spontaneous, dynamic energy. It is advised the reader or the student practice *long-pose figure drawing* while studying gesture, and vice versa, as both studies help to improve the other. When drawing gesture drawings over 3 minutes, or when laying in the foundation gesture lines that will become a more developed work—whether it is a finished drawing, painting, or full composition—proportions should be checked to ensure that the final idea does not suffer from any unintended proportional accidents. Proportions do not necessarily have to be realistic or naturalistic, but should be controlled and intended, so as to ensure the successful communication of our idea. When measuring, it is most common to use the actual drawing tool, usually a graphite, charcoal, or Conté pencil or a paintbrush. A stick of charcoal may be used as well, but if the physical size of the charcoal or stump is too small, it will be more difficult to achieve an accurate measurement.

The typical procedure of measurement is as follows: the artist takes the pencil or drawing/painting tool in hand; the arm is then fully outstretched; closing one eye, the artist lines the top or tip of the tool with the top of the subject's head, and then uses the thumb to mark the subject's chin. This is taking a head measurement, the most common unit of measurement in figure drawing; the artist can then count head units to create a ruler and may record with greater accuracy the position of key landmarks and structures. When drawing or painting from observation, one is not limited to head units for measurement; indeed, any shape or object may become a unit of measurement, though once chosen, it is advisable to refrain from changing the unit, as doing so may disrupt the consistency of measurements, and thus ultimately affect the overall accuracy of the drawing or composition. I find closed shapes to make the easiest units of measurement to use, though the artist may choose any shape or form he or she likes.

Alternately, if time is of the essence, one may use alignments on the x- and y-axes to develop the general geography of the subject or composition. In this case, the term *geography* is used to describe the 2D distance between things, such as the geography of the facial features on a head, or the structures of an individual's body. To measure using alignments: once more, the artist takes the drawing or painting tool in hand and outstretches the arm; instead of taking a unit of measurement and counting out a ruler, the artist uses the pencil as a straightedge to create a 180° horizontal line and a 90° vertical line, thus creating a scenario in which the artist is now observing the subject as a flat, graphic, 2D picture—in essence, using a vertical line and horizontal line creates x- and y-axes. We can then line up any two or more elements with each other to note the 2D distance between them. By matching slopes with the drawing tool, the artist may also check angles so as to obtain greater accuracy in a drawing, or in order to *exaggerate* those angles.

One may combine both measuring techniques to one's liking or incorporate other techniques to achieve the desired level of accuracy. Some students may find it helpful to take head measurements of the live model toward the beginning of the drawing session and create a ruler on the page so that they may draw their gestural lay-ins to the set proportions. If scale is something that must also be controlled, one may mark the top of the head and the bottom of the feet on the page in any scale one would like and utilize those marks—in conjunction with a ruler if so desired—to set the size of one's gesture lay-in.

The silhouette: One of the most useful concepts in observational drawing, it is the graphic, 2D representation of a 3D form (see Figure 1.14). The concept of the silhouette is often used in conjunction with the ideas of positive and negative space, and one may see the silhouette as the positive space the subject matter takes up in a picture plane. We read silhouettes constantly in life and use them oftentimes for the quick identification of objects—both living and inanimate. For the sake of visual clarity, we must define silhouettes as clearly and cleanly as possible, that is, we must not confuse or frustrate the audience (see Figure 1.15). Indeed, that is the very heart of the concept of visual clarity: striving for the successful communication of a visual idea so that our audience does not become confused and subsequently disinterested in whatever story we are trying to tell. This is why the silhouette must be taken into account before the first marks go down on paper. If using a gesture drawing as the initial lay-in of a more developed or finished work, constructing an effective silhouette will be the ultimate goal, as this will give the audience the first read of the story being told within the drawing.

Story: In order to complete story-driven drawings, we must first define *story* within the scope of our breakdown and application of it. The *Merriam Webster* definition of *story* includes the archaic definition *history* but also defines it as:

1. An account of incidents or events [much like the way a simple figure drawing describes a particular action or the way a set of storyboards provides a visual account of a script]
2. A statement regarding the facts pertinent to a situation in question [much like how a technical drawing describes factual information or

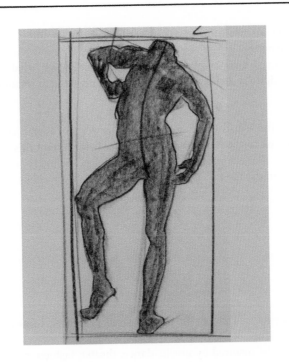

Figure 1.14

A silhouette.

Figure 1.15

A further example of a silhouette, though with more information within its construction than simply positive and negative space.

how an anatomical drawing describes placement and structure of parts of the body]

3. The intrigue or plot of a narrative or dramatic work [what we see applied in disciplines such as illustration, cartooning, and animation around the world]

We can use these definitions to help us define *story* for visual communication. We can also look to the humanities for further definition of this expansive and subjective term. For example, we can see how *story* is defined and used in literature, and we can use the following elementary concepts to aid us:

- Who
- What
- Where
- When
- Why
- How

These concepts will aid us in defining and providing context and subtext within our drawing.

We can also be inspired by music, dance, theater, fashion, architecture, furniture and product design, the culinary arts, etc., to develop our idea of what *story* is. Every time we observe the world around us, interpret the information we have inputted through our senses, and then communicate the meaning of those observations, we are telling a story. We are communicating a truth of the human experience. We are creating art. This mindset is not limited to the arts alone; we use the same curiosity, sensory observation, and quest for meaning and understanding in mathematics and science, and the habit of asking questions and looking for answers is also developed in these disciplines. When creating art and developing the craft of drawing, we must strive to create a mindset in which we are constantly seeking the underlying *truth* or story of our subject and attempt to capture, interpret, and communicate that story with *emotional resonance*. When we create something new, we endeavor to tell a story, whether literal or abstract, to our audience. The function of observational drawing and painting is to provide the experience or the emotional resonance to the story we are telling; a story with no emotional ups or downs is merely something that happened.

We will also be using the story concept of *beginning*, *middle*, and *end*, or chronology, to help us think in terms of sequence and subtext/context, and thus we can utilize certain ideas from the 12 Principles of Animation, as they are defined by their creators, Ollie Johnston and Frank Thomas, in their masterwork, *The Illusion of Life*. All drawing students are encouraged to pick up a copy of this book for multiple reasons: it is particularly useful to see the development and history of ideas, the trial and error involved in pushing oneself to create work with the spark of life, and to appreciate the artistry and passion involved in such a process. From an educational perspective, it is highly recommended to understand how and why the 12 Principles are useful, and to experiment with ways in which we can use them for inspiration for other media, such as illustration, painting, storyboarding, comics and graphic novels, etc. It is recommended to not only read and study this particular tome but also to produce master copies from the work contained within.

This brings us to the general outline or breakdown we will be utilizing throughout the course of this book, for drawing or painting, whether it is a single figure drawing or a full composition. One may see the individual figure drawing as a microcosm of picture-making, and as such use the study of life drawing to practice the elements of storytelling. Much like writing an essay, we will use a methodology that will allow us to organize our ideas into a cohesive, comprehensible, and visually clear product, while still retaining enough elasticity in our process to achieve different desired effects. In this way, we will control the story that we tell through our drawings. The following is the basic outline we will be utilizing and experimenting with throughout this study guide. This outline serves as a breakdown of the architecture or tools of a drawing. By focusing on one element of drawing at a time, we can see the myriad ways we can control, design, and experiment with it. The breakdown is presented in such an order as to build chronologically in terms of complexity. That is, the most primitive and basic ideas are presented toward the beginning of the breakdown, with more complex ideas presented toward the end. This does not mean that we must work in this chronological order every time we draw; instead, it means that we may shuffle or reprioritize the order in which we feel each drawing should be approached while still being aware of the relationships these elements have with one another, and the impact our choices have on each element. We will be looking at each Roman numeral as Key Topics or steps chronologically from this point on in building ideas, and once we've explored these elements individually, we will then be free to remix them for the sake of practicality and purpose.

Thesis Statement: the *Big Idea*

I. Primary line of action (major idea; internal construction).
   a. Supporting line of action: secondary gesture (major supporting idea).
   b. Supporting line of action: tertiary gesture (minor supporting idea; optional).
   c. Additional supporting lines of action/gesture (optional; only if necessary).
      i. Microgestures (small, minor supporting ideas; if applicable).
II. 2D shapes: positive and negative space analysis (the *protomannequin*; internal construction).
   a. Measurement and proportions addressed while in a 2D state (if applicable).
   b. Using simple shapes such as *tubes* to begin the traditional mannequin figure.
   c. Microgestures (if applicable).
III. Cylindrical or rectangular forms (introducing depth to the picture; setting the foundation for foreshortening; mannequin figure development; internal construction).
   a. This is a half-step to be used if necessary to develop depth (optional step).
IV. 3D forms (volume, depth, and the development of musculature and anatomy; mannequin figure continued; internal construction).
   a. Using geometric, organic, and abstract forms to develop the volumes of the subject while maintaining all previous gestural and proportional information.

V. Refining the silhouette of the subject (external construction).
  a. Utilizing the internal construction we have created up to this point, we will now finish the construction of our subject. We may utilize this silhouette for any number of things, and we may light and render it if we so wish.
VI. Lighting: designing shadow shapes.
  a. Utilizing both the internal and external construction of our figure, we may apply lighting if desired, mapping and designing the shadow shapes we see to further enrich our story and to echo the gestures designed and drawn throughout the subject.

Practically speaking, we can look at the above outline as follows: Roman numeral I deals with the concept of the one-dimensional (1D) line; Roman numeral II deals with the concept of the 2D shape; Roman numerals III and IV deal with the concept of 3D form; Roman numeral V deals with the concept of the silhouette and readdresses the graphic clarity and ultimate readability of an idea; Roman numeral VI deals with lighting and how we may design and approach it so as to aid us in the reflection of tone and mood, in addition to empowering the communication of 3D form and visual clarity. The subtopics beneath each Roman numeral (or Key Topic) are intended to show details regarding either technique involved during the application and construction of the major topic or important ideas to take into consideration that support it. Overall, we will move from large ideas to small ideas; simple to complex; and 1D ideas to 3D ideas, focusing on individual elements each step of the way, with the ultimate intention of combining them into a flexible methodology that allows one to draw with intent and a conscientious mindset. By focusing on ideas as individual stages or steps, the reader may choose to assimilate as few or as many ideas from this study guide into his or her own work flow or process; and, if desired, this manner of study can also aid one in troubleshooting one's work. Because of the sequence of the breakdown, it is best to take an ample amount of time comprehending and experimenting at each stage and seeing the results of each exercise or drill given. Our goal is to see and feel the relationships between each of these concepts and to see just how much interpretation each element can be subject to. Furthermore, the individual Key Topics—which we will refer to as *stages* or *steps*—of the breakdown can be manipulated to accommodate any given length of time (or duration of pose if the gesture drawing is completed during a live model session). As we will see in later chapters, for example, if one is completing quick-sketch gesture drawings, one may speed up the basic techniques presented and combine as many steps as necessary to get the pertinent information of the drawing completed or explored within a short time frame. If working with medium-length to long poses, one may explore each individual step more fully, taking ample time at each stage to think over choices and reflect before committing to putting the mark on paper. The basic techniques that we will cover may also be applied to different visual disciplines such as illustration, painting (either *alla prima*, *plein air*, or other long-term work), and sequential storytelling-based disciplines such as storyboarding, animation, comic books and graphic novels, etc. The applications are potentially endless depending on the ingenuity of the artist and the willingness to reinvent the basic techniques and breakdown for themselves. This is why such a great number of different visual artists use a procedure such as this to develop their drawings.

We will also be incorporating elements from the 12 Principles of Animation into this general breakdown at each step. Each Key Topic from the above outline will have its own dedicated chapter complete with examples that demonstrate not only the execution of each Key Topic but also HOW we may apply *story* elements to each individual step and drill/exercise ideas the reader may use to practice each concept.

Drills and Study Questions

Initial Warm-Up Drills: It is a good idea to develop the habit of warming up at the beginning of a drawing session. The following drills are generic enough exercises that the individual may manipulate or otherwise use as a jumping-off point to his or her liking.

Drill 1: Mass + Movement

In this initial drill, we are focusing on warming up the arm and the eye. We are not concerned yet with story, but rather simply thinking in terms of the mass of our subject and how it is moving in space (see Figure 1.16). We are thinking in the round here, being just conscientious enough to attempt to capture weight, balance, energy flow, and very loose proportions. We are not concerned with minor details, nor even recognizable 3D structures. These drawings are loose and should be executed entirely from the shoulder. We are simply asking ourselves *what* at the moment, and *how* that mass is moving in space. We are also

Figure 1.16

Mass + movement.

practicing the habit of working from large ideas and concepts to small ideas and concepts.

Recommended Materials: While the reader may choose to utilize any material for any exercise, there are certain materials that lend themselves very well to certain concepts and exercises. In this case, large, chunky, soft charcoals; large-tip markers; large flat or round brushes, etc., work very well. The idea is to impede our accuracy and fine motor skills enough to look at large ideas and to keep us from the temptation to draw small details first. Alternatively, the digital medium is available for the readers to use, should they choose to utilize it in lieu of traditional materials. However, if the resources are available, it is recommended that the reader practice using as many traditional materials as possible.

Drill 2: "Scribble" Gestures

In this iteration of quick sketching, we are still looking at mass, weight, balance, movement and energy flow, and basic proportions, but we are also introducing 3D volume by way of discernible shapes and forms, however simple they may be (see Figure 1.17). These shapes and forms will now enable us to record more information regarding the silhouette, the action of the pose, and rhythm and harmony. Ideally, these sketches are executed fast enough so as to forego any unnecessary detail. Typically, poses lasting between 30 seconds and 3 minutes (depending on the individual, of course) work well for this type of gesture drawing. When combined with story-derived design elements, this type of gesture drawing also works excellently when brainstorming or developing thumbnail sketches that

Figure 1.17

"Scribble" gestures.

will be used for a finished product or further application, such as a painting, illustration, sketch art, sequential art, etc. Because this type of gesture drawing can be interpreted, used, and applied in a variety of ways, it is listed here at the beginning of this book so that the reader may be reminded of such a simple but useful drill.

Recommended Materials: Again, any tools may be used, but for this particular exercise I am fond of utilizing General's charcoal pencils, in a softer range: 2B–6B work very well. Substratum is also ultimately up to the artist, but generally speaking I personally prefer smoother surfaces for this type of gesture drawing. Smooth newsprint is a good choice as far as smooth, affordable drawing surfaces are concerned; if using white drawing paper, certain colored pencils will give the hand a smooth, creamy feel. Prismacolor pencils are ubiquitous and of good quality, but Faber-Castell Polychromos pencils are a nice alternative if looking for a stronger pencil (one that can withstand more pressure from the arm) or one that is erasable. Use the provided photo reference of our model for this study guide, Ashli, to practice the basic technique of each drill to become familiar with the concept and procedure, before executing from the live model (see Figures 1.18 and 1.19). Figure 1.20 shows a simple gesture drawing, much like the kind executed during warm-ups.

The following are study questions meant to be completed after the reader has read through this chapter. The reader will find study questions throughout this book, and these can be completed in a sketchbook, along with one's daily sketches and doodles.

Figure 1.18

Use the reference photos provided to practice ideas presented throughout this book.

Figure 1.19

Reference photo of Ashli.

Figure 1.20

A simple gesture drawing embellishing action.

1. Introduction to Gesture

Study Questions

1. When beginning a life-drawing session, how do you normally start a drawing? What are the first things that go through your mind?
2. Do you prioritize information while drawing, or otherwise work with intent? Do all of your marks have meaning and/or logic, or are you simply trying to record what you see?
3. Do you think in terms of realism, naturalism, or cartoon, or all three? What way of looking at the world intrigues or excites you the most?
4. How important do you consider measurement and proportions to be while practicing quick sketch? Do you focus more on accuracy or exaggeration?
5. What do you use your figure drawings for? Do you consider gesture drawing to be separate from figure drawing, or do you naturally incorporate clear gestures into your observational studies?
6. From the breakdown presented, what aspects of drawing do you most enjoy to study? In your opinion, what are your strengths? What are your weaknesses, and as of right now, what do you think you could do to improve in those areas? (Come back to this question throughout the course of this book; you may find yourself changing your answers.)

References

1. LiteraryDevices Editors. "Tone" LiteraryDevices.net.2013. https://literary devices.net/tone/ (accessed May 28, 2016).
2. LiteraryDevices Editors. "Mood" LiteraryDevices.net.2013. https://literary devices.net/mood/ (accessed May 28, 2016).

2

Working with the Line

We will begin our gesture drawing by looking for our thesis statement, or the *Big Idea* of our intended subject. In the case of observational figure drawing, this is when we begin to search for the story behind the action the model is undertaking within the pose. If the pose is short and intended for quick sketch, we will spend most of our time thinking of the early stages of the process, rather than belabor ourselves with attempting to capture anatomy, detail, and lighting.

During quick sketch, we must prioritize, and if the focus of the session is storytelling and developing our sensitivity and efficiency in that particular skill set, then it is more important to focus on the early stages of our process rather than the end game, or finishing stages of our process. If the gesture drawing is a Lay-In for a longer drawing, painting, or composition, we can slow this process down and take our time, conscientiously focusing on each step, taking greater care to make good choices regarding the information we are inputting and how we are interpreting it—and thus giving meaning to it. We can also think of the first steps of our breakdown as being the *internal construction* of our drawing, with the intention of creating a drawing whose silhouette, or *external construction*, is visually clear.

Either way, Step 1 involves *defining the thesis statement*, and laying in *one-dimensional* lines that will set up the drawing to come. We are seeing and reducing our subject to its most simple, abstract, and purest form: The Line. In effect, we are building a *protomannequin*, which will ultimately become the more traditional mannequin figure. Our goal is for our mannequin to be designed and constructed entirely with intent, from the simplest linear foundations all the way through to the final marks made.

Using Ideas from Animation to Aid Us in Gesture Drawing

We will be adapting and utilizing certain Principles of Animation throughout this study guide in order to infuse more life and energy into all of our drawings. They are all based on observation and life studies, have been developed very thoroughly by their authors, and have been used around the world to create successful and emotionally moving animated performances. They help remind us of certain properties of physics as they relate to mass, volume, and weight in space, as well as the importance of draftsmanship and visual communication; further, they allow us to embellish acting and emotional resonance in drawings, which allows us to create works that feel more real.

The following are the 12 Principles of Animation [1], paraphrased and adapted for our purposes. They can all be found within Chapter 1 of *Disney Animation: The Illusion of Life*, by Frank Thomas and Ollie Johnson. While we will not be using all of the principles, we can use most of them for developing the story potential of any drawing. Readers are encouraged to look up and define the principles for themselves, in addition to the short adapted definition given here; readers are further encouraged to study the discipline of animation and to complete at least basic ideas, such as a bouncing ball, flour bag drop, jump or walk cycles, etc., ideally in an *instructed* introductory traditional animation class.

1. *Squash and Stretch* [2]: Used to show compression, weight, and gravity, this principle aids one in developing drawings with realistic volumetric and physical qualities. The most notable examples and exercises to learn this idea are the Bouncing Ball and Half-Filled Flour Bag. In both exercises, the goals are to indicate gravity and its effects on a volumetric object, as well as the compressions on impact with the ground. Doing so aids the artist in understanding gravity and acceleration and further provides practice with maintaining *consistency in volume* for the entirety of each exercise. Maintaining consistency in volume is one of the most useful disciplines the draftsperson can learn and become confident with, as it will allow one to stay on model and exaggerate and embellish drawings for more impact. Squash and Stretch is the most applicable principle of animation to the type of gestural work we will be looking at and executing throughout the length of this study guide.

2. *Anticipation* [3]: Refers to preparing your audience for an action to be performed by your character or subject. It is exactly what the name suggests: letting the audience anticipate the coming action, by using another one before. For example, if one were to jump straight up in the air, one would most likely have to crouch or squat before lifting off the ground. Without such an anticipatory action, the jump would be stiff and stilted. Much as we perform such anticipatory actions in real life, so too would an animated subject. While we might not be able to literally apply this particular principle, we can use it to help us embellish drawings or draw more specific character moments when exaggerating and stylizing from life. We can also

use it to help us think in sequence, which will allow us to explore characters and their motivations and personalities more intimately.

3. *Staging* [4]: The most broad of all the principles, staging deals directly with visual storytelling and the following issues: Composition and Framing; Shot Type and Placement of Camera; Action and Position of the character or subject within frame; Lighting; and any inclusion of additional ideas that provide Tone and/or Mood. We will be utilizing this idea in conjunction with the concepts of visual clarity and visual storytelling, as it is a crucial building block of both.

4. *Straight-Ahead Action and Pose to Pose* [5]: Animation-specific techniques. *Straight-Ahead Action* refers to the technique of drawing frames consecutively to achieve a more fluid or exciting sequence, while Pose to Pose refers to the practice of drawing key frames first while controlling different visual relationships, before completing the drawings between key frames, known as *in-betweens*. While we may not be able to literally interpret this principle for our work within this guide, we may use these ideas while sketching or thumbnailing possible animation, storyboard, or comic page sequences, and as such it should be experimented with.

5. *Follow-Through and Overlapping Action* [6]: This principle refers to physical laws such as inertia, gravity, and drag. Typically speaking, *follow-through* will refer to the continued motion of parts or clothing of a character or subject after their body has stopped moving, due to inertia. *Overlapping action* typically refers to the tendency of different parts of the body of a character or subject to move and stop at different rates. *Drag* refers to when those parts move at a slower speed than other parts, possibly due to wind resistance or friction, for example (the possibilities and adaptations are virtually endless). Included in this entry is the idea of the *moving hold*, which refers to keeping a subject or character predominantly still, save for a few indications of life, such as breathing, eye-blinking, etc. These ideas are important for developing the specific personality of a character or subject and allowing us to understand the flavor of the actions they are undertaking. We may borrow and adapt these ideas for gesture drawing, and the interpretations and applications are limited only by the imagination.

6. *Slow In and Slow Out* [7]: Another principle relating to a specific technique in the development of an animated subject. It refers to the acceleration and deceleration of an action of the subject or character drawn; it has to do with the quantity of frames at the beginning and end of the action and how close or far apart to each other they have been drawn. It makes sequences feel more real, since in real life our actions vary in speed. This is a principle that is more specific to the craft of animation and not necessarily applicable to the type of work we will be doing here.

7. *Arcs* [8]: Refers to the tendency for organic characters and subjects to move in arced paths, while mechanical constructs tend to move in straight paths. Arcs will be mentioned regularly, as they are used in the development of nearly every drawing in this study guide. They are used to understand trajectories and the potential paths of a moving subject, but we will also be using them in the development of the body of the

subject, as well. They will aid us in implying movement within single frame drawings, such as the typical gesture drawing.

8. *Secondary Action* [9]: Any action that supports the principle action of a character or subject within a sequence. This principle can be applied to a single frame gesture drawing, and we will be doing so throughout the study guide, in addition to other minor supporting ideas within a drawing. While we are not literally interpreting it, being aware of the importance of a strong supporting idea will aid us in embellishing our subject's actions and personalities, as well as his or her acting performance. It should be noted that we can use this principle to help us edit during life drawing: if at any point any secondary (or supporting) action does not emphasize or help the principle action, it should be left out.

9. *Timing* [10]: An animation-specific concept, it refers to the quantity of drawings needed for any particular action, which results in the speed of the action when it is viewed sequentially or on-screen. While it is an incredibly useful and necessary tool to practice for the craft of animation, we will not be applying this principle to our drawings within the scope of the study guide, as its usefulness is more apparent in an animated sequence. If the reader is interested in pursuing the craft of animation, this is a critical principle to become familiarized with and practice.

10. *Exaggeration* [11]: Simply put, *exaggeration* traditionally presents reality in a hyperbolic way, and the level and style are dependent upon the application of the drawing exaggerated and the style of the artist doing the exaggeration. Classically speaking, *The Illusion of Life* presents it as staying true to reality but caricaturing certain aspects of it, whether in the acting and actions of the characters/subjects or the situation the character is placed in. This is another broad term, and because there are so many ways to exaggerate, we will be utilizing this principle the most, and it will be seen applied to every drawing in some way throughout this study guide.

11. *Solid Drawing* [12]: The most important and fundamental of all the principles, and an absolute necessity for accomplishing work with visual clarity and meaning, *solid drawing* refers to the technical drawing ability of the artist. The artist should have experience with the fundamentals of Line, Shape, Form, Weight and Balance, Light/Value, Anatomy, Design, Perspective, etc., in order to achieve clarity and ease in communication via the medium of drawing. Any areas not comprehended will impede the artist, especially for a craft as disciplined and rigorous as animation or visual storytelling. The principle of solid drawing will be used throughout this study guide, and it applies beautifully to all types of drawing and applications of gesture and observational drawing skills. The artist simply must devote the time and mileage necessary to achieve solid drawing, and any weak areas or holes in their drawing education must be addressed, either through self-study or through instructed courses and workshops. Keep in mind that while self-study is a powerful tool when disciplined, sometimes we must take an instructed course, no matter what level we find ourselves in our draftsmanship or career.

12. *Appeal* [13]: Another useful concept and one that will also be utilized throughout this study guide, *appeal* refers to creating visual ideas that are aesthetically pleasing to the eye in some way. This does not mean everything must be cute and cuddly; rather anything one draws or designs

should be created with intent and harmony. Furthermore, *The Illusion of Life* points out how anything difficult to read lacks appeal, as the viewer will be unable to understand what they are looking at and subsequently lose interest. We must strive to create drawings that have some kind of aesthetically pleasing quality with visual clarity. The text also likens it to the idea of charisma, such as a live actor would have. We will be adapting and using this principle as well, though we are broadening the term to allow for more experimentation and investigation into what is visually appealing, what works, and what doesn't.

We can apply the following concepts at this initial lay-in stage:

- Line(s) of Action
- Rhythm
- Harmony
- Fluidity (or the Flow of Energy, or Life Force)
- Spontaneity

The following Principles of Animation may also be applied to this stage:

- Squash and Stretch
- Anticipation
- Staging
- Arcs
- Exaggeration
- Appeal
- Solid Drawing
- Follow-Through and Overlapping Action
- Secondary Action

These particular principles have been chosen as they are most directly related to the act of drawing. It should be noted that when utilizing the Principles of Animation during gesture drawing, we cannot always literally interpret the Principle being used; rather we are attempting to see our gesture drawing as part of a sequence, scene, or a story-driven scenario, of which our particular drawing is a component. Visualizing or seeing a single pose as a part of a larger story is particularly useful to those artists practicing drawing for sequential storytelling purposes, as it will aid in developing acting and creating diverse but emotionally relatable characterization, not to mention aiding in spontaneous creative problem-solving. The more variables we can play with in our drawings, the more fun and challenging our observational practices become. For those artists more interested in non-sequential work, we can still draw from the Principles of Animation to give our work more emotional resonance and ultimately truth, though the way we interpret individual Principles may not be as literal as when we apply them for sequential animation. Nevertheless, because they are based on observable logic, physics, and creativity, we may use them for inspiration, experimentation, and practice.

When defining our thesis statement, or Big Idea, it helps to look at the silhouette first. What is your initial response to what you are looking at? What jumps out? Is it the entire action being performed? Is it a small facet of the pose, such as the curvature of a finger or flick of a wrist? Is it the way the light wraps around the musculature? Is it the model's facial expression? If the model is acting as well as posing, what is our initial emotional response to that performance? We will be defining that gut instinct as our thesis statement, and it will become the backbone of the story we will develop in our drawing. When sharing a life-drawing session with multiple artists, it is always inspiring to see each individual's interpretation of that Big Idea, and it is recommended during such a session to periodically walk around the room and look at the artwork being created by the other artists. In this way, we can begin to understand how subjective our interpretation of reality is, which serves to inspire creativity in our own individual interpretations of our subject matter. This will further enable us to consider other interpretations of observable reality and develop empathy and creativity when deciding how best to communicate ideas to our audience.

Exaggeration

We must also decide on the level of exaggeration we are planning to use to develop our drawing (see Figure 2.1). We must ask ourselves how far we want to push reality; whether we plan on staying true to the reality we see, whether we will be exaggerating that reality within the scope of naturalism, or whether we plan on pushing our ideas to extremes, either exaggerating subtleties or over-emphasizing actions, expressions, etc. It is often recommended to overstate and overemphasize ideas from the earliest stages so as to compensate for any loss of vitality, energy, power, and intent later on. If the gesture drawing is being executed as the Lay-In for a more finished or fully realized work, the importance of overstating actions and exaggerating ideas becomes even more important; when polishing or rendering a work, it is easy to overwork an idea and muddle the thesis statement or lessen the gut reaction that was originally intended by the artist. Exaggeration at the early stages is even more crucial if the gesture drawing is being used for animating, as clearly expressed ideas are a fundamental component of bringing a sequence of drawings to life. Don't be alarmed if it takes time to think here, or if more warm-up time is needed; everyone works at their own pace, and this spontaneous decision-making only improves with more experience and drawing mileage.

Once we have deciphered our initial response and decided on what our thesis statement or Big Idea is, we must begin to lay our very first marks on paper. These marks consist of one-dimensional lines, and with them we will be

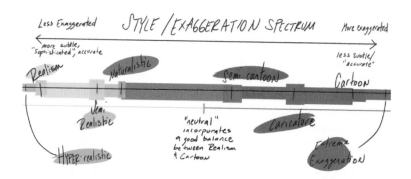

Figure 2.1

A spectrum of exaggeration.

defining our Line(s) of Action first. After we have defined our Line(s) of Action, we can then begin developing the groundwork of any rhythm and harmony we see as being pertinent to our Statement. It is also at this initial stage of the lay-in that we may decide if any Measuring is necessary. If it is, we have multiple options for attacking measurement and proportions, depending upon pose length and priorities.

Basic Technique: Step 1

We begin by defining our Line(s) of Action (see Figure 2.2). To do this and in fact to help define my story or thesis statement, I look at the silhouette first. It is common to utilize one line of action when practicing gesture drawing, but it is my personal preference to look at three (depending on the pose; sometimes it's only necessary to lay in one, sometimes only two, sometimes I may need four, but three tends to get the job done fairly well): a primary line of action; a secondary line of action; and a Tertiary line of action. I am developing a hierarchy of information, using the Secondary and Tertiary Lines to support the Primary Lines. In this way I am thinking of the strongest directional flow of energy within any particular pose or action and relatively weaker flows of energy that I deem necessary to tell the story I want to tell with a particular drawing. If I decide that one line of action is enough to tell a story I stop my one-dimensional design there. If I find I need supporting ideas so as to develop any other story-derived concepts—such as acting or any other contextual information, such as costume, props, staging/set, or even what will ultimately become lighting or texture—then I will find and lay down Secondary and Tertiary lines. Ultimately, it is up to the artist to decide in the moment the best course of action regarding the lay-in of a single line of action, or multiple Lines. I tend to limit myself to three ideas at this stage so as

Figure 2.2

Short-pose drawing constructed with limited lines.

to avoid muddling my statement, keeping in mind that I may want to add supplemental microgestures between Step 1 (where we are now) and Step 2 (which involves thinking in terms of two-dimensional shapes and geography. The artist should take care at this stage to focus on visual clarity and the communication of abstract ideas. I can develop these one-dimensional lines as S curves, C curves, and straight lines if I so choose, but they won't be physically small; because I want to think from Big Ideas to Small Ideas, they will be larger, more sweeping *arcs* that take on the general flow of an S or C curve. This will help me set up the larger, overlying Rhythms I see in the pose and will also aid me in keeping those Rhythms harmonious. I am keen on using arcs to set up the larger Rhythms of the whole figure at this stage, before I analyze the progressively smaller rhythms presented by the two-dimensional shapes (and later three-dimensional forms); this is why S and C curves and Straight lines come in so handy.

Concerning the Placement of the Head, Neck, and Shoulder Line

Before drawing, we must also decide whether we want or need to place the Head, Neck, and Shoulder Line early on, and, specifically, how early. We have two options: We can place the Head, Neck, and Shoulder Line at this stage of the *protomannequin*, that is: placing this information at the one-dimensional stage, or Step 1 of our breakdown, or waiting until Step 2, where we transition from 1D ideas to 2D ideas. We can further decide if it is necessary for us to lay in the Head, Neck, and Shoulder line either *before* laying in our Line(s) of Action, or *after*. There are advantages and disadvantages to both of these decisions. If we begin by laying in the head, neck, and shoulder line *before* laying in our line(s) of action, we have the following possible *advantages*:

1. Controlling the Placement of the Figure on the page and thus ultimately controlling composition and making it easier to avoid strange occurrences such as less than ideal cropping or tangents.
2. Setting Scale and a Controlled Unit of Measurement
3. Laying in a starting point for the torso
4. Controlling the relationship between one of the strongest *X*-Axes in the figure and the Line(s) of Action

The possible disadvantages of the above process include the following:

1. The possibility of not exaggerating the Head, Neck, and Shoulder line enough
2. Making the drawing too stiff by having laid in the two-dimensional structures of the Head and Neck too early on
3. Not being aware of or damaging the integrity of the thesis statement/Big Idea before laying in the Head, Neck, and Shoulders

Ultimately, one can choose either way to start one's lay-in and both ways are equally valid. There are some artists who choose to leave the Head and Neck last when developing their lay-in drawing, and that method works for them. It is up to the individual to choose the best starting method.

We can also decide to lay in the head, neck, and shoulder line *after* laying in our one-dimensional ideas; that is, when we move on to developing the two-dimensional representations of our figure. We will see an execution of this decision in the next chapter.

Now let us observe a demonstration of the basic technique as applied to a 2-minute pose. The photo referenced is included here (see Figure 2.3).

Demonstration

Using the picture of Ashli, I begin by first studying the silhouette for the statement I want to communicate about this particular figure (see Figure 2.4). I note where the foot of the outstretched leg is in relation to the head, on an invisible X-Axis. I also look at the feet and quickly gauge the distance between them. This is one way to visually measure without the aid of a tool: judge the two-dimensional distance between things. Because this is a quick sketch—that is, a pose in which one does not intend to go over 3–4 minutes maximum (depending on size; this demo is 18" × 24")—I know that I do not have time for actual measurements. This is where mileage comes in: the more you draw and observe from life, the more natural it becomes to quickly analyze an image and decide what marks should come first, second, third, and so on. Because of habit, I lay the head in first, so that I can place the figure on the page and thus attempt to control my composition as best I can. I say "attempt" because when practicing quick-sketch gestures like this one, I want to be sure to maintain the practice of studying composition, but I don't

Figure 2.3

Demonstration reference of Ashli.

Figure 2.4

Two-minute demo of the reference image.

want to worry too terribly about the boundaries the edges of the page represent. So I will split the difference and control to a certain extent the composition, while also making sure to give myself enough room to let my *shoulder* create long, sweeping lines. I draw from the shoulder and lay in strokes as broadly as possible, focusing on communicating action and—to a certain extent—geography, or simply where everything is. I am thinking in terms of movement and energy flow, while maintaining the integrity of the action presented by the pose. I am also watching how greatly I exaggerate this drawing; because I am keeping it fairly naturalistic, I will refrain from exaggerating to the point of cartoon or beyond believability. I tend to find my lines of action by studying the movement in the silhouette, which is represented by the red line (see Figure 2.5).

The lighter green lines are my major supporting lines of action: The longest uninterrupted line running from the top of the head down through the figure and out the foot is my primary line of action. If you're drawing using only one line of action, this line would most likely be the strongest directional force line. The additional movements I'm concerned with at this point are the weighted leg (since without it this action would not be possible); the straight line of the outstretched arm; and the crossed, foreshortened arm. This means that in this particular case, I am choosing to move slightly beyond only three major lines of action because of my desire to include the crossed arm. This crossed arm is particularly interesting because it places the hand so close to the face, and the elegant microgestures of the fingers (the smaller sweeping arcs of the moving fingers, that is) in both hands give this pose another layer of individuality and personality. Because I find that information so lovely and appealing, I will set

2. Working with the Line

Figure 2.5

Primary line of action in red; supporting ideas in green and dark green.

up my foundation in order to play with those microgestures, even if the pose is short and I know there is a slim chance of my having time for it. This is why short pose is such a powerful tool: we are forced to make moves *now* thinking of moves we might make 50 steps ahead. If we combine that kind of study with long pose, we can blend methodologies and techniques from that practice with these and be able to infuse carefully thought-out and designed structures with an extra spark. So while my goal at this stage is to look at my subject in the most abstract way possible, that is in terms of one-dimensional *lines of action* and directional force, I am planning in advance what I would want this drawing to look like and what ideas are most important and drawing in that order.

Now, let's speed up just a little and see what the same action may look like during a 30-second pose length (see Figure 2.6) and what happens to the basic technique, so that we may segue into variations one may choose to experiment with.

Variations on the Basic Technique

There are numerous ways to vary the basic techniques presented throughout this study guide, and readers are encouraged to use their ingenuity to reinvent and challenge themselves with different approaches to each concept. Let us look at some variations we might utilize.

1. The first variation relates to the relationship between *lines of action* and Angles (see Figure 2.7). We previously looked at what a gesture drawing might look like if we begin with the head versus placing the head after we've established our *lines of action*. One way to approach the

Figure 2.6

30-second gesture drawing of model Ashli.

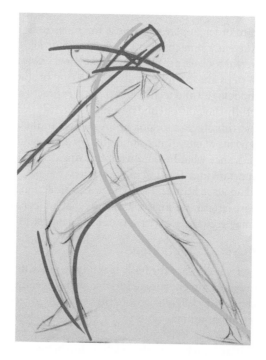

Figure 2.7

Primary line of action in light blue; head shape in green; supporting *lines of action* in red.

initial mark-making process in this case is to establish the primary line of action first (baby blue line), then place the head, neck, and shoulder line (in green), followed by any additional and necessary Supporting line of action (in red).

2. In the second variation (see Figure 2.8), we may place the primary line of action onto the page first, then follow up with the Shoulder Line, Hip Line, and end with any important and necessary Supporting line of action. In this case, the figure takes on more of a stick-man appearance. This approach allows one to have a very clear linear representation of the *action* of the subject. Furthermore, this variation directly relates the movements of each of the major masses of the figure to one another, allowing for an immediate inspection of the major overlying Rhythms presented by the figure. This approach also allows us to gauge proportions a bit more accurately than the previous variations, because we can immediately begin to see the geography of the trunk and limbs. It gives us freedom to aggressively alter proportions as we see fit and further allows us to exaggerate not only the curvilinear ideas of the lines of action but also the steepness of the angles of the shoulder and hip lines. These lines become more important when dealing with clothing and costuming; because we tend to drape and hang clothing from these horizontal lines (horizontal on a standing figure), we must know where they are and what they are doing during a variety of motions. This approach allows us to practice gauging those angles. This variation is also particularly useful to those of us who dislike laying in the head so early on in the construction

Figure 2.8

Primary lines of action in light green; shoulder and hip axes in orange; supporting lines of action in blue.

of a drawing: if we have what is essentially a dynamic stick figure, and we know how our major structures/masses are moving, we can develop the torso, legs, and arms first and lay in the head last. There are many artists who choose to place the head after constructing the 2D (and even sometimes 3D) structures of the rest of the body; procedural analysis of your own drawing method and subsequent experimentation will allow you to decide how you prefer to start a drawing and in what order you choose to develop the masses of the figure.

The above variations are just a couple of ways one can experiment with procedure. It should be noted that the second variation of the basic technique is especially useful to those students who are struggling with keeping proportions consistent, on-model, or accurate. One may combine that particular approach with a ruler drawn on the side of the page to be aware of what the ideal or heroic eight-head figure looks like and to compare and contrast from that model. Alternatively, one may take proportions during a standing or contrapposto pose and make a note on the drawing surface of the head count of the figure, from the top of the head to the bottom of the feet, then from shoulder line to the hip line to set the length of the torso. At this early stage of construction, it may be more ideal to disregard the lengths of the legs and arms and instead opt for long, flowing lines to describe the lines of action that represent such structures. Too much concern for proportion early on may interrupt or impede the flow of energy that we are looking for. We can place joints such as the knees, ankles, elbows, and wrists after we have completed the lines of action and before or after we have either *turned* those lines into two-dimensional shapes or used those lines as *guides* for our two-dimensional shapes.

Working with Story Elements at the One-Dimensional, Linear Stage

Now that we've seen the basic technique regarding the initial lay-in of gestural one-dimensional ideas, we can see what happens when we apply certain ideas from the Principles of Animation. Keep in mind that one need not limit oneself to only these Principles when exploring gesture; one can pull ideas from any other discipline, no matter how related or unrelated to drawing they may appear to be on the surface. Looking at these Principles will help guide us in thinking sequentially and therefore force us to think of the personality of the subject we are drawing, or of the scenario hinted at through the subject's choices in movements and poses. If character is something the artist wishes to explore during a life-drawing session, it is encouraged for the artist to speak to the model while they pose. Take note of the microexpressions in the model's face; observe the movements of the hands and feet; study the body language the model uses both on and off the model stand. A person is complex and infinitely interesting in a multitude of ways and worth studying, regardless of whether they are modeling or not. This approach to observational drawing studies causes us to practice empathy, which is a critical component of acting and will not only aid us in the development of figurative drawings with character and personality but will also help in developing the emotional resonance found in effective storytelling. We want our audience to feel something about our drawings (see Figure 2.9).

Figure 2.9

Exaggerated and cartooned character study focused on personality.

Why Work with Ideas from Animation, Even If One Is Not an Animator?

I am not an animator. I am what would be referred to as an *illustrator*: I make images that visually communicate an idea, narrative, story, or character. However, much like it is essential for the artist to experiment and take risks, it is also essential for the artist to broaden his or her mindset and appreciate not only the different types of drawing and storytelling but also the different applications of those disciplines and the learning potential they have to offer. Animation is one of the greatest art forms we as students of all levels have available to us; the discipline, creative problem-solving, imagination, and insightfulness necessary for animating are just as necessary for life drawing, as the animator must study directly from life in order to create it. Therefore, why not borrow ideas from animation? Or ideas from other visual art forms? Most art, as we define it, is our reaction to life, and as life is constantly moving and morphing it would be self-limiting to not appreciate ideas from sequential storytelling. The more we feel about our subject, the better we can compose our idea of what that subject is, and ideas from animation allow us to study different aspects of a character's choices in a scenario, the results of those choices on body language and physical expression, and how we may best communicate those choices to an audience. Furthermore, the study of animation requires keen observation and the constant reminder of the effects of Newtonian physics on mass. The ability to *feel* our subject and their actions is an integral part of gesture drawing; if we as creators cannot feel our subject or the story we are attempting to tell, we run the risk of our audience failing to understand the point of what we have created. This is part of how we bring a single drawing to life.

The following nine principles can come in quite handy while drawing from a live model:

1. *Squash and Stretch* will help us show weight, mass, and volume. This concept reminds us of the effects that mass and gravity have on the figure. Squash and stretch also allows us to embellish and exaggerate actions and helps with providing asymmetry and dynamism throughout the figure. Squash is alternately described here as *compression*.

2. *Anticipation* will help us think of possible sequences of action, which will create context. Specifically, this concept helps remind us of the setup of an action, which we can use to imply sequence or the feeling of a moment either before or after the pose we are currently drawing the subject in.

3. *Staging* must be thought of at all times when implying context. This principle is pretty broad and general, even by its definition in *The Illusion of Life*. Because it essentially boils down to visual clarity and the importance of making ideas as clear as possible, one may also see this concept as the point of illustration: when illustrating an idea, the more clearly we can put it together, the better for our audience. We simply do not want our audience to struggle to comprehend whatever we have just shown them. If they don't understand what they are experiencing, they may lose interest. Being mindful of this concept comes in particularly useful during life drawing, as it relates directly to the organization of ideas.

4. *Arcs* will be used in two major ways: using S and C curves (which are arcs unto themselves) to create fluidity, rhythm, and harmony; and to understand the range of motion of the figures we are drawing. Organic living creatures tend to move in arcs: that is, the path the limbs follow when in motion are not made of straight lines but rather sweeping arcs. To mechanically accomplish this in a gesture drawing, one *must* draw from the shoulder.

5. *Exaggeration* must be considered at all steps in the development of a drawing; it need not be explosive and boisterous all the time. It can be subtle as well and still be powerful. It is up to the creator to figure out what type or level of exaggeration is needed at any given time.

6. *Appeal* Generally speaking, this is most often described as *charisma*, but using the term broadly, we can attempt to make any movement, line, shape, form, or silhouette appealing through thoughtful and deliberate choice. Simply put, it comes down to making design choices that result in a work that someone will be drawn to look at and will want to spend time looking at it: the configuration of ideas so as to allow ease of communication of a concept while maintaining aesthetically pleasing design choices. For the scope of this book, and because we are borrowing ideas from animation for the sake of exploration, we will broaden this term to include nontraditionally appealing things as well, so that we may allow for all possibilities while brainstorming. I consider appeal to be subjective, though there are certain staples of appealing design that are timeless and universal, such as baby-like features and proportions in animals and characters.

7. *Solid Drawing* is necessary for successful visual communication and visual clarity. In fact, it goes hand in hand with appeal and staging. This principle is one of the most important, as it directly relates to not only understanding the tools at one's disposal but also how to use those tools comfortably and confidently. Those tools include understanding Perspective, Shape, and Form. It is recommended to understand both geometric and organic shapes and forms and how to use them together in a harmonious way. If drawing fundamentals are lacking, one will be unable to communicate using a visual language. One may see this concept in the way we learn to verbally communicate: when learning a language we are usually given small building blocks with which we may put together sentences. How well we communicate with those sentences is dependent upon whether we understand how to put the building blocks together, which requires an understanding of the building blocks themselves, as well as the general guidelines with which to put them together. For example, English speakers are usually taught the alphabet first, as it represents the most basic building blocks of this language. We are taught the properties of those building blocks, such as how each letter sounds by itself, as well as how letters sound when we combine them and how they affect one another to create the words with which we describe the world around us. We follow that up with learning grammar, or a system with guidelines and rules that will help us when deciding *how* to put words together to effectively communicate with others. Drawing is the same thing. It is a language that we use for visual communication. Classes such as Perspective, Vis Com (which incidentally is short for *visual communication*), and Life Drawing teach us the alphabet and grammar of drawing. This analogy should not be limited to only drawing. All disciplines—especially the Humanities—function in a similar way: we can see all of them as their own language with which to understand the world and to express oneself. It cannot be stressed enough how important the concept of Solid Drawing is and how we may continue to develop it to no end throughout our careers.

The following principles can be used as well, though not as literally as when we apply them to animation or sequential work. They serve to remind us of chronology (the sequential passage of time) and Newtonian mechanics, such as inertia, and their effects on mass and volume. Simply put, they remind us of everyday observations we may accidentally take for granted:

- *Follow-Through and Overlapping Action*—We can use these to imply action and liveliness, as well as show the effects of physics on a subject in motion, which in turn provides for environmental context and world-building, since the effect of gravity and weight can be felt here, which implies that the character or subject exists in a world such as ours. This provides a feeling of reality.
- *Secondary Action*—We can use this to support our thesis statement and provide character/personality/expression embellishment. It also functions as an aid to edit out any unnecessary ideas that may otherwise pollute the intended statement if we find our drawing is too busy to read clearly.

Now let's take a look at our initial photo reference and 2-minute demonstration and discuss how we may apply some of these principles in a pose such as this (see Figures 2.10 and 2.11). We shall systematically describe the

Figure 2.10

Demonstration reference of Ashli.

Figure 2.11

Two-minute demo.

2. Working with the Line

specific areas where we can place these concepts on the pose given in the photo reference and how we may compare and contrast a naturalistic drawing against an intentionally exaggerated one. The remainder of this study guide will refrain from systematically pointing out each and every principle in the works shown, so as to allow for a more fluid presentation of ideas and make the relationship between all choices more prominent. However, the reader should be aware that they are still being used, as abstractly interpreted as may be.

Squash and Stretch as Applied to a Naturalistic 2-Minute Study

There are a couple different ways we can interpret this particular principle, since we can apply it to nearly each stage of a drawing, as it relates to mass, volume, weight, and how those things are affected by physics, most notably gravity. Volumetrically speaking, our shapes and forms are being squashed— or *compressed* as it may otherwise be referred to—on the right side of the torso and stretched on the left side. We can also see squash in the compression of the breasts, and the muscles of the bent arm. one-dimensionally, the primary line of action running through the whole of the figure will be affected by how much we decide to exaggerate the squash in the torso. We can also see squash in the way the left leg (the model's right) is compressed and holding the weight of the action of the figure. We will visually relay this compression with the afore-mentioned C curve, with the level of exaggeration dependent on the artist recording the information. The stretch can be applied to the right leg; it is literally stretching to lift off the toes. To communicate this visually, we will make sure that when laying in the primary line of action, we keep that line straight and confident, making sure that enough directional force is implied. This will communicate the strength and power that this pose embodies. Because the straightened arm provides another layer of dynamic movement to this pose, we will lay it in as a supporting idea, as the fingers and face become bookends that provide personality and character in the microgestures they show. Again, to communicate the stretch of the arm, we will lay it in with a confident straight line.

Squash and Stretch in an Exaggerated Characterization Study

In this 2-minute character study, my primary line of action running through the figure is directly affected by the level of exaggeration I have chosen to utilize (see Figure 2.12). In this case, I have not stylized the drawing to the point of extreme cartoon. While it can be categorized as being a *cartoon*, it is somewhere between semicartoon and caricature, leaning more toward the former than the latter. Note what aspects of the drawing are more exaggerated than others: because I have chosen to emphasize the squash—or *compression*—in the torso, legs, and feet, my primary and supporting lines of action are laid in first; because I tend to keep exploratory drawings fairly sketchy for the sake of having freedom to explore ideas before committing to any, the lines of action used to construct this study are visible within the drawing. Note the exaggeration in the arc used to describe the primary line of action in this study versus that of the previous demo. The line of action of the bent leg also has a greater level of exaggeration applied to it than the previous demo: the arc has been pulled up, rounded out, and intersected abruptly by the straight line created by the bottom plane of the foot. The supporting lines of action created by the

Figure 2.12

An exaggerated and stylized study of Ashli.

outstretched arm and leg have been pulled from the torso with as straight a line as possible to contrast against the arcs of the torso and compressed leg and to further emphasize their stretch. The shapes and forms are built on top of the lines of action present. My impression of this particular pose is of a dancer; I see this pose as a possible moment of a dance. This is in part because I am familiar with the model and her particularly vivacious and fun personality, and I know that she participates in a variety of physical activities, including dance, which influences not only her physique but how she chooses to move as well. This is one of the reasons I used to decide on the level of exaggeration I want to draw with for this particular study: I still want her to look appealing and athletic, so I will exaggerate certain areas to a certain degree but will stop well before getting to the point of accidental monstrification of the model. This also happens to be one of the reasons pretty girls are amongst the most difficult subjects to draw: it's easy to accidentally make them unappealing if exaggerated to an extreme degree. My intention with this study is to avoid that. Drawing from a photo doesn't usually do the subject justice if practicing gesture drawing or story-/character-based explorations: the model's particular style of movement and the resulting effects of that movement style on our elements of drawing and visual communication are no longer communicated by a still image. This is why drawing from direct observation is such a critical part of learning how to communicate via this particular craft.

Anticipation, Follow-through, and Overlapping Action in a 2-Minute Character Study

Because this particular pose implies a lot of movement due to the number of diagonals present, we can interpret these Principles in a few different ways. In one instance, we can see this action as the anticipation pose for one that may follow in which our model has lifted off the ground, bearing the full weight of her action on her right leg (our left). In another instance, we can imagine an antic before this pose, possibly as part of a dance sequence; it is up to our imagination to create such context. This same type of thinking applies for both Follow-Through and Overlapping Action. We can imagine the arms and head in particular as almost swinging through space, until they reach the position we see now, and the legs themselves overlap in terms of shifting weight distribution. We can give an animated quality to the hair: has the hair just begun moving, will it move, or is it following through from a previous pose, albeit an imagined one? We are attempting to think in terms of sequence, using our previous experiences and imagination to fill in the gaps. This will directly affect our choices in exaggeration, tone, and mood, since now we are providing a narrative context to this still image. Again, it must be stressed that we are not using these principles in a literal sense but rather as a learning tool that we can use to embellish a drawing, to provide strength of expression and style, or simply to study a character and his or her choices. For this sequential study of Ashli, I have chosen to remain consistent with the idea of her being a dancer (see Figure 2.13). The reference pose is in the middle, with the action moving from right to left. Position A represents the before, while Position C represents the after. While my intention is not to animate a sequence, I do want to jot down ideas as to how a before and after might possibly look next to the reference image. Note the strong diagonals that make up the primary line of action of each figure, based on my previous opinions concerning the pose: Position B has plenty of compression on the bent leg, which makes me feel like Ashli may have just landed on it from a previous pose or movement. This forms the basis for what I think Position A may feel like. Position C uses the compression and

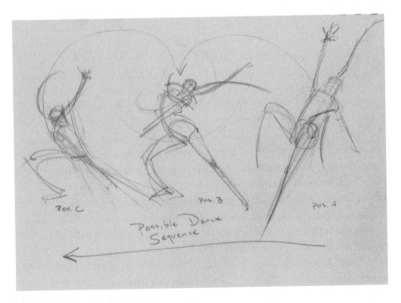

Figure 2.13

Exploratory doodles used to imagine how a character and personality may affect their sequential motion. These types of doodles can go in the margins of a larger life-drawing pad of paper, or in a sketchbook.

stretch of the legs from the previous position and emphasizes those ideas further to imagine some kind of follow-through of the energy of Position B. Possible positions of the figure's ponytail have been noted as well, and A and B both have more than one possible position. These positions merely represent possibilities without any in-betweens. To make the sequence possible, it would be necessary to work out the relationships between each pose, and each limb in each pose, possibly adding more keys where necessary, before developing any in-between drawings. So, while this is not an accurate representation of a true animated sequence, I can use this methodology to develop possible character explorations or even a set of storyboards or comic panels. Essentially, this is gesture drawing as utilized for brainstorming.

Arcs, Exaggeration, and Appeal in a Naturalistic 2-Minute Study versus a 2-Minute Character Study

Because organic figures tend to move in arcs, we can provide the implication of motion to our one-dimensional lay-in through their use. Indeed, the S and C curves we so commonly use in drawing are arcs in themselves. We can combine the ideas of arcs and appeal with exaggeration at this stage in order to define just what type of lines we want to use. This will directly affect the Tone of the ultimate drawing. For example, if we are feeling goofy, we might avoid the use of straight lines altogether and instead choose to define all of our *lines of action* (both the Primary Line and the supporting ideas) with nothing but exaggerated arcs. This will result in exaggeration that reads as cartoony rather than realistic, and we can choose to further design the tone and mood with our choices later on. Or, if we want to reflect a more realistic tone, we can downplay the exaggeration and focus more on accurately conveying the angles present in the figure. This means that our primary line of action, the one running through the length of the figure, may not have as steep an angle as we might otherwise choose to record if we were exaggerating greatly. The same is true for the steepness and degree of curviness in the arcs present in the nonstraightened limbs. When laying in the angles of the shoulder line and hip line, we can also choose to describe those in terms of straights or arcs, and again the degree of exaggeration is entirely subjective. All of these choices will have a direct impact on the type of appeal and the degree to which we are designing it. Our model is already very appealing in terms of shape and proportions, and the action present in the photo is an appealing one, as her movements are very controlled and graceful. We can use such ideas to our advantage: when deciding on what ideas are most important to us in any given pose, we can use what we find most appealing (subjectively speaking, of course, since all artists are different) and embellish or exaggerate those ideas further. The arcs of the character study have been exaggerated more than those of the naturalistic study, and the resulting S and C curves used in conjunction with the arcs of the *lines of action* present in both drawings have been exaggerated accordingly in order to maintain consistency in ideas. Because we use S and C curves to build visual rhythm and harmony and to embellish our lines of action or present supporting ideas, rhythm may be exaggerated or otherwise manipulated as well. Rhythmically speaking, the bounce in the exaggerated figure is much more apparent than in its naturalistic counterpart. However, certain rhythms are the same in both figures: for example, the S curve running down the length of

Figure 2.14

"S" curve in a straight leg.

the outstretched leg wraps around it virtually the same way in both figures, but it has been stretched more in the character study (see Figure 2.14).

Tone and Mood at the One-Dimensional Stage

Now that we've looked at possibilities presented by ideas from animation, let's look at ways in which we can explore line further, using it to practice Tone and vice versa (see Figure 2.15). One exercise that is both delightful and challenging is using the ideas of Dance, or other rhythmic kinesthetic movement, and Music. In this exercise, the artist is challenged to not only be aware of his or her own body but to also take into account the expressive qualities the line can possess and therefore can be utilized to describe their *attitude* to the subject by way of sensory experiences. The goal is to impart character, attitude, and personality to the one-dimensional line and to explore short pose in such a way that requires the artist to be inventive and spontaneous, much like when dancing. This basic exercise can be manipulated and varied so as to apply it in a multitude of ways and for different learning outcomes. For example, the same exercise can be utilized to explore shape and form, or, if playing and experimenting with lighting, the same exercise can become a study in mood. Mood can furthermore be explored by the introduction of Mixed Media, which will not only affect the Tone but can also be used to create atmosphere. The variations are endless and are meant to be an exploratory way to discover new methods of visual communication. Let's look at the basic technique for this particular exploratory gesture exercise, which will be included in the "Drill and Exercise" portion of this chapter, along with study questions and slight variations.

Figure 2.15

Sketch of a dancing life model.

Basic Technique

1. We begin by choosing music, which we will move to. This means, yes, you must get up and dance. If you do not like to dance or feel that you do not do it well, then move, using whatever parts of your body you choose, even if it is only your toes that you use to tap out beats and rhythm. For those artists and students who absolutely love to move, use as much of your body as is emotionally logical for each particular song, genre, or type of music. There is no wrong or right way to do this. The goal in this initial step is to become

   a. Spatially aware of your body in space
   b. Aware of your own anatomy and musculature and of what muscles are activated by what movements
   c. Aware of the *lines of action* present in each movement
   d. Aware of the resulting rhythms in your own body when you begin to move to a beat

2. After the preliminary kinesthetic exploration has been completed, we can resume our drawing positions. Keep the music playing as you draw through sets of short poses, focusing on drawing to the music currently playing. This can mean a couple of different things: we can either draw the subject while under the influence of the emotions we feel as a result of the music, or we can make marks literally using the rhythms we hear— that is, we are in a way dancing with our arms and drawing tools, laying

Figure 2.16

Model dancing to *Swan Lake*. The long lines embody the string instruments' sound in the symphony.

in marks in sync with the music. This will let us explore mark-making and line work that we may not normally be inclined to use, and therein lies the point: by becoming aware of different styles of movement and their relationships to emotion, we can design and construct drawings with different personalities and character qualities. Furthermore, our attitude toward the subject is directly influenced by the sensory input of sound (see Figure 2.16).

3. How the model may contribute: If you are completing this exercise in a life-drawing session or have a model who is willing to participate, ask him or her to pose thematically to each song or music type. One way you can accomplish this is to play music in sets, and break those sets down into smaller increments of time, or the pose lengths. For example, in class, we might change the style or genre of music every 7 minutes, utilizing 1-minute poses from the model. This means that every 7-minute set is thematically linked to a specific style, genre, type, artist, etc., of music. This is one way we can begin to study acting and expression utilizing the whole body (see Figures 2.17 and 2.18).

4. If completed in a group setting, a group critique is encouraged. For example, in class, we look at each individual's favorite page, *favorite* here meaning on whatever page they believe they visually communicated their reflections concerning the music and the model most success-fully. Each individual is then asked to express to the class key words that

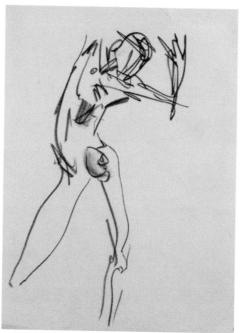

Figure 2.17

Music/dance exercise resulting sketch.

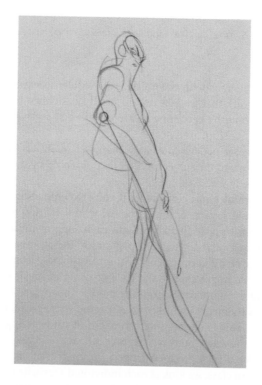

Figure 2.18

Music/dance exercise resulting sketch using a different style of music than the previous sketch.

2. Working with the Line

describe feelings or thoughts that came into their minds when completing the drawings being critiqued. Those who are not verbally inclined are encouraged to communicate their thoughts via kinesthetic movement or onomatopoeia. Again, there is no right or wrong way to complete this exercise, and it serves the artist more as an exploratory experience.

Variations

Variation 1 deals with the objective of the drawing portion of the exercise. In this case, we can play a set of music and shorten the pose duration to something like 20–30 seconds, in order to only focus on line of action and lay-ins and how we might approach those lay-ins from a rhythmic standpoint. So, instead of trying to complete the figure, we are only focused on our Strongest Directional Force Line, or primary line of action, and any pertinent supporting lines of action.

Variation 2 deals with a similar concept, but this time we are taking cues from the silhouette and attempting to communicate the entire action of the figure exclusively with line work. In this variation, we are seeing the effects music and rhythm have on the quality of the line itself, which will further communicate our attitude (Tone) toward our subject (see Figure 2.19).

These are only two of countless variations on this particular exercise. The reader is encouraged to explore the line in any way possible and to use

Figure 2.19

Line quality and expression as influenced by music.

inventiveness, ingenuity, and curiosity to explore the concepts of line and tone. This exercise can also be combined with other ideas and other elements of design or drawing in order to add more variables to the equation.

Exercises

Using the provided photo, complete the following Study Questions as you would homework. Additionally, you can use these Study Questions as a guide to create your own inquiries that you can use every time you draw, or if you find yourself in need of troubleshooting or critiquing your own work when another pair of eyes is not available. However, it is always a good idea to ask someone for critique, whether it be another artist you know and admire, a family member who is willing to give you the truth (be mindful of who you ask though), a colleague or collaborator, a student or instructor (if you are currently in school), or anyone else who can give you a thoughtful critique. You never know what you might find out, and it's always worth hearing someone else's ideas, opinions, and thoughts, even if you disagree with them.

Basic Technique Study Questions Concerning the One-Dimensional Line

1. Looking at the provided photo, can you identify the primary line of action? Think of this as the Strongest Directional Force you see in the pose (see Figure 2.20).
2. What supporting ideas do you find striking, if any? Can you define these with supporting Lines, without undermining the power of the primary line of action?
3. When drawing in general, do you find it more useful to start with the placement of the head Before or After placing the line(s) of action?
4. Looking at your drawings from your most recent life-drawing session, do you find that you have adequately communicated intent at the one-dimensional stage of each of your drawings? Is there a primary line of action or a Strong Directional Force within your drawings? Are the actions readable? If it is a scribble type of drawing, are there any indications of fluidity or any rhythmic properties? We will be looking at Rhythm throughout this study guide, so if you find yourself unable to answer this question at the moment, revisit it later.

The following exercises can be used during a drawing session to practice defining the Line(s) of Action:

Single Line of Action Drills (10 Seconds): Identify and lay in the line of action within a 10-second pose (see Figure 2.21).

Multiple Line of Action Drills (20–30 Seconds): Identify and lay in a primary, secondary, and tertiary line of action, making sure the integrity of the thesis statement (your Big Idea) is not damaged (see Figure 2.22). Your Big Idea should not be muddled for the sake of visual clarity. The Secondary and Tertiary Lines should not only support your thesis statement but also serve or compliment the primary line of action in some necessary and fundamental way.

Figure 2.20

Reference photo of Ashli.

Figure 2.21

Ten-second lines of action Drills.

Figure 2.22

Multiple-lines of action Drill.

Follow these drills with 1-Minute gesture drawings, focusing on visual clarity and Fluidity. Look for any S and C curves and any Straight lines that will serve as a beautiful contrast to those curves. Additionally, if you find yourself with time remaining, place the angle of the shoulder line and the angle of the hip line. For the sake of the exercise, do not concern yourself with proportions or measurements: 1 Minute is much too short for such analysis. While some artists may find themselves able to measure in such a time length, it is not absolutely necessary to do so at the moment.

Exercises and Study Questions for Applying Story Elements, Namely the Literary Concept of Tone

1. Before drawing, create a playlist featuring music you currently listen to and enjoy. Dance or otherwise move rhythmically to each song on your playlist. Do you feel the different tempos of each song? Are there highs and lows, or does the song move in a straight line? When moving rhythmically to each song, can you feel which muscles in your anatomy you are using? Do you use different parts of your anatomy or move differently depending on which song you are listening to? Do you move differently depending on the theme, tone, or mood of each song in your playlist? Can you feel the *lines of action* within your own body?

2. Now, draw to each song on that playlist, keeping in mind what you felt when moving rhythmically, remembering how you moved your own anatomy. How does each song affect the one-dimensional (Linear) aspects of your drawings?

3. Now repeat both exercises using music you don't normally listen to, music from around the world, music you don't like, or a mix of all. How do you move differently to music you are unfamiliar with or dislike? What are the effects on your drawings? Do you find your own personal reactions reflected in the lines of action you choose to define your figure with at this early stage of construction? What effects might establishing tone this early on have on your choices down the road?

Ideally, these exercises are best performed when drawing from observation, either in a live figure-drawing session or from photographic reference. It is most enjoyable and interesting when performed in a group. If possible, put together your own figure-drawing session, with a group of friends or other peers, and take turns modeling. It is not necessary for the model to be nude, nor even experienced, as long as the person modeling can hold a pose anywhere between 20 seconds to a full minute. It should also be noted that one may repeat this Music-based exercise with each Stage of drawing we look at: What are the effects this exercise has on how you develop two-dimensional shape? Or three-dimensional form? You may also manipulate this exercise to create your own. What are some ways you can change this exercise to suit your particular needs?

Study Questions That Relate to the Principles of Animation, As Applied to Observational Studies

1. Which of the 12 Principles can you see as being most applicable to your own drawings? How might they affect your own process? How might they affect your own style or design taste?
2. Can you think of other ways in which you can interpret and apply these ideas to static drawings—that is, drawings that are not part of a sequence, but rather stand-alone or single-frame drawings, such as an academic figure drawing?
3. Can you think of ideas beyond the 12 Principles that you can use to guide your drawings? These ideas can come from any discipline.

Figure 2.23 shows a continuous contour line drawing technique that may be used for warm-ups in addition to quick sketches.

Figure 2.23

Continuous contour line short-pose drawing.

References

1. Thomas, F. and Johnston O. 1984. *Disney Animation: The Illusion of Life.* New York: Abbeville Press; pp. 15–37.
2. Ibid., 15–19.
3. Ibid., 19–21.
4. Ibid., 21–24.
5. Ibid., 24–26.
6. Ibid., 27–30.
7. Ibid., 30.
8. Ibid., 30–31.
9. Ibid., 31–32.
10. Ibid., 32–33.
11. Ibid., 33–34.
12. Ibid., 34–36.
13. Ibid., 36–37.

3

Working with Shapes

Basic Technique: Step 2
Setting Up Geography/
    Placement
Demonstration
Rhythm and Harmony

Explorations in Story with
    Shape and Gesture
Demonstration
Study Questions
Exercises

We may now move on from the one-dimensional linear architecture of our idea and continue the development of our *protomannequin* with two-dimensional shape ideas, again making decisions with intent. While any two-dimensional shape ideas may be used at this stage, the technique will be described utilizing tubular constructs, since we will be looking at a naturalistically drawn figure for the demonstration (see Figure 3.1). This two-dimensional tube is simply a cylinder without the top or bottom, eliminating the ellipses and elliptical cross contours that provide the three-dimensional form of a cylinder. In this way, we can begin to control what our three-dimensional forms will be and how they affect our thesis statement before we develop them on paper. The reader should be aware that there is freedom of choice at this stage: it is not necessary to use the tube shape, nor the eventual cylinders that they will become. The reader is invited to use as much creativity and experimentation with their shape choices as is desired, such as squares/rectangles, or circles. It should be noted that at this stage the tube and the square/rectangle may look fairly similar, and if circles are utilized, they will have to be manipulated depending on the level of realism or naturalism desired. The tube is utilized here because it represents a cylinder at the two-dimensional level, and cylinders describe the major structures of the human body fairly well. It is recommended, however, not to focus too greatly on the three-dimensional aspects of the subject just yet. We want to be able to control the graphic nature of our subject and understand how our two-dimensional shape choices affect what our audience feels or is reminded of when looking at our work (see Figures 3.2 and 3.3).

Figure 3.1

Simple quick-sketch gesture drawing predominantly built with "tube" shapes.

Figure 3.2

A short-pose gesture drawing with value.

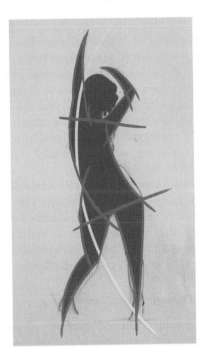

Figure 3.3

Positive/negative space breakdown using the silhouette and tube shapes with lines of action built into them.

We will be utilizing the following concepts during the development of Step 2:

- Line(s) of Action
- Rhythm
- Harmony
- Fluidity (as it relates to harmony and rhythm)

We can also utilize the following concepts from the Principles of Animation at this stage:

- Squash and Stretch
- Anticipation
- Arcs
- Secondary Action
- Exaggeration
- Appeal
- Solid drawing (of two-dimensional ideas and shapes at this stage)

Basic Technique: Step 2

Utilizing the initial lines laid in on paper, I complete the *protomannequin* by laying in additional line work that will turn those initial lines into tubes. Essentially, I drew one side of the (subjectively) most important structures of the figure during the initial abstract lay-in. My additional line work at this stage should complete those ideas, providing the other edge of the aforementioned structures. During this step, I may also incorporate any additional one-dimensional ideas that further support and embellish my Line(s) of Action from Step 1, but *only if I can ensure that any additional ideas do not lessen or otherwise negatively impact the power and visual clarity of my thesis statement/Big Idea.* (At no point should the story of the drawing be sacrificed for aesthetic purposes; instead, the goal is to make the aesthetic choices work for the story.) If necessary, I can choose to measure during this step, by using either the traditional head-unit measuring system or alignments. Because this drawing is still only two-dimensional, it is much easier to measure here using the idea of an *X* and *Y Axis* system, or a 180-degree horizontal and a plumb line. Once finished, I should end up with a two-dimensional Mannequin that retains not only the exaggeration of my initial 1D lay-in but also the proportions of my choosing, whether measured or manipulated with intent. Because prioritization is crucial to the organization of ideas in our drawings, there are a couple of variations on this basic technique that we must look at, dealing with the slight reshuffling of ideas from Steps 1 and 2 of our Breakdown.

Setting Up Geography/Placement

I may also set the geography or general placement of major landmarks/structures, without developing any volumetric forms (see Figure 3.4). The following front-view landmarks may be indicated at this stage (and if measuring is necessary, now is the time to do so):

A. *X*- and *Y*-Axes of the head/face and ears or ear line

B. Pit of Neck and Clavicle (if desired or appropriate, the Shoulder Line can temporarily double as the Clavicle, though if time is not an issue, the Clavicle should be addressed separately from the Shoulder Line)

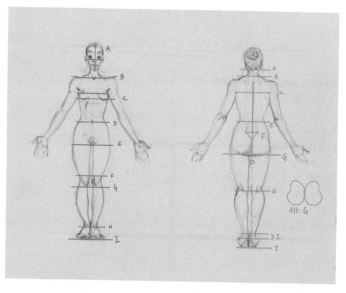

Figure 3.4

Landmarks on the body. You can use as many or as few as necessary to help with measurements/proportions.

3. Working with Shapes

C. Breast Line or Armpits (if necessary)
D. Belly Button
E. Crotch
F. Top of Knee (if necessary)
G. Bottom of Knee (if necessary)
H. Ankle
I. Bottom of Feet

Back View Landmarks
A. Hairline or Nape of Neck
B. Base of Neck (not always easily visible)
C. The Armpits (if necessary)
D. Spine
E. Waist (if necessary)
F. Sacrum
G. Gluteal Muscles (the bottom horizontal line created by the gluteus maximus, or the whole butterfly shape created by the Gluteus Medius and Gluteus Maximus)
H. Back of Knee (if necessary)
I. Ankle
J. Bottom of Foot

If locating landmarks on the body is for any reason difficult, search for vertices or corners instead; they are relatively fixed points in Positive and Negative space that may be used to assess distances and therefore help with setting up general geography/proportions.

The preceding list of Landmarks are not in order of priority; they are simply listed from top to bottom of a standing figure. Not all of the Landmarks listed are necessary; indeed, some of them are optional, but it is up to the individual to decide when and what information is important and/or necessary enough to place at this early stage. Keep in mind that it will be much more difficult to place volumetric forms while maintaining the integrity of the Line(s) of Action of the drawing later on, and any measuring necessary to place major structures will be easier while the drawing is flat or predominantly two-dimensional.

Concerning the Placement of the Head, Neck, and Shoulder Line

We can now further explore when best in our drawing to place this structure. Typically, I refer to these three ideas as a unit, and rarely do I lay in one without the others. There is also the option of placing the Head dead last (but still while in Step 2). Wherever in the process the head is placed, it should be somewhere within Step 1, Step 2, or in between. We want the graphic, two-dimensional shape of the head to be designed as well, and utilizing the eye and/or brow line and ear line, and the center front Y-Axis of the head while in a two-dimensional state will make it easier for us to place the structures and features of the face. If any measuring on the face is necessary, we can measure it at this stage along with any other measurements we need, keeping in mind to measure only if the pose is held long enough to adequately do so, if the proportions are not as accurate as you would like.

Demonstration

For this demo, the picture of Ashli that has been chosen is something more reminiscent of a character pose, rather than what we might find in a traditional classical figure-drawing session (see Figure 3.5). The challenges presented by this pose are a wonderful opportunity to explore how we might define our primary line of action and how to relate it to the supporting ideas of the limbs. In this pose, the entirety of the body is activated in such a way as to embody a character, and it lends itself well to embellishment, both contextual as well as within the body itself. Before I begin drawing a pose such as this, I take a moment to reflect on the silhouette of the subject. Disregarding any and all of the details, I immediately take note of any feelings or key words that float into my mind. Sometimes I even write those key words down, so that I may have a direction to take my study. In this case, I do feel an animalistic—perhaps even predatory—quality to the action: much like a cat raises its back in an arch to appear as large as possible, Ashli arches her upper torso and raises her arms in what could be described as an attack stance. We could even see this pose as an anticipatory pose before a lunge forward, an attack driven by the spring of the compressed, or recoiled, leg. There are different ways to feel this pose; my interpretations are just a few of many, and dependent on my point of view. Indeed, this pose may read differently if I were to see it from another angle. We will come back to interpretation and how it affects our choices in the next section of this chapter.

To decide on my primary line of action—that is, my Strongest Directional Force—I choose to use movement from the torso: because I feel that this pose feels spring-loaded and I anticipate an attack to follow immediately after this action of recoil, my primary line of action is a sweep backward and upward, from

Figure 3.5

Reference photo of Ashli.

Figure 3.6

Two-minute demo of reference image.

Figure 3.7

Primary line of action in light blue; shoulder and hip axes in light green; supporting *lines of action* in red; the purple lines complete the tube shapes begun by the supporting lines of action; the head appears in blue as a simple shape; microgestures in green provide flourishes to the action; and geography is indicated via orange cross-contour or otherwise arced lines.

the ball of the model's left foot, through the torso and out behind the ear (see Figures 3.6 and 3.7). In this case, my primary line of action can only be incorporated as a part of the structure of the upper torso. Note that the center front line of the torso would be an ineffective line of action, as it is nearly a straight vertical line from the crotch, through the belly button and up to the pit of the neck. While I can utilize the center front line for geography, I deem it unexciting for any other use. In drawing a pose this complex, I do not usually draw in a primary line of action; instead, I opt to incorporate it directly into the construction of some part of the torso. We will see other instances where the line of action is addressed in slightly different ways. This is also an instance of a pose where I deem it important to lay in the two-dimensional shape of the head first, to set the scale of the figure and to place the figure on the page so as to be mindful of composition and positive/negative space. So, while I may intake the entirety of the pose (the overall 2D silhouette) first, the first marks I actually put down on paper are those of the head, keeping it two-dimensional and dynamic. Note the curvature of the lines that make up the basic shape of the head. I next place the Shoulder line so that I know where to begin the torso; this is crucial at this point since I plan on using my primary line of action to construct the upper torso and use its direction to build my rhythms. I will construct the torso now as a flat, two-dimensional shape; in this case, it takes on the appearance of a triangle sweeping up from the crotch, since the hips are weighted in such a way as to pop the model's left hip out. This pop-out has been implied as movement within the shape of the torso. Once I have the triangle of the torso laid out, I can then move on to the supporting ideas of the limbs. I have prioritized thusly: Head, Neck (in this case, obscured but felt), Shoulder Line, Torso, Legs, Arms. It should be noted that the arms and legs in this case could be thought of as interchangeable in terms of importance; where I feel that the legs are a critical component of balance and the recoil I see implied, another person may deem the arms and hands as being more important than the legs due to the personality and character present in their actions and therefore place them earlier. I place the legs using the longest unbroken lines I see, so that I may begin to set up visual rhythm in two ways: large, sweeping rhythms, and smaller, bouncier, rhythms. The large rhythms are being picked out from the longest, unbroken lines in the forms, and the smaller rhythms are being picked out from shapes. Both legs are laid in with arcs of varying characteristics, and the knee of the model's left leg is implied by completing the arc in two strokes, with the resulting vertex where the knee would be. These sweeping lines of the legs include what will be the structures of the feet, included so as to not break the flow. The arms follow, using the same general guidelines of looking for the longest uninterrupted lines. The model's bent right arm is constructed with three lines: starting from the armpit, the first line sweeps upward in a slight arc toward the elbow; the second line of the forearm sweeps in an arc from the elbow to the wrist; and the third line sweeps in an arc from the wrist and follows the index finger outward. The index finger in this pose is interesting and points directly toward the face, an action that can be utilized to direct the viewer's attention. To finish constructing my tube shapes, I need only complete ideas with additional lines, since I have my preliminary construction halfway completed. These lines should further support the movement and rhythms already present so as to provide the structures with harmony and appeal. I complete the structures in order of priority: the torso is completed by providing the information of the pelvic structure; the legs are completed by providing the arcs of the bottom of

Figure 3.8

Comparison of silhouette of reference image versus demo drawing. I will often "see" real-life objects as flat, 2-dimensional images first when beginning the lay-in of a drawing. Controlling the graphic image will ultimately affect your final statement.

the model's left leg and the outside of the model's right, recoiled leg; the arms are completed in a similar fashion. When completing the legs, it should be noted that while the bottom arc of the model's left leg is drawn the same way as the upper part of that leg, the recoiled leg is approached a bit differently. While this leg may also be constructed as a simple tube shape, I find that particular approach to be too stiff for this pose. Instead, I opt to describe the remainder of the leg with more rhythmic arcs, constructing a B curve (you can choose to use any kind of curve or arc you feel is most appropriate for what you are trying to communicate) and overlapping those lines to imply what will be a foreshortened form. To embellish the hands, I may choose to lay in microgestures—that is, the implied movement of individual shapes found throughout the body. The shapes of the fingers in this case directly impact how I feel about this action and are therefore included in this quick sketch. Note, they were placed *after* the larger structures were addressed. I can now begin to lay in the position, or geography, of further structures, such as the breast line, belly button (here, laid in as a gestural line rather than a dot or hole), and the knee of the recoiled leg. I can furthermore separate out the graphic shape of the hair from the overall shape of the head. A note concerning Positive and Negative space: This is one of those poses in which Positive/Negative space can come in handy (see Figure 3.8). Here, I used it to gauge the distance between the legs and to understand the relative position of the hand for placement. When looking at hands and fingers, we can use negative space to gauge the movement and any foreshortening present.

Regarding Foreshortening

Because we are attempting to think only in terms of Two Dimensions at this stage, I flatten the image I am looking at in order to think in terms of X- and

Y-Axes, which allows me to gauge distance or how long something should be. This way of visualizing was useful in completing the preliminary structures of the arms and legs, which all contain varying degrees of foreshortening. The torso does contain compression and thus a minimal amount of foreshortening, though not enough to greatly impact my drawing in this iteration. From a stylistic or Tonal (as we've defined Tone for this text) standpoint, the drawing is Naturalistic, or idealized realism. In the proceeding section of this chapter, we will see how our choices may be impacted by implementing a higher degree of Exaggeration, and how our Tone is further refined by making choices based from a story point of view, in which we will address context, subtext, and character.

In Chapter 2 we looked at the effect of placing the Head, Neck, and Shoulder Line in Step 1, while in the one-dimensional state. Now we shall see what happens when we place this unit in Step 2.

After the lay-in of our initial line work in Step 1, we may proceed to place the Head shape in relation to our Primary (or only, if the case may be) line of action, or in relation to the supporting ideas. This depends on the pose, but typically the Head, Neck, and Shoulder Line tend to have a direct relationship with our Line(s) of Action; this is not always the case, however, and we must proceed with the placement of the head while keeping in mind our thesis statement. After we draw our two-dimensional head shape, we can then draw the two-dimensional representation of the neck. The aforementioned tube shape is particularly useful here, as the neck column can be most accurately described as a cylindrical form, and the 2D tube shape will allow us to control both the height and width of what will eventually be the neck. It is useful to follow up the neck shape with the shoulder line for multiple reasons: primarily, it defines the starting point of the torso and thus gives us the position of the head/neck in relation to the torso; it also gives us one of the strongest axes in the body, and later when dealing with costume or props it allows us to drape the figure. Furthermore, we can set the width of the torso—specifically, the upper torso—while working in Two-Dimensions, letting us control proportions at an early stage. After laying in the Head, Neck, and Shoulder Line, I may complete the two-dimensional structure of the torso by finding the end point: on a frontal standing figure, this end point is the crotch, and either a V or a horizontal line will suffice in marking off the end of the torso. I like to use a V, usually in conjunction with a horizontal line, simply because it lends itself well to the anatomy of the groin area on both male and female figures, and it is usually laid in at the starting or attachment point of the male genitalia (see Figure 3.9).

When completing the two-dimensional Mannequin, it is common to prioritize the order in which the figure will be developed. Ultimately, the order in which ideas are stated and completed is based entirely on the story being developed, on the thesis statement or Big Idea. For example, if the pose is one in which the head is partially or completely obscured, it may not be the most prudent choice to lay in the head so early on in Step 2. It may suit the artist to instead focus on the structures that matter more in that particular pose. If, however, the partially obscured head is a key element to the thesis statement, the artist may then choose to lay it in early on in Step 2 or even Step 1, as long as the introduction of a two-dimensional element in no way mars the integrity of the one-dimensional abstract lay-in or otherwise lessens any exaggeration being employed (see Figure 3.10).

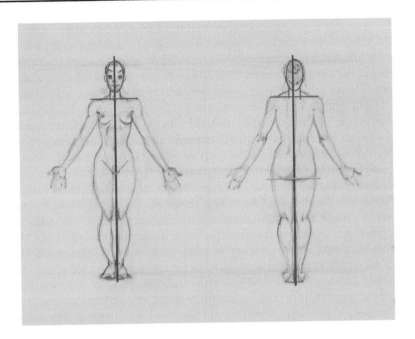

Figure 3.9

Vertical axis/plumb line running down figure in blue; head/neck/shoulder line in red; end of torso marked with "V" or horizontal line. These are quick tools for indication of start and end points of a torso which may aid one when "eyeballing" proportions during quick-sketch gesture drawing.

Figure 3.10

Figure with head obscured but felt.

My personal preference for the prioritization of structures tends to be as follows:

- Head, Neck, Shoulder Line
- Torso
- Legs (with feet)
- Arms (with hands)

This is merely a go-to prioritization and must change depending on the pose the model takes or what action or scenario the subject is undergoing or participating in. While developing these two-dimensional structures, you must also decide whether or not any measurement is necessary to complete the relative placement. You may choose to utilize your pencil as a horizontal or vertical axis to quickly note the alignments of structures, and mark off on your drawing key landmarks, such as the pit of the neck, the navel, the elbows, and knees. Alternatively, if the pose is long enough (such as 3–5 minutes), head unit measurement may be employed, though the speed and accuracy vary depending on the individual.

It should also be noted that the hands and feet have already been accounted for with the completion of the two-dimensional tubes noted above. Instead of drawing the figure piecemeal, we instead complete the ideas of *whole* structures, such as the whole torso, taking care not to separate the upper torso from the lower torso, nor separating the whole limbs into upper and lower sections. When drawing the limbs, we are drawing the whole limb as a two-dimensional shape, before we separate the upper sections from the lower sections, before separating the hands and feet, before developing the individual fingers and toes. We are developing *large ideas* first and gradually working our way toward smaller and smaller ideas. This is how we will control the drawing's rhythm and harmony.

Rhythm and Harmony

At this stage, we may begin to plan out the Rhythmic aspects of our drawing, which will help us establish the Harmonious flow of energy that will dictate the movement of the structures of our subject (see Figure 3.11). The anatomy of living

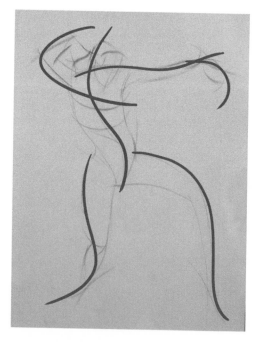

Figure 3.11

Major rhythms of the 2-minute demo.

3. Working with Shapes

creatures tends to naturally flow in what we generally consider an appealing or aesthetically pleasing way, and this is why S and C curves are used consistently to aid us in the construction of anatomical structures, helping us to provide the continuity we see in organic, living forms. The concepts of fluidity, rhythm, and harmony are not limited to only organic, animated matter but can also be applied to inorganic, inanimate objects and subjects as well. For the scope of this study guide, we will focus predominantly on organic, living subjects and, later, only the inorganic objects we typically see during life drawing, such as costuming, props, and any set pieces that convey environment, setting, or additional context to the story of our images. When thinking of how to apply rhythm and harmony to our drawing, we must first take into account our thesis statement, and the story we are striving to tell with our drawing. We must also think about how the Rhythmic and Harmonious choices we make ultimately impact the Tone and Mood of our piece.

We can begin to break down the rhythmic elements of our drawing at Step 1, while we are still only looking at one-dimensional ideas and the abstraction of our subject. The rhythm should be dictated by the thesis statement (though in some cases one may choose the Rhythm of a particular drawing to be the thesis statement itself). After we've decided on our Line(s) of Action and we are comfortable with moving on to the next step of our workflow, we can begin to design how our supporting ideas actually move on the paper. We can utilize S curves and C curves—as well as any necessary straight lines—to design our supporting ideas. We can also decide if any counter-rhythms are necessary and where they will be placed. Typically, it is visually pleasing to provide counter-rhythm in a drawing, as visual patterns can get a bit dry and boring if not occasionally broken or varied in some way. To achieve Rhythm, we are looking to create a pattern or chain of simple, one-dimensional ideas (line), with enough variation to keep the pattern from becoming droll and predictable.

Once we set the Rhythm of the piece, we can complete Step 2 utilizing whatever two-dimensional shapes we choose, striving to use our rhythmic line work to create those shapes. In this way, we are beginning to infuse our shapes with life, motion, and character. It should be noted that we can interpret Rhythm subjectively, and we can use the ideas of tempo from music to do so. It is a good idea to consider reinterpreting preconceived notions regarding visual communication and drawing through a different lens than one is used to. By using the analogy of music to describe visual Rhythm, we can explore different ways to feel what a drawing might look like. For example, we might describe the Rhythm of a particular drawing as Largo (very slow) or Allegro (brisk or lively). We can also slow or speed up parts of a drawing like we do in music, or even use the concept of the Fermata, which causes us to hold a note or pause (much like a moving hold, the Fermata's visual counterpart). Furthermore, we can affect Rhythm later on in the drawing by reinterpreting and utilizing the concept of Dynamic Markings as seen in sheet music; the individual characteristics of the marks we make can embody the concepts of *legato* or *staccato*, or the concepts of *forte* (Loud), *crescendo* (Growing Louder), and *diminuendo* (Growing Softer). We can see line variety as a means to communicate such abstract concepts. The Rhythm and rhythmic choices we make throughout the drawing process ultimately affect our statement—our story—and the Tone and Mood of that story. The accompanying life drawing was a 20-minute study using a Naturalistic/Realistic approach, meaning my level of exaggeration was downplayed, and instead I focused on more subtle, realistic rhythms and

Figure 3.12

Line quality and edges controlled so as to heighten the aesthetic quality of the drawing while not calling attention to the marks themselves.

utilized marks of different qualities and characteristics to loosen and soften edges and to tighten and crisp up others (see Figure 3.12). In this case, my tone—or attitude and subsequent approach—is an academic one, because I have completed this drawing with an academic mindset. It is much like writing an essay, in which the tone will be felt by the reader due to word choices and how those words have been put together (diction and grammar).

Once we've set the Rhythm of our drawing, we can then see whether we've begun to create harmony; if we have constructed our 2D shapes with rhythmic intentions and kept our major structures whole (instead of breaking them down into anatomical pieces), we can begin to see whether those structures are moving in such a way as to not only complement each other but also support our Big Idea/ thesis statement. At all stages of our drawing, we should continually check the flow of ideas and whether at any point that flow has been disrupted in any unintentional way. We will continue to address the concepts of rhythm and harmony throughout this study guide, in the later steps of our breakdown. As with most, if not all, of the concepts explored throughout this study guide, we can employ any level of exaggeration and appeal we like to Rhythm.

How our rhythmic choices affect the tone of our drawing

The tone of our drawing will usually reflect our attitude as creators toward our particular subject. *Our attitude toward our subject is reflected by the choices we make at all stages of the development of an image.* The Rhythm we see in our subject and how we interpret it will affect the way the architecture of our subject moves on paper. This is part of the *how* of our interpretation of the action of our subject: the *how* will also give us clues as to what kind of acting—if any—we must incorporate into our drawing. For example, if one develops the primitive architecture of a drawing to reflect the concept of staccato, we can expect the Tone to be sharp, whereas a drawing utilizing the concept of largo might feel more languid or relaxed in tone (see Figure 3.13). We will see Tone be impacted further by the two-dimensional shape language we employ in Step 2. If we choose to develop the concept of staccato, we will not only utilize a Rhythm or bounce of energy that indicates this at the one-dimensional level but also utilize two-dimensional shapes that give us the idea of *stunted* or *sharp*, or *punctuated*. We could exaggerate that idea even further and affect the proportions of the figure as well so as to visually relay that message in an even clearer manner. If dealing with *punctuated* and *sharp*, shapes with vertices such as triangles and squares/rectangles may more precisely indicate this idea than, say, a circle. (So, instead of using *tubes* to develop the architecture of what will be our mannequin figure, we may use squares/rectangles, though at this stage those shapes look very similar.)

Mood may be influenced at this stage as well, though it may remain more abstract than in later developmental stages of a drawing or composition. To develop Mood this early on, we think about the context of our subject. This will also impact the thesis statement and the story of our drawing. To develop context, we may ask ourselves the following questions during a figure-drawing session, the answers to which will inform the decisions we make throughout our entire drawing process:

- Is the model acting while holding the pose? How does this impact the story or your interpretation of your subject?
- Can you imagine the model in a story-driven scenario, and whether this scenario is character-driven or event-driven?
- Can you imagine the pose in sequence? Where in this sequence does this pose belong?

Figure 3.13

Drawing while under the influence of candy.

We can also utilize subtext to further inform and/or enhance our choices:

- What do you think the Model is thinking of or feeling while performing a particular action or pose?
- What do *you* feel when looking at your subject?

By constantly asking questions during drawing, we can think and feel our way through our workflow, ensuring that our choices are driven by emotional resonance, which will ultimately be reflected in the drawing as Tone and Mood. We may ask ourselves the above questions at all stages of the development of a drawing.

Explorations in Story with Shape and Gesture

Now let's look at ways to explore the demo photograph. My concern with the next set of explorations is no longer merely directly replicating what I see; my focus in this case is no longer only academic (i.e., drawings that attempt to realistically communicate a subject completed for the express purpose of developing technical draftsmanship). Instead, my goal is to practice ideas used in storytelling in conjunction with concepts from visual communication. I am now using the tools from drawing to practice telling a story via quick-sketch drawings focused predominantly on gesture. The academic purpose of this kind of practice is to become more illustrative in everyday drawing; it is imperative to think critically while practicing both disciplines of drawing and storytelling. Why not practice both simultaneously in order to become more confident in complex, creative problem-solving and provide oneself with multiple challenges? When practicing drawing with story-driven motives, one should not necessarily be concerned with *good* or *bad*; rather, one should choose to free oneself of preconceived notions of what constitutes a good or bad drawing. At the end of the day, a good drawing is really just one that successfully communicates an idea utilizing a visual language. We stumble and make mistakes using verbal language every day, and the more we read and write, the better we become at verbal communication. The same concept holds true for drawing and visual communication: we must make mistakes and explore ideas freely in order to learn what works and what doesn't. story is something that comes naturally to most of us, even if we don't necessarily realize it; we need only to realize how we already approach it, what the different components of story are, and how we might better understand them in order to improve how we visually communicate with other people. Now is our chance to start putting the puzzle pieces together and see the different ways we might begin to incorporate story ideas into our figurative work.

Demonstration

For this demo, I will be utilizing the same picture of Ashli provided earlier in this chapter. As previously stated, my initial interpretation of this action is *animalistic*. In fact, I feel as though this may be a humanlike or anthropomorphic creature stalking her prey. I still want her to feel feminine, but perhaps reptilian. A lot of this is due to the fact that I talk to my models and learn about them as people, not just professionals for learning observational drawing skills. I do not feel that I can properly study a model unless I see them talk, move, or otherwise express themselves; if I don't know what they look like while moving in space, I will not understand how they use their whole bodies and anatomy to communicate different ideas and the complex relationship between actions, body language, and personality/character/emotion. Without this context, I feel as though I only have half of my toolset available; I only have my tools for visual communication and drawing but not my tools for creating an idea that is more than just the sum of its parts. My intention for every drawing is to feel some kind of emotional truth about my subject. That is the essence of story: it is the emotional truth behind every experience. In this case, because I have drawn Ashli before with her bearded dragon Mango, and I am aware of her professional studies in Biology, I naturally associate her with nature and animals, reptiles in particular. I appreciate her fondness for cold-blooded creatures. This association is what drives the following choices; all of my choices will be made with the intention of communicating that initial context: reptilian.

My focuses for this particular study are the following: Movement + Shape. Within these two focuses are subtopics that must be dealt with in order for me to organize ideas within this drawing that maintain consistency—or harmony, if you prefer. I want to choose Shapes that will work with the characterization I have in mind of Ashli while in this particular pose, but while being aware of the action of the pose itself and what context/subtext the action is telling me. The resulting study is presented threefold: the first image is the pencil drawing (with yellow marker lay-in) itself; the next is the Shape breakdown; followed by the movement breakdown (see Figures 3.14 through 3.16).

While I do think in terms of movement/gesture first at all times, I do consider the graphic shape of the silhouette before I lay in any mark, as I tend to

Figure 3.14

Stylized character sketch of reference image.

Figure 3.15

Line of action and shape analysis.

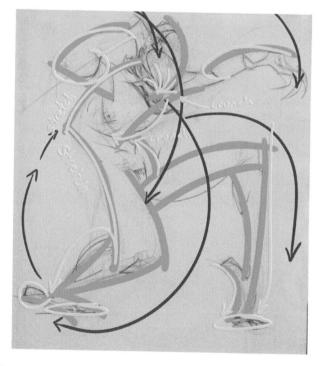

Figure 3.16

Squash and stretch and movement analysis.

find ideas of how to relate movement in different areas of the body to each other by using the silhouette and positive/negative space itself. This is an example of working from Large to Small ideas. The whole should be considered first, before being concerned with consecutively smaller and smaller ideas.

Let's look at the Shape breakdown first. The silhouette has been laid in graphically in purple. Apart from the exaggeration of the action and exaggerated stylization of shape/concept, the pose has been changed from that of the reference photo. There are a couple of reasons for this. I want to keep the arms raised in that type of action, but I realize that certain areas may not read the way I want them to in silhouette. Namely, these areas are Ashli's right hand and right leg. I don't necessarily want all the negative space between the fingers, and I realize that for clarity, another solution would be to place the hands well above the head entirely, but I feel that particular choice may not result in the whole of the silhouette reading the way I want it to (I want a lot of crunchy compression in this action). Because I want to capture my initial reaction to this character, I don't want to overthink it—as it may result in my energy being dampened—but I also want to avoid being lazy in my problem-solving, so I choose instead to overlap the right hand over the head, with the gestures of the fingers pointing directly to the face. While it is not the only solution, it does what I need it to for this initial exploratory sketch. The same problem is presented by the right compressed leg; because of the position it is in, the crunch or compression of that leg is not as clear as it could be when seen in silhouette. Therefore, I will opt to reorientated the leg, so that the center front line of that leg now faces the viewer's right, rather than head on (I orientated the leg from a front view to a three-quarter front view). This is one way I'm using the graphic Shape of the silhouette. I'm using Exaggeration in conjunction with this idea to develop readability. I'm also using the graphic shape of the silhouette to decide upon one dominant directional force, or primary line of action. This is represented by the solid red line running through the entirety of the figure; the whole figure will be based on the compression of the action and will therefore be exaggerated to support that idea. The green line represents the overlying rhythm of the pose. This is based on the crunchiness of my assessment of the pose as I see it in the silhouette, plus the attack/pounce quality I see. Before moving on to the shape ideas I will be using to build the structures of the body, let's look at the movement breakdown, as I consider those ideas to be larger and more important than the individual structures of the figure.

The movement breakdown represents ideas of the energy flow present in this action and the attempt to capture and reinterpret them so as to support my Reptilian characterization of Ashli. The yellow lines represent areas where I apply squash and stretch to my masses. This is not necessarily planned out in advance; because we normally execute gesture drawings during quick-sketch or short-pose sessions, we are limited to the amount of planning we can complete. So, while I am thinking of where I want to add compression and stretch, I will build it into my shapes as much as possible, especially because squash and stretch directly affect mass and volume. While I am not necessarily worried about volume at the moment (since I'm not focusing on three-dimensional ideas specifically for this study and merely want to imply them where necessary), Shape represents mass; therefore, I cannot ignore the effect of compression on my shapes. This is in part why this demo happens to include a marker lay-in: while I don't always lay in the one-dimensional (linear) gestural analysis (at least not in bright permanent media), I find it helpful when I'm creating an exploratory drawing—that is, one in which

I am not entirely sure of the character or story that I'm working on, but I have some inkling of an idea and want to find the character as I draw (or in this case, in my Shapes). Because this study is based on exploring the relationship between Shape choices and character/personality/narrative, I don't want to risk losing the gesture while I experiment or find my way through those Shapes. So, to avoid losing energy flow or, in this case, a guide as to where squash and stretch may be placed, I have opted to complete a gestural lay-in in yellow marker (it may not be easily visible in the pencil drawing, but that's the point). This method of using a gestural lay-in for a short-pose drawing is quite handy for those still practicing the organization of ideas in drawing within a limited time frame or for those interested in exploratory drawing (where one goes into the session or each pose with no predetermined ideas). The orange and deep blue lines represent the arcs I have used in this study: the orange lines are the arcs that make up the major rhythms of the Shapes used and follow an S or C curve and, where I deem necessary or interesting, a straight line. These rhythms are thought of during the initial gestural lay-in (the yellow marker lines beneath the color pencil) and during my Shape construction pass. The arcs all have some degree of exaggeration, and appeal—none of them move in such a way as to disrupt the energy flow. The deep blue lines represent the possible range of motion of this pose: I am imagining the arcs that make up the path of the motion of the arms/hands and the legs/feet, in addition to a possible arc of movement of the torso. I am thinking not of a possible anticipatory pose for this action, but rather an *anticipatory motion*. This is related to the primary line of action.

Now that we've looked at the larger ideas represented by this character exploration, let's look at smaller, structural ideas and how they relate to the larger ideas mentioned. In this study, I have utilized the concept of laying in large structures as graphic tube shapes; this is an example of how a flat tube (which is a cylinder without the top and bottom, and therefore no circumference/volume) looks nearly identical to a rectangular shape. This is why during the early stages of a drawing you have a chance to consider what types of shapes you want to use and in what configuration. While thinking of those flat shapes, I decided to play up geometric angles and vertices, while downplaying organic, gooey, soft shapes. I want just a little bit of goo in this study because I find that idea humorous and appealing, but in terms of amount, there should be more sharp angles and vertices than rounded gooey shapes. I am choosing to play up geometric ideas and vertices because I want this character to feel a bit predatory. My initial response to the action was, "That looks like a predator ready to pounce or grab their prey"; as a result, all of my choices up to now have been made in an attempt to support that specific thesis statement. My shapes should read as threatening but not scary. My limbs are constructed knowing that the anatomy will be based on a bipedal, humanlike frame, so proportions haven't been affected too greatly. (I'm also opting to keep to fairly naturalistic proportions instead of playing with them too much, simply because I'm more interested in the idea of Movement + Shape.) To keep the figure slightly gooey and goofy, I'm opting to include rounded ideas in my sharp shapes: while my figure is predominantly made up of squares and triangles, I have included enough round shapes to allow for a humorous squash in parts of the anatomy. At the moment, I am not sure whether or not this character is a straightforward villain—there are enough sharp ideas to make this an acceptable identity—or if the character has merely taken on this temporary expression due to the action they are currently involved in—say, she is only preparing to pounce on her next meal because she needs to eat, as do we all, but her inherent nature is not necessarily *villainous* nor *bad/evil*. This is one function of an exploratory drawing: it allows us the freedom to explore character and its relation to the many choices we face when deciding to put our next mark on paper. To continue with this exploration and to see how we may extend our study of story based off a preliminary, exploratory sketch, we will next look at examples of the types of drawings we may follow up with this study.

The next set of sketches are a continued exploration of expression of movement and personality of the character we have just created with the exploratory sketch. At this point, I am no longer working with a photo reference, and I'm not necessarily concerned too much with the quality of drawing but rather expressiveness. This is also why for these sketches I have opted to use an ink pen; it allows me freedom for detail, but controls the number of marks I can make on paper due to its permanence, which means that I must subconsciously consider the necessity of each mark before it is put to paper. Ideally, working with permanent media keeps me from hay-stacking by accident than by stylistic choice. These sketches are loose, and again, my primary focus is movement and its relation to character and narrative contexts.

Why Am I Including these Character Studies Here, Even though they Are No Longer Based on Observation?

These studies are an example of the types of doodles I might do during a life-drawing session while the model is on break, or immediately following a pose. I often find myself doodling margin notes of this type when I'm studying characters/narrative from life; it helps me understand the story ideas I'm attempting to develop in such a limited time frame, and my intention is to use these character/story notes in conjunction with my drawings from the session for possible application in the future. This is why we take notes while studying; why we annotate while reading; why we jot things down in general: so we may remember certain ideas for possible future development and use. Because now we are dealing with Visual Communication, the notes that I'm jotting down are predominantly visual in nature. In addition to doodling, I will oftentimes include bits of the character's imaginary dialog, or if the model happens to say something while modeling that strikes me as revelatory or relevant to the character, I will jot that down, too. Key words can come in quite handy as well, and their advantage is that they can be jotted down quickly, spontaneously coming from one's gut reaction. For those who are not comfortable with verbal vocabulary, in lieu of key words, onomatopoeia functions fantastically.

We see my initial exploratory personality sketches in the first page of the next set of studies (see Figure 3.17).

I'm still mostly trying to stay on model but allowing myself to exaggerate as much as possible so as to make ideas clear. It is on this page that I decide to give this character more reptilian features, borrowing the idea of a tail, head crests, and further spiky embellishments reminiscent of iguanas and other reptiles. I definitely have a little bit of Ashli's bearded dragon Mango popping up here and there, and instead of questioning those ideas, I'm letting them show up on my paper. I won't know if it's a good idea or a bad idea until I physically see it in front of me, and these sketches are executed so quickly that it doesn't cost me too much time or effort. Preconceived notions of what is good or bad will only slow me down if I question everything for this type of study; I'm practicing brainstorming in this case. I like the idea of a tail for this character because I see the possible

Figure 3.17

Character doodles.

ways one might apply the ideas of Follow-Through and Overlapping Action if this character were animated, and the idea of using it almost as a secondary character is very appealing. The tail in and of itself could be designed as a character full of its own mischievous appeal, and could potentially act autonomously, make its own choices, etc. If so, instead of describing its actions as secondary actions that support the primary action/pose of the character, the tail's secondary actions may in fact be REactions to the body. This presents possibilities for visual gags and jokes, which would be an excellent opportunity for pantomime. This is an example of how quickly one may use a simple exploratory life drawing as a spring board for myriad storytelling possibilities.

The second page of these character studies further explores possible range of motion, exaggeration, and full body expressions of this character (see Figure 3.18).

I am still concerned with Movement + Shape; however, I'm allowing myself freedom of exaggeration. This can be seen in the *lines of action* used to describe the major movements of the character. I have gone so far with these quick pen sketches as to begin imagining possible sequence. Moving down the page clockwise and starting at approximately one o'clock, I have sketched the figure as imagined in midjump, possibly in the process of throwing a spear. Below it are tiny silhouette sketches of different actions, exploring the primary line of action in each, and how the tail might appear. There are sketches of the character in both a crouching position (based on a downward dog position from yoga) and the follow-through to upward-facing dog. Next to those are quick little notes exploring what that character's jump and pounce on prey might look like, followed by a dynamic sketch of the character's figure. While on the surface they don't look like much, they are necessary for understanding what ideas one might want to work

Figure 3.18

Further exploratory character doodles.

with as far as developing a character's personality and the subsequent expression of their body. Body movement and how one chooses to physically emote are based on personality, character, mood, and circumstance.

Continuing with this idea, I cap off this preliminary character study with a third page in this study, this time choosing to quickly sketch a short narrative-infused picture (see Figure 3.19).

This is what would be considered more of a brainstorm illustration, where I'm actually trying to develop some kind of simple story on the page, while still

Figure 3.19

Character/narrative context sketch. It's oftentimes a lot of fun to create these types of sketches after a life-drawing session. What kinds of stories might you envision?

utilizing the same ideas and tools that I utilized during the observation-based sketch. I'm still predominantly thinking in terms of Movement + Shape, but now I'm wondering how to further explore the character as an individual. Based on some of the exaggerated ideas from the previous pages, my attitude (Tone) toward the character has changed, though I'm still predominantly using the same vertex-heavy shapes (boxes and triangles) in conjunction with arcs and enough rounded ideas to describe thicker, meatier parts of the anatomy. I still want a little bit of a crunchy feel to this character, but I want to pump up the appeal a little bit so I'm mindful of my shape relationships. This is why exploration is so important while practicing ways to experience, understand, and create narrative. We won't know *our* particular attitude toward the character until we have experienced that character in more thorough scenarios. It was while exploring this character via quick little doodles that I realized Reptile Ashli is humorous. This attitude or Tone I have as a creator is influenced by a few different factors and may be described mathematically in a way: How I Know Ashli as a Person + The Action (Pose) Ashli Uses + My Initial Response to the Action (Pose) + Exploration + My Sense of Humor. In this case, my own sense of humor comes out in a lot of these sketches, as is evident by including breasts in the design of Reptilian Ashli, even though reptiles do not have mammary glands; we as creators always come out in the work in some way. In some cases, it's obvious (as it is here); in others, it's subdued. This is why we must work with the ideas of Tone and Mood; we should understand how much of us is showing up in our work and how. It is part of the creation process. This particular drawing is a result of those factors: I am fully aware that a lot of this expression is coming from me directly rather than the model, but that's the point. Let's pick apart this little doodle a bit: we see Reptile Ashli (no, she doesn't have a name yet, but while you create characters, you can keep a name in mind if it helps you) coolly sipping a martini while lounging on her heat rock. Around her are the little insects that are her dinner. I am imagining this character as living in a glass reptile aquarium/cage. She's pretty comfortable in her life and appears to be content; there's a warm lamp above her and all the bugs she could ever want. She doesn't live in the wild, so she wouldn't really have a reason to be too predatory. Reptile Ashli can relax and enjoy the finer things in life, while her tail skewers her dinner. I imagine her as possibly having one little insect friend; maybe he/she is really smart, or funny, or otherwise worth not turning into a midnight snack. I'm borrowing a little bit from Ashli's real-life pet bearded dragon Mango for this sketch. My students and I are fortunate enough to have models come in with their animal friends for additional studies during life drawing, and this is why it's so enriching: we can use the relationships between humans and their animal friends as well as characteristics/personality traits of the animals themselves to influence us while we draw. So, instead of merely taking note of proportional and anatomical differences between species as we would when we are studying life drawing academically, we are going a bit further and annotating personality traits and individual characteristics as well. My previous studies of Ashli and Mango are predominantly what informed me while sketching this idea out. Mango is a funny little guy. Yes, we project on animals. Why not use it to our advantage while drawing, even if only for the sake of exploration?

Why Am I Including this Type of Illustration-based Study?

Perhaps I will develop a full story idea from this concept and proceed to brainstorming story and plot, followed by additional supporting characters, which in turn will be visually developed, or perhaps I will only use this for a single finished illustration; perhaps I'll keep it in my files for future reference, or let it appear in another form, possibly combined with other ideas. There are many possibilities for application when utilizing life drawing to practice story; these are just a few. Again, the goal of life drawing is not always to study what one sees in terms of academic goals to improve draftsmanship. Yes, that is crucial and necessary for adequate visual communication, but we must also learn to see beyond what our own two eyes record. This is part of creating ideas with emotional resonance that our audience can relate to. We are essentially filing away not just visual ideas but visual ideas with some kind of narrative, story, or character notes built into them for experience, mileage, and potential future use. Much like we collect reference material for the refinement of strictly technical visual ideas, we are now putting together our own story reference material.

The following sketch is a reassessment of the reference pic (see Figure 3.20):

Included at the top left corner are key words that I jotted down quickly before proceeding to sketch this reimagined iteration. Again, my focus is predominantly on Movement + Shape, and I'm keeping in mind the overall graphic idea of the silhouette, positive and negative space, line of action, and using tube shapes to begin constructing my masses. I'm not necessarily worried about developing three-dimensional volume, but I am using overlapping shapes to imply anatomy and foreshortening where necessary. I'm not using cylinders as I would if I were intending on thinking of this character in the round. Instead, I am focusing on using shapes that are squishy, round, organic, soft, and appealing. This pose is no longer predatory in nature but cute and playful, and ever so slightly flirty and

Figure 3.20

Alternate character sketch.

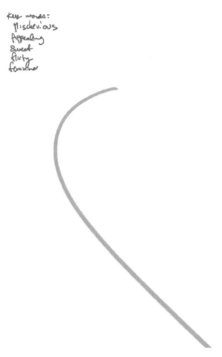

Figure 3.21

primary line of action.

mischievous. I still have vertices, but I no longer need as many sharp ideas, and the crunchiness has been minimized to more of a sashay. Included are the passes as layers: the first layer to go down is the primary line of action (which I'm leaving as the only line of action in this sketch) in yellow ochre (see Figure 3.21).

The second layer to do go down is the Rhythm layer, which is built up from the line of action (I use very swirly, bouncy shapes to develop this layer) in green, with the abstraction of motion of the arms and legs in yellow ochre (one could argue that they are in fact supporting lines of action; I include them here to remind myself of the larger ideas present) (see Figure 3.22).

The third layer down is the *tube* layer (as opposed to rectangles from earlier, since now I want more round shapes than pointy ones) in yellow (see Figure 3.23). Note the discrepancies between the yellow tube layer and the green rhythm layer: during the lay-in of the rhythms, I decided to restructure the silhouette slightly to pull the hand away from the face. In this case, I wanted to make greater use of the positive and negative space present to keep from obscuring the face, since I want to draw the expression and make the silhouette read a bit more clearly.

The following little painting is included here to show how we may utilize Movement + Shape + Mixed Media to create a character from life during a predominantly short to medium pose length session (see Figure 3.24).

This watercolor sketch was created during a Sugar Plum Fairy–themed life-drawing workshop where the models came dressed as different faeries, complete with props. This is another case in which the character was developed with very specific ideas in mind: I was explicitly concerned with the ideas of *cute, cuddly, adorable, round, doll-like,* and *sweet.* Using these ideas as the basis for my

Figure 3.22

Supporting ideas and rhythm of figure.

Figure 3.23

"Tube" layer; part of the "internal construction" of a drawing.

Figure 3.24

Simple tube shapes and circles make up the majority of this study. Simple shapes make it easier to work fast, allowing one to reserve time for color, value, texture, or any other finishing techniques. Do you ever reserve time in a pose for such explorations?

approach, I chose a medium that I felt best reflected these ideas; the end result was a watercolor sketch based predominantly on simple, tapered tubular constructs. There really is no volume nor three-dimensional structure in the lay-in drawing; it has been developed entirely out of Shape alone. Any impression of volume has been painted directly onto the tube shapes that make up the initial lay-in. This is a case of how Tone and Mood have started to be developed using movement, rhythm, shape, and mixed media, as well as being an example of being able to *finish* a drawing using only lines of action, Rhythm, and Shape.

Study Questions

The cartoon is my preferred method of communication as I use that medium to think, and I find that I express myself most adequately through it. Knowing this about myself helps me understand what kinds of choices I automatically make versus the kinds of choices I might otherwise make if using a different style of communicating. This allows me to push and pull a drawing with different stylistic choices and approaches and to experiment with choices that are not my normal way of doing things. This in turn allows me to broaden my own personal styles and techniques, and it positively impacts my learning outcomes. *How do you prefer to think? Realistically or in Cartoon? Do you make the same choices each time you draw? What other styles have you come across that you would like to experiment with?*

Exercises

Warm-Up Drills: You may recognize these drills from a previous chapter. It is generally a good idea to reinforce finding the line of action during observational drawing from time to time, or if it is something that is central to the kind of work that you do or are interested in, it is advisable to do it often.

Ten-Second Line of Action Sketches: Draw the Dominant Directional Force line of the subject. You are only drawing one line (one one-dimensional idea).

Thirty-Second Line of Action Sketches: Draw not only the Dominant Directional Force line of the subject but also decide on whether any supporting ideas call to you or are important enough to be laid in. Lay in the Dominant Direction Force line first, then lay in additional supporting ideas while working only with lines (one-dimensional ideas).

One- to Two-Minute Poses: Begin to develop your two-dimensional *protomannequin*. Begin with one-dimensional, linear ideas and move into two-dimensional ideas. You may use primitive shapes here when necessary, choosing shapes and graphic ideas with intent.

Three- to Four-Minute Poses: Same basic technique as before, but now begin to question the *context* of your subject. Alternatively, you may explore the *subtext* of your subject (which can be seen in minor actions such as facial, hand, or feet expressions). How does either context or subject affect your choices at this stage? Explore how your choices and priorities are affected by thinking of these two concepts so early on in the drawing process. *Tip:* Think of the *who, what, where, when, why,* and *how* of your subject. What comes to mind?

Pastiche Exercise Focusing Predominantly on Shape: Another fun and challenging exercise is the Pastiche, where the goal is to imitate another artist, style, genre, etc. It can be executed in any discipline or medium. For example, some readers may have already done a pastiche in an English class, having perhaps written a poem, short story, or essay imitating another writer. The Pastiche is a great method of self-motivated study, as it can be used in conjunction with any lesson plans or classes to more fully explore concepts, in addition to serving as an imaginative and creative problem-solving exercise. It is highly encouraged to do many master copies and Pastiche works to more intimately explore visual ideas.

General Method

1. Begin by deciding which concept you will be focusing on. In this case, because this chapter concerns itself with thinking in terms of Shape + Gesture, this exercise may be executed with the study of Shape in mind. This is your learning objective.

2. Once you have an idea of what the focus of the study will be, find an artist you admire who masterfully executes that particular concept in their work. This will require you to really pay attention to the artists you admire and figure out just what it is about their work that appeals to you. So, if continuing with the focus of Shape, find an artist who understands how to use shape to successfully visually communicate different ideas. This may mean that you look at Graphic Designers, or Cartoonists; you could even look at Old Master paintings and begin to analyze how they've used Shape in their work.

3. After you have selected at least one artist to look at for this study (you could choose more if you like and compare and contrast them against each other), proceed with completing Master Copies. When assigning Master Copies for Pastiche assignments in-class, I will usually ask the students to complete as many Master Copies of their selected artist as is possible during the week for homework. The idea is that you should get a fairly large cross section of their work and see how they've used concepts to complete different visual ideas. Taking notes is often recommended as well, and they needn't be legible to anyone but you.

4. Once you have completed as adequate a number of Master Copies as you think you need—keeping in mind that individually everyone may need a different amount—complete a life-drawing session *entirely in that master's style*. The goal is to attempt to problem solve using concepts in a way you imagine your selected Master would. The challenge is twofold: you must quickly analyze what your subject matter is as well as interpret it through a filter or lens that is not your own; you are attempting to see the world the way another artist would. This will ideally result in creating work that you might not normally do and gaining a greater understanding of different ways to observe, analyze, interpret, and relay visual information. If an actual live, nude model is not available to you,

Figure 3.25

A character page using simple shapes due to the quick-sketch format of the drawing session.

opt instead to use online resources for photo reference. There are a great many reference resources on the Internet, and many are available at no charge. Alternatively, if direct observation is strongly needed or desired, ask a friend or relative to pose for you; even if that person cannot perform nude or dynamically enough, at least you will have the benefit of studying real three-dimensional forms in space and translating them to a two-dimensional picture plane—with the additional challenge of completing a Pastiche. The translation alone is worth annoying someone, and if no person is available, you can always opt for animals, vehicles, objects, etc. You could even watch a movie and pause it when your favorite characters come on screen and complete the assignment that way.

Master copies are recommended with use of this study guide, as they are one of the most insightful tools artists have at their disposal, especially if classes or instruction are not so readily available to the reader.

Figure 3.25 shows character drawings focused on using simple shapes for ease of sketching during a short amount of time.

4

Using Cylinders and Exploring Shape

At this developmental stage of our mannequin, we can focus on building the general volumes of our figure (see Figure 4.1). Step 3 in our workflow deals with building cylindrical three-dimensional forms from our two-dimensional tubes in Step 2. Step 3 can be thought of as a half step or a transitional step; it can be completed either toward the end of Step 2 (while working with two-dimensional shapes) or at the beginning of Step 4, when we more fully realize our three-dimensional structures.

The development of cylindrical forms is included here as its own step only because the translation of three-dimensional space to a two-dimensional picture plane does not always come so easily to artists with less mileage, and Step 3 is presented for those who may need to take their time with this translation. The reader should decide for themselves whether Step 3 can be blended into either the preceding step, the following step (Step 4), or both; or whether additional care should be taken in developing depth (or z-space) in their figure. In terms of the concepts utilized during this step, because our cylindrical forms are entirely dependent on the previous step and may even be developed as part of Steps 2 or 4, the concepts from either Step 2 (the previous chapter) or Step 4 (the following chapter) may be applied here.

Basic Technique: Step 3

Utilizing the two-dimensional tubes from Step 2, we will add cross contour lines, and, if necessary, the elliptical or otherwise circular tops and bottoms to create cylinders that retain not only the gestural information set up back in Step 1 but will

Figure 4.1

A quick-sketch figure. Tubes and cylinders were the predominant shape/form ideas utilized.

also reflect the general volume and perspective of the major, primitive structures of the figure. It is not necessary to utilize cylindrical forms here. If one so chooses, one may utilize rectangular forms instead, or if the tubes from Step 2 have been tapered, one may even describe these primitive three-dimensional forms as *cones*. We use these basic 3D forms to aid ourselves in developing the depth necessary to communicate z-space, and the cross contour lines aid us in understanding the perspective and volume of not only the whole figure but also parts of the figure as well. Additionally, this step gives us the opportunity to double-check proportions, both height (Y-Axis) and width (X-Axis) (see Figure 4.2). Furthermore, if utilizing a particular gesture drawing as a Lay-In for a more finished purpose (such as a rendered figure drawing, painting, or otherwise fully realized composition), we may check the depth relationship of our figure to other figures, set pieces, environments, props, etc. present in our composition.

This is also an opportunity to add the demarcation of the joints. Because joints are not always the most important landmarks, depending on the pose of the figure being developed, they may be lower in the list of priorities than other, more structurally—and universally recognized—critical landmarks. If we are utilizing cylindrical forms to develop our mannequin, we may use the elliptical gesture of a cylindrical cross section to mark off the major joints of the limbs, such as the following:

1. The Armpit
2. The Eye of the Elbow (inside arm)
3. The Elbow (outside arm)

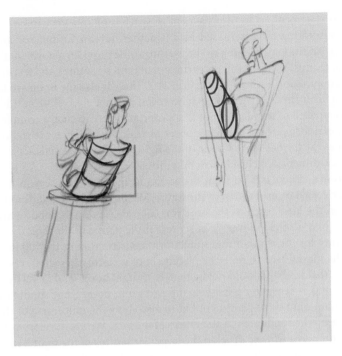

Figure 4.2

X- and Y-axes and cylinders can be used to quickly gauge foreshortened limbs or features present in a figure during quick-sketch gesture drawing.

4. The Wrist
5. The Knees
6. The Ankles

Because at this point the figure is still predominantly two-dimensional in nature, we may measure if necessary. Again, the proportions of the final figure do not have to be based in reality if this is the artist's intention. When marking off joints, we are using smaller microgestures that are inherent to the structures making them; we are looking at the movement inherently present in the three-dimensional, volumetric forms we see before us. In effect, we are creating cylindrical forms simply by marking off the joints of the figure. In turn, we can even incorporate these microgestures into the *rhythm* being developed in the drawing, as small flourishes to enrich our song or story being told.

Heads, Hands, and Feet

At this stage, we may also continue the development of hands and feet. Up until now, they have been only loosely laid in—as is the case with the head—or loosely indicated, as with the hands and feet. To continue the development of the head at this stage, we must begin to apply three-dimensional ideas to the previously laid-in shape. The Eye Line (and/or Brow Line if being utilized) should have a definite 3D direction to it; that is, it should describe the elliptical cross contour of a cylinder, giving us direction in 3D space. In fact, the Eye/Brow Line may be laid in with cylindrical perspective as early as Step 1, or whenever the artist first lays in the two-dimensional head shape. Doing this early on will aid in developing the thesis statement, as head placement in space is often a very important facet of communicating a figure-based idea (whether human, animal, or anthropomorphic). Additionally, laying in the eye/brow line provides a horizontal axis for the head, aiding in the overall construction of both structures and features when used in conjunction with a y- or vertical axis. There is also the option to lay in the head as a 3D form as early as Step 1; however, it is not always the best idea—the reader is advised to decide when it is appropriate to lay in such a complex three-dimensional form. There are some poses in which it makes sense to do so, and sometimes the flow or story we see in the figure may even be dependent on placing a three-dimensional head form first thing (see Figure 4.3).

As always, it depends on what the action is, the story one sees in it, and the characterization or expression of the figure. We may also place additional information on the head, such as the nose line, muzzle (optional), mouth, and mandible. We may also lay in lines that represent the planes of the face, creating the architecture for the three-dimensional form construction in the following step. Again, the marks used to note the placement of such features should be *gestural* in nature; that is, they should not be merely straight horizontal or vertical marks (unless it makes sense to do so given the particular pose). They should rather be drawn to not only show placement but to also show the movement of the forms that make up the fundamental structures of the face. We are developing the head and face the same way we develop the larger structures of the figure: in an organized manner, moving from large ideas to small ideas, holding off on detail until we deem it appropriate to think in terms of the smallest parts. While the facial

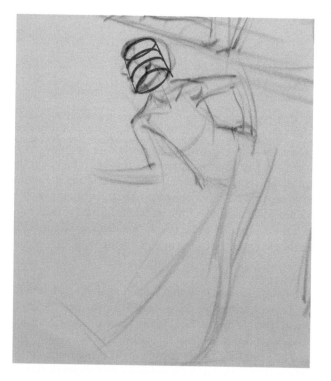

Figure 4.3

The head was laid in early on using a cylindrical base form to capture the tilt present.

4. Using Cylinders and Exploring Shape

features give us important information, we must think in terms of the big picture first, so as to ensure visual clarity at the simplest level. Even in the event that the artist chooses to specifically study only the head in any particular pose, it is still recommended to move from large ideas to small ideas, starting with the overall silhouette of the head, then moving through progressively smaller ideas to achieve a head study, reprioritizing steps and/or ideas as necessary. The hands and feet up until now have been laid in as part of the whole arms and legs, respectively. This is to ensure the uninterrupted flow of energy throughout the whole body of a limb; we can even think of the limbs as having their own distinct predominant directional force (a line of action, if you will, not to be confused with the primary line of action that defines our thesis statement); this directional force line provides the harmony of the forms that make up the musculature of the limbs. Now is our chance to mark off the major joints of the limbs so that we may define the portions of the tube shapes that will make up our hands and feet. Specifically, we will mark off the wrists and ankles first (again, with marks that describe the cross section of a cylinder), then mark off knuckle and toe lines, moving to even smaller ideas if desired. Measurement should be included if necessary and if time permits. After marking off the joints, we may lay in the two-dimensional shape of the hands and feet, keeping fingers and toes grouped together as large shapes. We can keep the shapes of the hands and feet as two-dimensional ideas for now and develop the three-dimensional forms in the next step. The hands and feet are developed after the larger, more massive parts of the body, but if one needs to reprioritize the drawing at all, the hands and feet may be more fully realized earlier on. The previous chapter demonstration included portions of this half step toward the end of the lay-in, while still focusing only on two-dimensional shapes. In that case, we used the ideas of marking off the general geography of the figure, such as the breast line and other landmarks. We also incorporated the idea of the microgesture to further refine our rhythmic properties. Now we can take those two-dimensional tubes from Chapter 2 and quickly mark off their elliptical cross sections so as to gain a better understanding of space and depth. While the cylinder is an important and necessary form to understand, when developing cross contour marks, do not be concerned with the technical accuracy of the cylinders, nor the degree of their cross contours. The goal is to indicate volumes while controlling gesture and movement.

Demonstration

Working with this pose, we will see how quickly we can give ourselves an implication of volume by utilizing cross contour to develop a cylindrical mannequin (see Figures 4.4 and 4.5). I once again utilize the silhouette of the figure to lay in the longest uninterrupted line I see in the body because, in this case, it is also my primary line of action. The next strongest line I am aware of is the swoop of energy running across the arms, but I will not be placing it into the lay-in. However, I will be keeping that directional force in mind as I continue on this drawing. This is an example of how one need not physically draw every force line in a drawing, even if they are important. This is an advantage of mileage: knowing what lines must be placed in order to keep the energy flowing, and what lines to be aware of that do not necessarily need to be drawn in. For me, the exception to this would be the lay-in of a longer, more finished work: in that case, any flow of energy that is crucial to the idea being communicated will be laid in, since it

Figure 4.4

Demonstration reference photo of Ashli.

Figure 4.5

Demo drawing of reference image.

4. Using Cylinders and Exploring Shape

will eventually be covered up, and it will aid in overall compositional decisions. After placing the primary line of action running down the left arm through the body and down and out the left leg, I then mark off the termination of the torso at the gluteal muscles with a sweeping arc moving in the general direction of the gluteal shapes. I can then return to my starting point of the top of the left arm and complete the tube of the shape, using the Negative space I see in the pose to gauge the length of the arm. I then lay in the head and neck shape, starting at the base of the neck upward toward the head, again creating a moving shape out of the column of the neck, before placing the overall shape of the silhouetted head, again with dynamic, arced marks. To complete the shoulder line, instead of opting for a simple horizontal line, I choose instead to indicate it using the arc of the trapezius, then move down the arm, laying in one side of the right arm, then the other to create a tube shape. In this case, the hands have not been included in the long lines—and resulting tube shapes—of the arms because both hands change flow direction. I will instead choose to drop down to the legs and complete those as tube shapes before returning to lay in the hands as simplified graphic shapes. Regarding the legs, the compressed right leg is completed by drawing from the arced line of the gluteus through to the knee, then from knee to ankle; the foot is placed separately from the tube shape of the leg, since it too changes direction and has perspective applied to it. The stretched left leg is completed by running a line from the glutes down and out through the foot, and a termination mark for the toes is laid in, as is the bump of the heel. The torso can be completed as a tube shape by connecting the gluteal mark to the armpit created by the lay-in of the right arm. I lay in microgestures next so that I may communicate twist in the torso, as well as any other rhythmic notes I find interesting, such as the compression in the right side of the torso and the compression of the left shoulder. I can also address the finger gestures, separate the shape of the hair from the shape of the head, provide the bump of the right shoulder, separate the left gluteal muscle from the right, and lay in the spine. At this stage, the fingers can be further blocked in, but I choose to keep them as gestural marks in this drawing. Instead, I move down the body marking off the separations of forms, using marks that are cross contour in nature, effectively turning the two-dimensional shapes I have just completed into cylindrical forms. These forms will give me an indication of space, which when combined with further refined ideas of three-dimensional forms and plane breakdowns, will communicate form and depth. It will be much easier to light a figure for which we know what forms we want to use to relay information than one that is still predominantly flat. At this point, keep in mind the perspective on the feet: pay attention to the bottom plane of the foot, where it makes contact with the ground. The angle there will give important information regarding eye line and perspective. This angle becomes more noticeable if and when the model wears shoes. The feet are great indicators of perspective and are expressive and important for defining and embellishing character; therefore, they should never be neglected entirely. It should be noted that this half step of moving from tubes to cylindrical forms happens quickly, and the reader already most likely uses the idea of cylindrical forms to describe the human figure. It is brought up here as a reminder that sometimes there are poses in which marking off cylindrical cross contours or elliptical cross sections can aid immensely in the development of a drawing, especially if perspective and foreshortened forms still present issues, either during quick-sketch studies or while completing longer, more finished

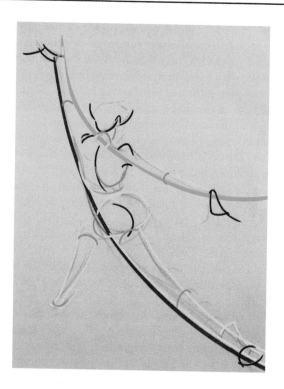

Figure 4.6

primary line of action in dark green; secondary line of action in light green; supporting actions in light blue, constructed first as lines of action, then completed to create simple tube shapes; microgestures in dark blue; cross contours in orange to indicate direction of motion.

studies or works. Use as many or as few cross sections as you need, or none at all if unnecessary. Included here is a simplified overview of the major gestures and rhythms of the figure as drawn in the demonstration (see Figure 4.6).

Head, Hands, and Feet Demonstration

Now let us look at how one might construct and define the head, hands, and feet as Shapes and ideas to be aware of (see Figures 4.7 through 4.9).

When laying in the head for either a short-pose or long-pose study, I tend to look at the silhouetted shape of the whole head structure, including the hair, while also taking into consideration the neck and shoulder line for reference (see Figure 4.10). I lay in a large shape, constructing it with curving, sweeping lines. The whole shape is laid in this way before I begin to indicate the placement of smaller structures, again with arcs. I want to avoid using too many straight lines at the moment, as the face is full of round, appealing forms that are in constant motion. A living model will never sit perfectly still, so we must work quickly to capture the placement of the expression given. When I draw a head, I am not looking to draw a generic mannequin head; instead, I want to construct an image that captures the sitter's character and personality, no matter how subtle or how briefly it stays on the face. This is why I am searching for the gestural qualities of the face. We can think of it the way we think of constructing the figure,

4. Using Cylinders and Exploring Shape

Figure 4.7
Head reference.

Figure 4.8
Hand and arm reference.

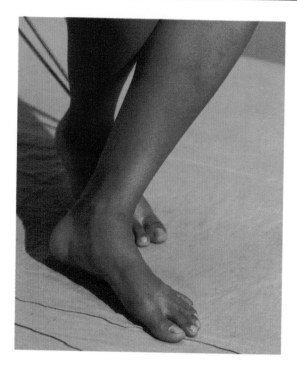

Figure 4.9

Feet and lower legs reference.

Figure 4.10

Head lay-in.

4. Using Cylinders and Exploring Shape

remembering that we can exaggerate wherever and whenever we want or feel it is appropriate. After carving out the hair shape from the rest of the head, I lay in the eye line, using an arc that indicates perspective on the head; I will do this for the nose and chin as well. I add the ear and add additional mass to the jaw of the face. I can also place the tube shape that will be the volumetric column of the neck.

I start hands and feet in the same general way as the head, looking at the silhouette and separating the positive space from the negative (see Figure 4.11). For a form as complex as the hand, it helps immensely to take note and advantage of the negative space present, and to develop it as a moving gestural shape. This is an example of how shape can be drawn in without necessarily laying in a line of action: with mileage comes the ability to prioritize the marks that will be laid down, and one can draw directly with shapes that have line(s) of action built in. This is why the silhouette is such a useful tool. I lay in the hand with the longest lines present in both the hand and the forearm. I have never been much of a fan of drawing only pieces of the figure unless it is for sheer drawing practice or some other specific reason; it is much more useful to see the relationships between forms and how rhythms are interconnected. The rest of the hand is laid in as overlapping shapes, again constructed with sweeping arcs. If one so desires, the negative space between the figures may be cut out here, while still dealing only with graphic shapes.

The feet are laid in primarily as silhouetted shapes, keeping toes grouped together, and utilizing negative space to judge placement and overlaps (see Figure 4.12). The angles of the toes are noted, as are the gestures of the heels. The arch of the foot is laid in as an S curve ending at the big toe of the front foot. We will keep building off of these shape lay-ins in the following chapters.

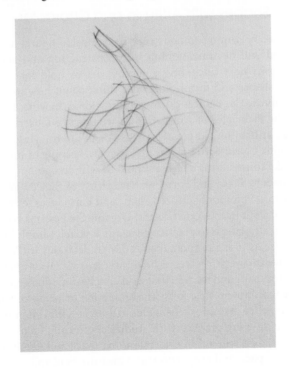

Figure 4.11

Hand lay-in.

Figure 4.12

Feet lay-in.

Developing Shapes with Attitude and Character

Now that we are beginning to construct recognizable figures with simplified shape ideas and will be transitioning into constructing and applying three-dimensional forms next (including anatomy), let us hold for a moment and explore simple shapes and forms alone and think about how we may manipulate them to improve our choices during observational drawing. If necessary, we may refer to the Principles of Animation as we practice (observational studies and ideas from animation aid greatly when it comes to drawing/experimenting with/and designing *form* with volume and weight), keeping in mind that all the choices we make constructing a figure should be with intent.

When it comes to Shape and Form, we have plenty of choices. We will be looking at the two most commonly utilized Shape and Form ideas for figure drawing and observational studies: Geometric and Organic Shapes and Forms. The very nature of gesture drawing is to practice it via quick sketch (simply because quick-sketch challenges us to make spontaneous design decisions while retaining the power of the gut reaction). It is in our best interest as visual artists to develop an understanding of shape and form so that we do not become flustered or frustrated when drawing with time restrictions. The animation principle of Solid Drawing describes this practice. It is an excellent idea to draw still lifes often and to balance out one's figure-drawing practice with studies specifically focused on geometric shapes/forms, as it will aid in understanding space and depth (perspective), positive/negative space, and proportions and measurement and in developing the ability to recognize geometrics within organic living forms. Conversely, plein air and outdoor observational drawing (nature-based studies, that is) will also help with recognizing gesture, rhythm, harmony, movement, form, and perspective in inanimate but living organics (such as a tree, a plant, or even a rock, though it would depend on one's philosophical outlook whether a rock is *alive*). Ideas from nature such as a rock may be described and constructed using rhythms found in more obviously organic, living creatures, with structures based on geometrics to provide volume, perspective, and plane changes, all the major characteristics of a rock (surface texture is as well, but for the sake of simplicity we will consider that a rendering issue). To push this idea a bit further into the story realm, we can develop a drawing of a rock to embody a specific idea, character, or mood to create world building—such as when an environment artist chooses what major visual ideas will contribute to serving the story of the piece, regardless of whether there are any characters present within. As long as the tools of visual communication are regularly sharpened and experimented with, the possibilities for visual storytelling are virtually endless.

Exploring Simple Shapes and Forms

Let us start by looking at the most common basic geometric shapes and forms (see Figure 4.13). The square, circle, triangle, and rectangle—which can also be viewed as a two-dimensional representation of a cylinder since the lack of depth restricts our ability to view the ellipse that would describe the top and bottom—may be considered building blocks, and we may create further geometric shapes by combining them with each other, adding more planes, etc. We may consider using polygons as well, though they are not included here, since one may extrapolate them from the four shapes mentioned. As far as basic forms go, we can use

Figure 4.13

Basic shapes and forms.

the same shapes but with depth (Z-Axis for those mathematically inclined): we have the cube, the sphere, the pyramid (which may have a base comprised of three or four faces), the cone, and the cylinder. Notice that the two-dimensional triangle may become either a cone or a pyramid, and a cube may also be stretched in proportion to become more rectangular. A sphere is usually denoted by placing a shadow that indicates turn of form or by simply adding a core shadow where appropriate, but in the event of quick sketch (or if there is inadequate lighting), one may use cross contour or the ellipse to denote or imply form, rather than leaving it to read as shape if need be. When it comes to drawing the cylinder, cone, or sphere/circle, it is generally a good idea to practice the ellipse, which is a circle in perspective. The ellipse in itself is another shape idea that is extremely useful for communication. These shapes and forms as-is are merely informational. It is up to us to give them the breath of life, so to speak.

Organic shapes and forms are imperfect and irregular and are usually reminiscent of nature and life, as opposed to geometrics, which feel perfect, mechanical, or mathematical in character. Incidentally, I have found through teaching a variety of students that some people prefer to work with organic shapes/forms, while others prefer to work with geometric shapes/forms. This is not always the case; however, it does seem that some people have a natural inclination toward one shape type versus the other. I note this here in case the readers find that they favor one type of shape over the other, and they wish to balance out their usage, understanding, etc. It is worth analyzing your own work to see if ideas are being communicated with the most effective shapes/forms and if it is necessary to conduct further experiments with shape/form. It is important to be reminded of what we feel when we see shapes and forms and what context they are provided in. If we can feel the individual nature of every shape or form we use, we will have a better understanding of what will happen when we use them to describe visual ideas. Shapes and forms are never meaningless. We use shapes constantly for everyday communication: when driving we know to stop at octagonal stop signs (yes, the red color helps, but recently a fully color-blind person reminded me of how important *shapes* are when driving or going about everyday life); we use them to read the silhouette of a person walking toward us, so that we may quickly determine whether they are friend or stranger; we use them to pick out clothes when going shopping; one may even argue that the alphabet we use is nothing more than symbolic shapes. They are simply everywhere, in everything, at all times, and if one is observing a man-made subject (such as a car, building, interior, or garment/clothing, etc.) then every decision made concerning the shapes used has been made with intent or for a purpose. The same is true for forms: they will most likely read in the same or a similar way as the shapes they are based on, though one can manipulate proportions to a greater extent since there is now a third dimension to play with, and they are incredibly important for building solid drawings that reflect the physical properties of the world we live in (such as gravity, weight, volume, inertia, etc.).

Let's play with our basic shapes a little to see how we may *activate* them in space utilizing the line of action (see Figure 4.14).

Using the square/rectangle, we begin by looking at its neutral expression. Instead of opting to use the line tool to create this geometric, I've opted to draw it free hand, as the neutral pose of a living character would be neither perfect nor absolutely still (much like the moving hold), much less *mechanically* so. (As a side note, it is nice to contrast *mechanical* or *man-made* visual ideas with organic ones, as it creates

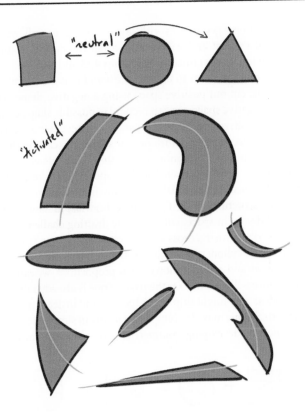

Figure 4.14

Shapes activated with a line of action.

greater variety and visual interest.) This neutral pose may even be described as wonky in nature, since it is imperfect, and the faces of the square have a slight arc to them to imply the ability to move, and to further assign it a *living* characteristic. I can manipulate a shape's proportions and line of action alone to activate the mass it represents. On the same image, one will find our other basic shapes played with in such a way; each activated shape has been assigned its own single line of action. When working with such simple ideas, we need not concern ourselves with supporting lines of action; instead, it is more effective to limit ourselves to only one: the strongest directional force line we see within the shape. We may think if it as: LINE OF ACTION + PROPORTIONS + SHAPE, with each section of the *formula* being variable. In terms of the Breakdown presented, this formula is essentially Steps (or Key Topics) 1 through 3 (we will get to cylinders and 3D forms shortly). Note that the moving rectangles drawn are essentially those 2D *tube* shapes I am fond of constructing a life drawing with, and if tapering at either the top or bottom of that shape is necessary, it may be applied to a rectangle or one may simply use a triangle that has been manipulated, such as the curvilinear small triangle found on the right side of the page next to the ovoid. Notice that a circle when squashed and stretched becomes an Ellipse. Once we move into 3D forms and weight and volume become an important part of bringing a figure to life, the ellipse will become incredibly useful to denote compression/stretch, as when thinking sequentially it is crucial to understand that volumes (or the amount of mass present in the subject) must remain consistent. We can further combine basic shapes to better illustrate ideas and we can combine geometrics with organic shapes as well, which will further enhance visual interest and will aid the artist in communicating complex visual ideas, as seen in our next image (see Figures 4.15 and 4.16).

We can either combine them to create *additional* mass, or combine them to *negate* mass—that is, cut out positive space using a negative shape. This how we read Positive and Negative space: we can recognize possible shape configurations that make both the Positive and Negative space of whatever we are observing and use those shapes to describe the nature of that space. We can furthermore contrast size between shapes to create more interesting visual ideas.

Now that we've activated and played with Shapes, let's make the transition to three-dimensional forms. As previously stated, my favorite basic forms for beginning the volumetric structures of the figure are cylindrical in nature. They are easy to manipulate and design in space, with the only drafting challenge present being the ellipse that describes either a cross section (or cross contour, if you will), or the top and bottom of the cylinder. If we design them first as simplified *shapes* with assigned *lines of action* and consideration of their proportions, we can quickly begin to see what our figure will look like on the page. If one is already fairly comfortable with volumetric ideas, one might skip the shape step and instead move directly into cylinders; alternatively, one may also jump from laying in simple shapes (in my case, tubes or rectangles) to developing volumetric, three-dimensional forms without

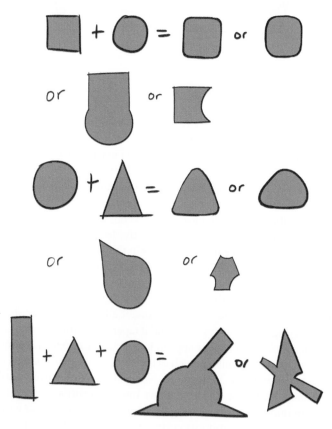

Figure 4.15

Shapes as mass.

4. Using Cylinders and Exploring Shape

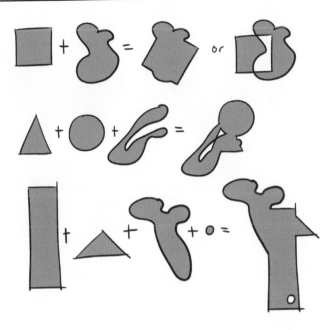

Figure 4.16

Shapes as mass.

indicating cylinders. It is entirely up to the individual. For thoroughness, the reader should practice utilizing cylinders, as these forms do aid in clothing or draping a figure and should be considered while developing a life drawing.

In our next image we see our tube shape on the left, moving laterally; again, if it helps, one may think of it as moving across an *X-, Y-*Axis system, but it is not necessary to do so (see Figure 4.17). Simply thinking in terms of movement and direction is enough.

In this case, I have laid in a green line of action through the center of the tube/ rectangle shape, but keep in mind that my normal tendency is to build the primary line of action of a figure into as much of the construction as possible. This is partly why arcs are so useful. The tube next to it has been transformed into a cylinder, moving upward and to the right but also away from the viewer. I have also chosen to utilize two different ellipses to cap the ends. This is one way we can accelerate or decelerate the steepness of a foreshortened limb, for example, or contort the volume throughout. The invented figures on the right represent simplified mannequin figures and have been completed in a quick-sketch style; that is, they are not belabored, have been completed within a short time frame, and are indicative of the type of drawing one might use for brainstorming or thumbnailing. My procedure through this figure is as follows:

- Action/Pose (this will determine the silhouette)
- *lines of action* (both primary and supporting ideas for individual actions of the limbs)
- Tube or two-dimensional Shapes (based on the *lines of action* previously laid in)
- Cylinders

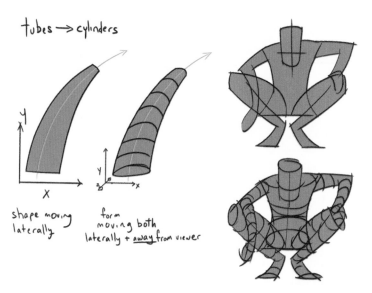

Figure 4.17

Playing with cylinders to describe forms. It's easier to measure them while flat—that is, 2-dimensional, or graphic.

A note concerning the digital medium: Because of the nature of the medium used to complete this sketch (digital), I may develop this figure in *passes* or stages, with each step on its own layer, much like I would do when completing invented work (an illustration for example), and have completed it sequentially (step by step, with each step being a Key Topic) following the Breakdown presented in Chapter 1. This is an example of using the Breakdown as a *process*, building each step directly on top of the previous one. Note that the hands and feet have been left as very simple shapes, each with their own subtly different and much more minor lines of action (supporting ideas). One could quickly develop a mannequin figure based off cylinders alone, and it would succeed in conveying visual information; however, cylinders alone are often too generic to adequately capture volumetric ideas such as compression (squash) and stretch, or inertia—this limits our visual storytelling potential with each individual figure study. Furthermore, cylinders do not adequately convey enough anatomy/musculature to create a striking silhouette, nor provide enough varying intervals of ideas. While these ideas could theoretically be accomplished with cylinders alone, and they function extremely well for construction, they do present limitations to use on their own. Their advantage in construction is how informational they are: the cylinders used in the bottom figure retains all of my gestural notes from the two-dimensional pass, as well as proportions and measurements, and further provide spatial information so that I am aware of what direction in space the whole figure and its limbs are moving. The next pass would consist of applying three-dimensional forms of my choosing to the preexisting cylindrical forms in order to more fully realize musculature and anatomy and would make it easier to clothe my figure afterward if desired.

We will now take a look at applying Narrative, Expression, Attitude, and Characterization (elements of story, and the building blocks of Acting) to a simple three-dimensional form. For this demo, we will use a rectangular throw pillow, as it fulfills the basic requirements of being a fairly primitive form and, because it is stuffed with cotton, having volume. One of the most fun things about this kind of exploratory drawing is experimenting with personalities and characterizations, and the artist is invited to make any and all academic exercise as fun as is desired. The more of a challenge, the more fun and ultimately rewarding the exercise will be. Those of you already incorporating animation exercises into your drawing studies may already be familiar with the famous and beloved *half-filled flour sack* and the range of motion, expression, and attitude such a simple form may possess. (It is essentially a configuration of a rectangular cube and a sphere, and only half filled so as to present specific challenges concerning the communication of weight and the physical ideas of gravity, in addition to understanding further Principles of Animation such as timing, slow-in and slow-out, etc., which are not easy to practice with stand-alone or single frame drawings, yet incredibly useful and enriching concepts.) One of the reasons the flour sack test/exercise is so effective is that it forces the artist to retain consistent *volume* for the entirety of the exercise. It presents excellent learning opportunities and is greatly recommended along with studies in animation—particularly traditional, hand-drawn animation—as part of a drawing exercise routine. The more often an artist practices different disciplines within drawing, the better his or her understanding of the craft of draftsmanship, visual problem-solving and communication, and visual storytelling.

Demonstration

For this particular demonstration, I have chosen to produce what I call an *exploratory drawing/study*, much like in the previous chapter (see Figure 4.18). By *exploratory*, I mean a drawing or study that is not preplanned or has been neither brainstormed nor figured out before marks are put on canvas (in this case, a digital canvas); it is spontaneous in nature—much like a quick-sketch study from life. Typically speaking, an artist usually does not know what challenges or problems will arise during a life-drawing session, so it is useful to practice drawing spontaneously and creatively at home. The challenges I have set for myself with

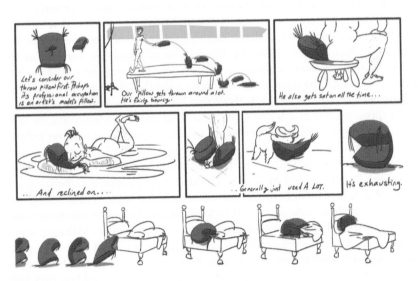

Figure 4.18

Exploring a character concept via basic shapes and forms.

this study are to (1) define a narrative with which to understand possible characterizations of my throw pillow; (2) explore the throw pillow's reactions to its environment. I already know the general character design of my throw pillow: it's a puffy rectangle, meaning that it definitely has a structure, but can be squashed, stretched, thrown, sat on, or otherwise manipulated. This means that I must pay attention to the following:

1. The Volume and Form characteristics of my pillow
2. The Scale of the shape of my pillow (notice that I define *scale* as a two-dimensional issue, since it is easier to measure horizontally and vertically, before depth is introduced)
3. The pillow's gesture during each action performed
4. The pillow's reaction to external forces, circumstances, etc.

One may define the first three issues as *drawing* or *draftsmanship* issues, meaning that solid drawing is necessary in order to explore less tangible concepts, such as a character's thoughts and feelings. The fourth issue deals entirely with developing my throw pillow as a sentient, feeling, living creature. This is essentially what *anthropomorphism* is, and it is an excellent creative thinking challenge to assign inanimate objects with personality and character, as it forces the artist to deal with solid drawing and the issues that may arise with visual communication, and what effects characterization and narrative context have on drawing choices.

As I laid out my ideas on the canvas, I realized that it would be helpful for me to see vignettes or possible sequences of my pillow's daily life. This is what gave me pause to consider developing a one-page comic or another type of hybrid study in lieu of stand-alone emotion expressions (or what one might call a *model sheet* or *expression sheet*). This decision further inspired me to write little notes into my study, much like in a comic strip. I generally recommend that visual artists read and write as often as possible, as it aids in the organization of ideas/concepts and further helps us practice different types of expressive and creative communication. Comic strips and sequential work are wonderful vehicles for this type of creation and practice. First, I considered what type of environments one might find a throw pillow in; this led me to remember our pillows that are used in life-drawing studios or classes. Those pillows have seen *quite a lot*. I thought it would be interesting to wonder what the life of one of those throw pillows would be like and think about that lifestyle's effect on characterization and expression. My first frame establishes what my pillow looks like for reference. From there I developed panels, each depicting scenes of how our pillow is commonly utilized; essentially it becomes a "day in the life" narrative. I realized that a throw pillow such as the one depicted would be exhausted, both physically and mentally, after a hard day's work. Underneath my panels is a small sequence study of how our small hero tucks itself in to bed at night. From offstage left, our pillow waddles into scene and tucks itself into bed. This particular study began as a study in expression of basic forms, with particular challenges kept in mind. It's not meant to be finished (as in rendered); it doesn't have to be pretty or particularly good in any specific way. It's meant to force myself to solve specific drawing and story problems: Solid Drawing, Narrative, and how they influence each other. Furthermore, there are additional subchallenges presented, such as composition and staging, both of which must be exercised to improve visual clarity. I am using specific tools in my tool belt to solve specific problems and by doing so improving my grasp and comprehension of those tools.

Exercises

The following exercise ideas are for the reader to practice recognizing both geometric and organic shapes and forms during observational studies so as to further solidify draftsmanship. This is crucial for successful visual communication. We must be comfortable with simple shape and form ideas before we can activate and assign life and attitude to them. The goal with this type of academic study (rather than story-based) is to minimize time spent solving drawing problems rather than design problems. This is why the concept of Solid Drawing is universal rather than merely a principle of animation only, and all artists should periodically review their understanding of fundamental ideas in order to gradually master them. I have heard other artists say both online as well as in real life that there is really no such thing as advanced drawing, but rather a deeper understanding of the fundamentals of visual communication and draftsmanship. While I cannot attribute this idea to any single origin, I find the concept to be very truthful and indeed have found through the study of artists of a much higher experience level than myself that, yes, they indeed have a deeper, more intimate understanding of the basics, such as line, shape, form, value, color, design, and composition, etc. Essentially, it is up to us as individual artists to draw anything and everything all the time. These exercise ideas are meant to inspire you to do so.

Still Life, Three Variations

1. *Geometric Shape and Form Still Life*: Using the most basic geometric forms you can find at home, at school, in the studio, or office, draw each form from multiple viewing angles (see Figure 4.19). Rotate the form,

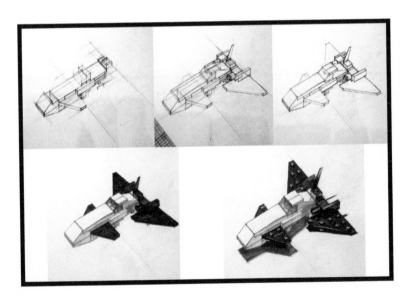

Figure 4.19

Geometric still-life study.

place it on surfaces of different heights, look up at it, look down at it. You will do two sets of drawings: for the first set, focus on drawing only the silhouette (two-dimensional graphic shape) of the form, constructing the shape as necessary, blocking in the large rough shapes that make up the positive/negative space of whatever form you have chosen and progressively refining it until the positive shape of the silhouette of your subject appears accurate. For the second set of sketches, focus now on drawing your subject as accurately as possible to reflect plane changes and perspective. Ideally, depending on your comfort level with geometric forms, you may start with a simple form, such as a box, candle, roll of drafting tape, etc. As you progress and feel the need to challenge yourself, move on to more complex forms, such as a wrist watch, a camera, a radiator, a shoe, etc. From there, if desired, you can combine forms to create a geometric still life with multiple subjects, with the intention of creating a composition out of them. If needed or wanted, you may light it much as you would a figure, so that plane changes are more easily seen and understood.

2. *Organic Shape and Form Still Life*: Same exercise as the previous one, swapping out geometric subjects for organic ones, such as a fruit or vegetable, house plant, animal (such as a sleeping cat or dog, though this would double as life drawing), tree, other types of food, etc. (See Figure 4.20.) Again, begin with the silhouette, focusing on accuracy. Afterward, move onto drawing that form in the round, with the focus on communicating *volume*. As you begin drawing your organic subject, you may find yourself indicating plane changes or using cross contour to aid with perspective and volume. Draw the form multiple times, from multiple viewing angles, until setting up a still life full of different organic forms (for this type of still life I usually opt for fruits and vegetable or other foods, all at varying shapes and sizes; the more variety the better). Your recognition of geometric ideas within organic, living subjects will begin to improve.

Figure 4.20

Organic still-life study.

4. Using Cylinders and Exploring Shape

3. *Combination Organic/Geometric Shape and Form Still Life*: For this variation, you may use any combination of both organic and geometric forms together. Instead of drawing them each one at a time, put together an interesting and challenging still life for yourself that incorporates both geometric and organic forms, varying size and general shape. This exercise is what one would consider a traditional still life, and you have freedom of choice as to your composition. It is recommended to light your still life, so that you may see plane changes and volume. While it is not necessary to render, you may choose to do so if you are already comfortable with value and would like the additional challenge of lighting composition/staging. (Note that staging is another principle of animation that may be considered universal in nature, and the still life is an excellent way to practice that concept.) For those who crave a further challenge, you may add as many lights to your still life, render the individual textures of each object

Figure 4.21

Quick sketch utilizing simple shapes, silhouette, acting and action to study a character, in this case a pre-teen girl at a sleep over in the early 2000s.

Figure 4.22

Different narrative and personality variations of the same pose.

(since texture may be interpreted as the effect of light on shapes, only at a smaller scale), or opt to place a colored gel for your light source. While color will not be studied within this guide, it is part of the fundamentals of art, design, and visual communication and must also be practiced as it further refines and communicates Tone and Mood.

Figures 4.21 and 4.22 utilize simple shapes and silhouettes to explore characterizations and acting during quick sketch.

5

Working with Forms and Volume

We may now more fully develop our drawing utilizing the preexisting information from the previous steps of our breakdown and utilize three-dimensional Forms to more specifically describe the nature of the story we are telling. We will be *wrapping, inserting,* and *overlapping* shapes and forms Around, In, and On Top Of (respectively) our cylindrical forms and each other. We can utilize any ideas from studies in Perspective and Visual Communication to communicate both literal and abstract concepts, choosing and designing shapes and forms that more accurately represent our intent or bring more life to our stories (see Figure 5.1).

We will be applying the following concepts to our drawing at this stage:

- Rhythm
- Harmony
- Exaggeration
- Acting
- Tone (as derived from Literature)
- Mood (as derived from Literature)

We can also apply the following Principles of Animation:

- Squash and Stretch
- Anticipation

Figure 5.1

Quick sketch focused on acting, using simple forms for construction.

- Follow-Through and Overlapping Action
- Arcs
- Secondary Action
- Exaggeration
- Solid Drawing
- Appeal

At this stage, we may also develop the three-dimensional forms of the heads, hands, and feet to a greater degree, and we may develop as much or as little anatomy as is desired or necessary to support our thesis statement. For example, if our story is heavily trenched in *realism*, we now have the opportunity to develop the idea of realistic anatomy, having kept in mind the idea of realism throughout our process, ensuring that every stage of our drawing's development reads realistic. (That is, our Line[s] of Action and other components of our drawing so far are not so exaggerated to the point of cartoon; instead we opt for sophistication in movement.) If we instead choose to heavily stylize our drawing, we may have added exaggeration to whatever degree at every step; now we can follow through and exaggerate our forms as well. Typically, the more stylized or exaggerated the drawing, the more applicable the Principles of Animation, though we can apply them even lightly to works based in realism to heighten the Tone and Mood of the piece and to further provide weight, character, personality, and unique style of movement. If we have successfully designed the rhythms of the figure in an earlier stage, and we are pleased with the planned harmony of our cylindrical forms, the resulting *mannequin* figure after the completion of this stage should closely resemble the final Idea, complete with movement and harmonized anatomy. The drawing will look more finished at this stage of development, and, should the artist deem that there is enough information recorded, he or she may end the drawing here, or, if lighting is desired and necessary for whatever reason, there should be an adequate amount of structural information to apply lighting and rendering (also, if time allows) (see Figure 5.2). If further evolution is required or desired, we may continue the development of the drawing past this stage.

Even though we are not worried about lighting at the moment, we use it to be able to see the forms of the body present. We must begin squinting our eyes to pick apart the light and shadow shapes; this is typically why in class I specifically use only one strong primary light and the fill light of the

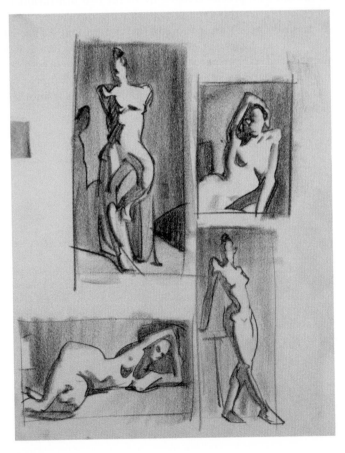

Figure 5.2

Short-pose composition studies completed by utilizing silhouettes, simple forms, and value organization.

fluorescent light strips of the room. This is to make picking out forms simple and fast, and in effect may be thought of as *chiaroscuro*. This is not the only way to light a figure for life drawing, but it is the easiest way to see forms quickly, especially for those who do not work from long pose very often or currently have trouble remembering anatomy.

Basic Technique: Step 4

Using previously established information from Steps 1–3, I can now Insert, Wrap, Overlap, or otherwise combine forms of my choosing and/or design with the cylinders from the previous half step (Chapter 4) to build a Volumetric Figure.

If Cylindrical (or other three-dimensional directional) information has not been indicated up until now, it is recommended to lay in any that is needed, so as to maintain consistency in the perspective the forms are to follow. If no such information is at all necessary and one chooses to develop one's drawing in a more two-dimensional style, Step 3 regarding cylinders may be skipped; however, perspective should not be disregarded but communicated instead with precise Geography, or the two-dimensional distance between objects. We see this type of two-dimensional Perspective communicated successfully in 2D animation, both Western and Asian, where the graphic shape of, say, an eye or an ear has been foreshortened without the use of volumetric ideas. Perspective is not always stated directly but rather can be implied by spacing and *graphic overlaps*—that is, simply overlapping multiple 2D shapes on one another (see Figure 5.3). This is another facet of foreshortening.

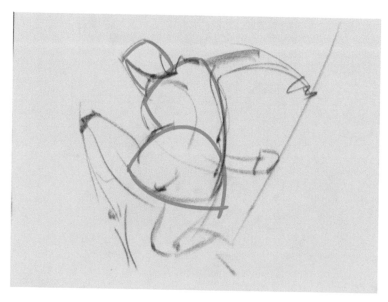

Figure 5.3

Foreshortened forms indicated by overlapping shapes.

Tone and Mood

We may combine, recombine, and design any configuration of shape and form at this step, and the resulting combinations will ultimately affect the Tone and Mood of the drawing. We must keep in mind that different shapes and forms communicate different ideas, and we feel them as much as we see them. Typically, we think of squares and boxes as being very stable and masculine; circles and spheres as being safe, warm and feminine; triangles and cones/pyramids are often seen and felt as aggressive, strong, and sometimes even threatening. Aside from Geometric ideas, there are also Organic shapes and forms, which tend to feel warm and familiar; and Abstract shapes, which represent ideas rather than literally communicate them, such as a stick man representing a human being. These are just a few examples; there are myriad subconscious ideas that spark in the mind when looking at shapes and forms, and we can combine and recombine them to create more fully developed visual ideas, feelings, and meanings. These feelings and meanings are what we use to create a sense of Tone and Mood in our drawings (among other elements of design, such as color and lighting) and bring emotional resonance to our thesis statement. We can use the Actions of our subject to help inform our decisions as to what shapes and forms would be most suitable to develop our story, and if we are also developing any Acting in our drawing, we can further use those shapes and forms to communicate expressions.

A Note Concerning Tone and its Relation to Style

Because we are interpreting the concept of Tone through a visual artist's lens rather than that of a writer's, one might think of it in a few different ways. Firstly, we are defining it as the creator's attitude toward their subject. This means that no matter how we feel toward our subject, we as creators will always show up in our work. It is simply inevitable. This is why there are so many different artists, with different outlooks on life, with different life experiences that influence how they feel when confronted with different subjects or concepts and their subsequent choices during problem-solving, and why different styles exist. Secondly, we are using it to remind ourselves of all the possible choices we might make each time we sit down to solve a visual problem, whether that problem is one concerning itself with solid drawing and draftsmanship (an academic pursuit, if you will) or a story problem, where now we are using our drawing skills and draftsmanship to develop a character, environment, prop, costume, vehicle, etc., that is thematic and emotionally charged in nature. When dealing with that type of problem-solving we are essentially finding and developing the emotional resonance necessary to connect with an audience. We do this subconsciously as well, but when drawing for a specific application that is meant to be viewed by a specific audience (such as Illustration, Storyboards, Comics, Entertainment, etc.), we must be more conscientious and aware of what the effects of our choices are. This idea is absolutely crucial to believable world building and is why it takes a team of creative individuals to produce large artistic endeavors, such as Animation, Film, and Comics (though this particular medium happens to be one of the few that may be large, complex, and produced by an individual rather than a group). This is why experimentation is necessary for the visual artist, particularly the drawer/painter. We do not want to make the same choices every time we draw simply because different stories or narratives evoke different

Themes and Moods. To effectively communicate those Themes and Moods, we must change or alter our attitude toward our subject in order to more adequately arrive at the emotional truths of those Themes, and to develop Mood appropriately. Style is usually considered to be *how* the artist has chosen to express a Theme or idea. We can see Style as being dependent upon both the Theme of the Narrative or story told or evoked within a drawing, and the creator's attitude toward their Theme, Subject, or both. To simplify, we may look at Style as Theme + Tone. We could add more elements to this formula to create even more complex approaches to a work. As a visual artist who practices storytelling in as many disciplines as I can find time for (without neglecting the continued development of the craft of drawing), I find Storytelling to be one of the most challenging crafts a person can pursue. It requires artists to be aware of the following:

- Their own life experience and how that affects their attitude toward any given subject/scenario
- What effect that attitude will have on design choices at every stage in the development of a drawing, whether quick sketch or long pose
- The emotional truth or resonance behind both the artist's attitude *and* the choices made
- The Stylistic effects on the artist's work (*how* one has put the puzzle pieces together)

The result of this conscientiousness is what we can consider a building block of Style. I personally consider Style to be something that should always be thought of in terms of *serving the Narrative or story at all times*, though it is absolutely recommended to experiment stylistically from time to time. We should constantly pursue furthering our understanding of visual communication, and practice arriving at solutions we may never have thought of if we hadn't taken risks in experimentation. This improves our creative problem-solving and further aids us when thinking on our feet during quick-sketch gesture drawing. This is why experimental or nontraditional drawing exercise ideas have been included in this study guide.

How Can We Relate this Pursuit of Emotional Truth to Observational Studies?

In terms of the Breakdown we are using for this Study Guide, we may see our thesis statement or Big Idea as the result of Theme (the emotional truth) plus Tone (our attitude toward our subject) and Mood (the atmosphere created for the viewer) for our drawing, influencing every single choice we make. One of the major and important ideas I have learned from different artists and storytellers, both in and outside of class, is this: essentially, Plot is *what* happens; story is *why* it happens and *why* we as an audience care. This is why our working definition of story throughout this Guide is so loose: just as different people experience, interpret, and relate to story differently, different types of stories and storytelling exist around the world, and our approach to it is influenced by a number of variables, such as life experiences, taste, and preference for how we express it. In terms of a life drawing, story manifests itself by *what* we have chosen to put on paper and *why*.

Demonstration

So far the previous two demonstrations have been completed with the intent of showing slightly different ways of laying in drawings based on prioritization and the problems presented by different poses. Now, we will see how to overlap, insert, wrap, or otherwise develop our volumetric ideas based on a two-dimensional lay-in (see Figure 5.4 and 5.5). This two-dimensional lay-in is a more accurate representation of what I shoot for during a quick-sketch lay-in: developing graphic shapes with Movement, Expression, and Character. Typically speaking, I find anywhere between 30 seconds and a minute an adequate amount of time to lay in shapes that already incorporate movement, before moving on to further problems such as volumetric forms, mapping in light and dark shapes, rendering, and finishing (as one might during a 3–4 minute quick sketch depending on size, speed, and accuracy). This procedural method of drawing with lay-ins and passes (as opposed to drawing directly, with no block in—which should also be practiced from time to time) presents the artist with a huge amount of control and is adequate for both short pose and long pose. This is, however, merely a go-to or autopilot process for getting something down on paper. Every time we sit down and draw and the model's pose changes, we are presented with a new array of challenges or problems to be analyzed and solved; therefore, we should remain flexible enough in our own methodology so as to allow for improvisation and the reprioritization of ideas. Therefore, my goals for the initial lay-in lines for any drawing relate to infusing my shapes with character and personality, including my primary and supporting *lines of action*. Because I have a lay-in that now has most of my two-dimensional shape information, I can begin the demo

Figure 5.4

Demonstration reference of Ashli.

Figure 5.5

Shape analysis of reference image.

directly with my volumetric form construction (see Figure 5.6). The primary line of action runs in a diagonal from the top of the head, upward and to the left. Because of the limitations of the paper, the drawing surface has been flipped horizontally to accommodate the pose. Note also that because this is meant to be drawn quickly and spontaneously, the lay-in has been completed in a short time frame, much like in a

Figure 5.6

Form analysis of reference image.

5. Working with Forms and Volume

regulated life-drawing class or session. Because I am racing against the clock, less priority will be given to proportions and more to the overall flow of the drawing. If this were a lay-in for a 4-hour drawing, the first two passes—that is, the gestural pass, dealing only with line and movement, and the shape pass, dealing only with two-dimensional graphic shape ideas—may be given a greater amount of time to develop the accurate geography of the figure and to ensure proper proportions, perspective, and overall structure. I begin my form lay-in at the head and work my way across the form, ending with the legs. This form lay-in is not timed so as to give a clear idea as to how we may place the volumes on the preexisting shapes. I already have a shape for the head, hair, and neck laid in with marks that indicate the direction the head is moving in: away from me and to the right. This allows me to build the head as a cylinder, then place the form of the cranium and the jaw, then the forms in the neck, overlapping as necessary and observing plane changes. The more realistic the drawing, the greater the attention paid to form, volume, and plane changes, so as to more accurately address and communicate three-dimensional structures. The hair is kept as a graphic shape: if we squint our eyes, all highlights drop out of focus, and the hair becomes a dark, graphic shape. I can then develop the shoulder line, and the torso. The arms are both cylindrical and boxy in nature, as are the legs. That is, they may be described well as cylinders, but because of the human figure's anatomical configuration the legs—and arms—may also be adequately described as rectangular boxes or, more accurately, a hybrid of both ideas. Because of this, it is important to consider plane changes when developing the musculature/anatomy of the figure. In this reference image, we can feel the wrists flatten out in more of a rectangular form. I make sure to indicate this idea using cross contour marks that describe the plane changes of the forearm, rather than use cross contours that evoke a cylinder. The hands are developed in the same manner, completing any two-dimensional shapes that must be addressed before proceeding to developing the volumes. Moving down the torso, we can draw in the forms of the breasts, developing the upper torso to reflect more volume, then move to the pelvis, using perspective cues to place the box of the pelvic structure. The legs are then completed, using both the preexisting shapes, then cylindrical ideas, then using more of a rectangular form to define the model's right foreshortened leg. The plane changes on this leg are more easily visible than on the model's left leg, since the left one faces the viewer broadly and as a result has shallower perspective on it: it reads a bit more flat than the other. We can still sense the volumes, though, so marks are laid down to describe the forms in the upper leg, and across from the top of the pelvis to the insertion of the leg. I then complete the volume of the box of the knee, including overlaps where needed, move down the lower leg, and complete the foot, paying attention to the perspective on the ball of the foot. The right foot is left mostly implied, with the form of the heel developed more than the remainder of the foot, keeping it more of a graphic shape than a finished form. This drawing now has forms set up in such a way that I feel I have enough information of form present to light, map, and fill in values if I so desire, or if it is a quick sketch I can end it here, if time is up. Note that this pose will be further utilized in the proceeding chapters to develop into a longer study, building off the information we lay in with each pass. Because this drawing is developed based on a quick-sketch lay-in, accuracy in measurements has been semineglected (an example of prioritization). In this case, because proportions are not as high on my list of priorities for this specific study, I've chosen to sacrifice their absolute accuracy and opted instead to let myself focus on other aspects of drawing; I'm more concerned with developing volumes and the subsequent breakdowns of planes and values.

Heads, Hand, and Feet

We now have an opportunity to further refine the action(s) and character of the head, the hands, and the feet. If we have already laid in the general placement of the features of the head, we can design the shapes/forms of the face and—to a certain degree—the features. Before we look at plane changes, we will develop the large shapes of the head and facial structure, utilizing shapes and now forms that describe the subject as we seem them in that instant. If Facial Acting is involved, we can manipulate those forms to reflect facial expressions, contorting and organizing them as we see fit. The same is true for the hands and feet: we now have the opportunity to address the individual character of the subject's hands and feet, clearly stating the actions of those parts of the body by not only using the harmonized gestural architecture that is already there but by further developing those ideas with appropriate shapes and forms. In this way, we can give even our subject's Hands and Feet character, personality, and clear expression and will ultimately affect the story we are drawing.

Demonstration

Using the lay-ins of the previous chapter's demos of the head, hands, and feet, we will see how to develop volumetric forms to these ideas. Much like an entire figure is approached in terms of staying true to the fluidity of the original movement lay-in, the same approach is taken for smaller—yet more complex—ideas, such as the hands and feet. The head is approached similarly, but one has more options with a form as complex as a head and face. The hands and feet are constructed with volumes and simple forms in mind, paying attention to negative space where necessary to break apart individual units of fingers and toes. Because the original lay-ins were developed as they would be for quick sketch, measuring is not always possible during a short pose. Therefore, I will choose to develop the forms based on the movement originally captured, rather than trying to correct geography or minor measurements. Similarly, during class sessions dedicated to long-form studies, I will often advise the students not to chase the drawing; that is, if at any point during the long pose the model has shifted and corrections to the pose have already been made, it is a better idea to roll with any inconsistencies between your subject and your drawing, and instead *leave your initial gestural ideas intact.* If we continuously chase the drawing during our long pose, we run the risk of losing the power of our initial gut reaction, which ultimately affects the integrity of the thesis statement. Measurements and proportions should be addressed if corrections are necessary, but do try to retain the initial impact and punch of your initial gestural ideas. If at any point during the development of a quick-sketch drawing I find proportions/measurements lacking too greatly in accuracy (depending on how accurate I am intending on being), rather than correct them I will start over, either on the same page or another. If these lay-ins were being developed for a final, longer piece, I would make corrections *prior* to developing volumetric forms but with the intention of maintaining as much movement and harmonious flow of ideas as possible. One can see this decision as a sort of compromise and it is visible in the development of the volumes of the hands and feet; accuracy in the positive/negative space is not as important as the general gesture of the hands and fingers (see Figures 5.7 and 5.8).

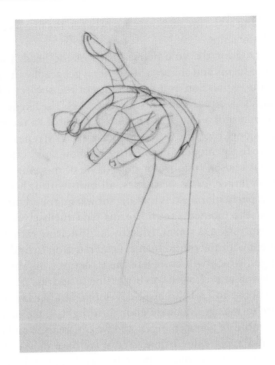

Figure 5.7

Hand form analysis and lay-in.

Figure 5.8

Feet form analysis and lay-in.

Rather, I am looking at the arc of movement between the fingers and controlling volumes and relationships.

The same is true for the volumetric forms of the head: I am looking to develop the major forms and shapes with general geography in mind and looking to capture the expression and personality of the subject with my forms, rather than shoot only for a likeness (see Figure 5.9). The likeness is secondary in this case. Be reminded that it is absolutely possible to recognize a model via their poses alone, regardless of whether a facial likeness was captured. This speaks more to the model's *personality* and how this personality dictates *how* he or she has chosen to move or pose (style of movement). The features are thought of as larger forms or shapes, all built with inherent movement. My focus for this particular head is looking for warm, round forms rather than plane changes at the moment; round forms lend themselves well to Ashli's face, since her expression is warm, friendly, and inviting rather than neutral. Once I am content with the round forms, I can move on to finding and depicting plane changes, which will complete the structures. Again, during quick-sketch, one may find oneself with too little time to address plane changes and might instead choose to end the head development after laying in volumetric forms. These forms are adequate enough to light, since mapping shadow shapes will also indicate plane changes, and we can analyze and indicate those plane changes and apply value in one step if we have to. As always, there is variety in how one may choose to prioritize and approach each individual study or drawing. We will continue to look at the development of these same hands, feet, and head studies in the following chapters.

Figure 5.9

Head form analysis and lay-in.

5. Working with Forms and Volume

Depending on the intended application of our gesture drawing, we may choose to end our ideas at this step and proceed to *finishing*: bringing a drawing to a *finished* level of refinement, using such tools as final, weighted line work; refinement in the silhouette; lighting and rendering; or color; etc. Ideally, there is an adequate amount of information in our drawing at *this stage* to proceed to finishing tactics. If our desire is to bring our gesture drawing or figurative study to a higher degree of finish—keeping in mind that the level of finish necessary or possible is entirely dependent on application, taste, and time—we can move on to the next step of our Breakdown, in which we readdress the silhouette and refine it as thoroughly as necessary or desired to ensure successful visual clarity, before proceeding to ways in which we may incorporate lighting into either a quick-sketch or long-pose drawing while retaining gesture, rhythm, and harmony throughout the figure.

Thinking in Terms of Style and Approach

Now that we've explored how we might build a figure from life using the first four Key Topics from our Breakdown as consecutive steps or passes in order to build a figure that retains all of the initial gestural information and shape analysis we see in our subject, as well as how to further develop the volumes and musculature/anatomy with forms chosen with intent, let's see how we might approach another pose now with story and characterization in mind. Because we are now going to begin dealing with more complex ideas, I will be providing the formulas I use to think my way through a drawing. This is not something I do all the time, but when faced with particular challenges or analyzations it helps me to think this way and makes it easier for me to communicate how I think while drawing.

Demonstration

Let's look first at our initial photo reference for this particular demonstration (see Figure 5.10).

Because this demo is from a photo and not real life, note how high our eye line is. I am keeping this in mind as it will help me develop forms with perspective, most notably on the feet and legs. This photo has been chosen because it provides enough negative space to make gauging measurements quick, which is suitable for a quick-sketch demo—again, use negative space to help yourself gauge proportions when you simply do not have enough time to measure. Furthermore, it is a type of pose I consider a *character* pose versus a *classical* or traditional life-drawing pose. We will look at the formula I use for studying variations in my approach during drawing, and we will now introduce media and how I choose it depending upon my approach, dictated by my attitude toward my subject (Tone) and/or the Theme present, even if that means I have chosen the Theme for myself.

Demonstration Drawing 1

Demonstration 1 shows a figure built in a more *naturalistic* style: it functions as a study in slight exaggeration of foreshortening and forms (see Figure 5.11). The drawing is fairly neutral. When thinking through this preliminary quick-sketch, my thinking went something like this:

Thesis Statement = Tone (Lines of Action + Shape Analysis + Form/Anatomy Analysis)

Figure 5.10

Demonstration reference of Ashli.

Figure 5.11

Naturalistic iteration of reference.

5. Working with Forms and Volume

My attitude toward the drawing (Tone) is a Naturalistic one; that is, it is fairly realistic but idealized. In order to get myself into this particular mindset, I opt to listen to *nature sounds* such as running water and animal sounds, from an online source. I want my attitude to be a relaxed, easygoing one. This attitude affects each of my choices; in effect, I have multiplied each of my drawing steps by it so that they are each directly informed by my attitude. My thesis statement (Big Idea) is the direct product of my drawing steps from the breakdown passed through a naturalistic view. I have created a primary line of action that harmonizes all of the parts of the figure to communicate the action of my subject; laid in the supporting lines of action of each of the limbs; developed the rough block-in of the silhouette based on those linear ideas; and subsequently laid in the volumes first as cylinders with cross contours to let myself feel perspective on the limbs; and lastly finished by quickly developing the forms that imply musculature. The resulting drawing has a clean silhouette with a clear action. However, because my attitude was one of simply wanting to reflect the action (naturalistic), there is no implication of character or story; it simply functions as a life drawing. I can use the same base formula to experiment with different attitudes toward the reference photo, with slight variations. This drawing was completed with a soft charcoal pencil sharpened to a fine point on smooth newsprint. The medium chosen was a direct product of my attitude, since I first take into account the Tone used to approach a drawing before I choose the medium necessary to best reflect it. This in part is what results in Mood, which will become more apparent with the introduction of mixed media. There is no Theme influencing the reference photo, so for this particular study I need not worry about it, nor its effects on my choices.

Demonstration Drawing 2

Because I feel that the first drawing lacks any particular characterization and does not imply enough story/characterization (however loosely interpreted and implied), I decide to slightly alter my base formula:

$$\text{Thesis Statement} = \text{Tone (Lines of Action + Shape Analysis + Form Analysis)} + \text{Medium}$$

In this case, to alter my attitude (Tone) toward my subject, I choose to execute this quick sketch while listening to Scandinavian death metal (see Figure 5.12). The reader might recall this particular exercise idea from an earlier chapter. Listening to this wildly different cacophony of sounds directly after completing the first demonstration results in a drawing with a slightly different narrative context: now my subject is more aggressive and notably more forceful in her full body expression. There is no delicate line work featured as my approach results in choosing a *different* stylus for the completion of this study. I opt for a thick, chunky, extra-soft charcoal stick, in lieu of a finer tool. I do not want to dwell on details, as I feel that the music that informs my mental space does not allow for my consciousness to pick out musical details. Furthermore, my volumetric forms are directly affected: while I still opt to use cylinders to describe the volumes of the limbs, the forms of the musculature are gruffer and not as refined and delicate when compared to the first demonstration. The marks themselves are harsher and bolder, and the figure in general is more *crunchy*—that is, the lines present are not as long and fluid as the previous demo.

Figure 5.12

Variation under the influence of Scandinavian death metal.

Demonstration Drawing 3

In this third iteration—still a quick sketch—my Tone is changed yet again to result in a different characterization (see Figure 5.13). This time I have opted to change the Tone of the drawing to a sweeter one, and my intent is to make the subject feel more sweet and feminine but strong nevertheless. Instead of Scandinavian death metal, I choose a more uplifting pop song that is fun and much lighter and easy to listen or dance to. I am still using the same formula:

Thesis Statement = Tone (Lines of Action + Shape Analysis + Form Analysis) + Medium

My approach is now altered because I have chosen to alter my attitude once more, which means that I will choose a medium to best reflect my new attitude. I switch out my paper so that now I am working on smooth white paper rather than smooth newsprint and opt for a thick and soft color pencil instead of charcoal. I want the marks themselves to feel smooth, crisp, fresh, and light; and I want to be able to work in more swirling, sweeping, longer marks (ligado) than rough, scratchy, short ones (staccato). In this drawing, my forms are smoother, and longer, with considerably more S and C curves than the previous sketches, and the anatomy has been very idealized to mostly show volume but not over-developed muscularity. My goal for this drawing was to create a traditionally appealing idealized female hero, and the face, hands, and feet have also been developed to express that. The face is round with large features; the hands and feet are large so that they feel strong, balanced, and more than capable but have

Figure 5.13

Variation under the influence of Erasure.

also been sketched with very round ideas. Overall, this drawing is markedly different than the previous one, and the only difference was my attitude, which helped form the basis for my approach.

How I Define Approach: When I participate in a life-drawing session, whether short pose or long pose, I decide before starting what my Approach will be. Why is this important? It allows me to create a clear objective for the drawing session and further allows me to think of what style I would like to practice working in, and what media. This allows me to use life drawing as a learning tool to better not only my drawing skills, but also my visual communication and storytelling skills. If I only need to practice drawing a human figure with realistic proportions, my Approach for the session reflects that objective. Conversely, if I feel I sorely need to practice some facet of visual storytelling, my Approach changes. I think of my Approach somewhat like this:

Approach = Theme + Tone + Mood

My Approach dictates what my media will be and what Style I will want to use to reflect the particular story I want to explore and tell for the session. Keep in mind that I will often think of Style as Theme + Tone. Mood is included here because I oftentimes practice Illustration during life-drawing sessions, and different illustration techniques are very efficient ways of developing Mood in a work. If the poses are long enough, one may complete simple illustrations during a typical 3-hour session. My ideal pose lengths for this type of drawing study are what I consider to be *medium length* poses, ranging from 5 to 25 Minutes.

Anything longer than 25 minutes I consider to veer toward long pose. When working from life for myself (that is, noninstructionally), I usually bring a variety of media with me for experimentation.

Study Questions

What do you typically do in a regular life-drawing session? Do you always do the same thing? Do you always use the same media?

Let's look at the effects of different attitudes and approaches to short-pose character sketches (see Figure 5.14).

This page of life drawings from class highlights the exaggeration and appeal that may be applied to the volumetric, three-dimensional forms that make up the anatomy of a human figure. Each figure has a slightly different characterization of the head and face. Stylistically, I chose to approach the session that day with caricature in mind. I consider caricature to lean toward cartoon, though the goal is to base one's exaggerations on the most prominent or idiosyncratic features of the subject. This approach informed my decisions the whole way through the construction of each figure; my intent was to not leave any stone unturned. The muscularity itself is developed most notably with the ideas of squash and stretch in mind, as well as appeal, exaggeration, and arcs. The arcs can be felt in the cylindrical volumes of the limbs, and the shapes and forms themselves have been carefully thought out to not only flow harmoniously through the body in accordance to the initial *lines of*

Figure 5.14

Cartooned forms and exaggeration allow actions to read clearly.

5. Working with Forms and Volume

action laid in but to also feel warm and inviting, friendly rather than overtly masculine—hence the rounder, *softer* forms, instead of boxier, *harder* forms. My attitude toward my subject and the desire to reflect his figure with warm appealing shapes and forms was a culmination of my objective for the session (focusing on caricature and exaggeration) and the model's charismatic personality. This particular model, Jee, is always happy, uplifting, warm, and friendly; his personality is what I attempted to capture during that session. This is also an example of how a drawing may feel finished even though there may not be any lighting or rendering applied to it; the figure on the bottom has a little bit of value added to it, but because of the nature of quick sketch it's not always possible to add value, so it was not a priority during this session. My priorities were as follows: *lines of action*; Shape and Form; and the results of having a specific Tone or Attitude in mind. Note that because I emphasize thinking of the silhouette early on, these full figures do not necessarily need to have the silhouette readdressed to feel finished, and the marks used have variance to them to feel as such. Even when working in a style such as this, solid drawing is absolutely needed to recognize ideas, even if they are not drawn in exactly how one sees them.

Using the same idea of attempting to capture personality, we will expound upon that concept further to begin exploring Acting to a deeper degree. Acting is effectively the most obvious way we see story during life drawing: even if we had no costume, props, or even decent lighting and all the model has to interact with is themselves, we can see story and narrative implied by the *Actions they choose to perform*, and *how they've chosen to perform them*. If faced with a model who does not act, it is up to the artist to imbue their drawings with acting. This is why we must practice from life, working with models who excel at acting, as well as practicing it ourselves. Acting is a craft and discipline unto itself; we must respect it as artists and learn as much as we can about it and how people are in order to emotionally touch and resonate with our audience. The first aspect of acting that most students tend to think of is the head and face. While the head and face provide an excellent opportunity for expression, it does not do to neglect the hands and feet, nor the full body itself. This is why we must keep in mind our *lines of action* when developing acting and full body expressions; a human being emotes with the entirety of the body, not just bits and pieces (though there are some individuals who are more introverted and their body expression will show that idea through body language). First, let's look at facial expressions (see Figure 5.15) and how to simply imply them through gestural marks, rather than belabored drawings—which, while important and recommended, falls outside the scope of this study guide.

This image is a compilation of two different sessions from in class. The head studies to the left are all very short studies. My goal for these was to study how this specific model interprets different emotions and how he expresses them. I asked my students to take turns calling out different emotional ideas, or scenarios, and the model reflected for a moment before he took each pose. His face is particularly great for studying the squash and stretch present on the forms when emoting. The features are all directly affected by the movement in the muscles of the face, and each different emotion or scenario results in a different configuration of movements. Anatomically speaking, there is a lot of information going on in the face, and we are capable of a wide range

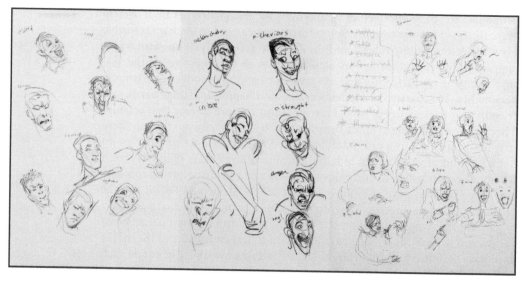

Figure 5.15

Facial expressions and acting studies.

of subtle microexpressions. Instead of worrying about getting a likeness, or even worrying about developing each form as solidly as possible, I instead opt to sketch the expressions using the inherent gestures of the shapes and forms present, meaning they are implied rather than explicitly stated. This means I am

1. Using the graphic shape of the head
2. Separating out the shape of the hair
3. Laying in the features, thinking of geography and the relationships between the features based on the *lines of action* of the face

The head and face may be thought of as having its own distinct primary line of action, which helps dictate orientation when used in conjunction with vertical and horizontal axes, and minor *lines of action* of each of the major portions of the face and the major muscles activated therein. Without the understanding of basic forms, these quick sketches would have felt more labor intensive; this is the advantage of solid drawing and understanding simple geometric forms within an organic figure. The cluster of female sketches on the furthest right is another set of facial expressions but with more hands and upper torso present. In this case, the model found it nearly impossible to facially emote without the use of her upper torso, and arms and hands. She found it unnatural and difficult to adequately express the emotions we called out (which are seen on the left, checked off) without the use of her hands and torso. This is why we should execute this type of study often, with different subjects: we all emote and react differently, and we all use our bodies to reflect those emotions differently.

The next page of studies shows two models acting off each other (see Figure 5.16). Disregard the fact that they are clothed for now, as the same approach can be used for both nude and costume.

5. Working with Forms and Volume

Figure 5.16

Exaggeration used to study acting and distinct expressions.

This session delved specifically into studying two different characters acting and reacting off of one another in spontaneously created narrative scenarios. The characters featured are a butler and maid; the models provided
their own costumes and props. My concern for this session was to show the
proportional differences between the two, as well as isolated acting studies. The top cluster of drawings focused on sketching the two characters as
quickly as possible while still retaining a clear action and expression. This
means that my forms were simplified and downplayed, and the figures were
constructed based more on Lines of Action + Shape/silhouette. Their expressions have all been exaggerated, and the use of arcs is very apparent throughout every figure. The bottom section of the page shows isolated studies of
the disgruntled butler. Here, because I was only concerned with one figure,
I was able to slow down just enough to indicate form more solidly, which
was necessary in order to show the tilt of the head of the drawing to the left
and the effects of perspective on the facial features, and to show the figure
sitting on the chair to the right, with proper volumes to make the figure feel
clothed and with some sense of weight. Weight is one of the most important
aspects of making something feel alive and should be studied often. Even if
forms are only implied, we can still evoke weight by exaggerating a figure's
actions (pose).

Building from the ideas we have looked at so far, let's now see the effects of Style and Tone and how they form the basis for the approach used for a drawing session based on developing characters (see Figures 5.17 and 5.18).

Both of these drawing compilations were completed from the same model during two differently themed short-pose drawing sessions at my studio. To give the reader some background as to how I typically set up a drawing session, I will briefly overview how I plan one. First, I think of either a theme or objective for the session or the model I have in mind. In the case of the first set of drawings, I knew that I wanted to hire this model, Toni, for the session, but did not have a theme or objective in mind. Therefore, I asked her for some character ideas based off her costumes, and we decided on The Green Fairy. Toni is an excellent character and story model, so I know that I can rest easy

Figure 5.17

Simplified forms and volumes allow one to stay more or less on model during a short-pose format life-drawing session, allowing one to design and explore a character in a single session.

Figure 5.18

Mixed media allows one to begin exploration into tone and mood, and their influence on style and vice versa.

5. Working with Forms and Volume

that she will provide the session with interesting poses that evoke story. My personal drawing objective for the session was to develop a simple, stylized characterization of Toni and, once having decided on a stylized model, to attempt to draw on model for each pose. This is something I do often from costumed figures to practice the discipline of *staying on model*, which is useful when drawing sequentially, such as for comics, animation, or storyboards. My formula for this session was the same as earlier:

Thesis Statement = Tone (Lines of Action + Shape Analysis + Form Analysis) + Medium

where Tone (my attitude toward the subject) directly influences my Approach, since here I am thinking in terms of Approach = Theme + Tone + Mood. Furthermore, since I consistently think of style as Style = Theme + Tone, I am able to decide what style I would like to experiment with based on the Theme of the evening and how I find my attitude toward it. Sometimes, I have no idea nor reference as to what kind of style I would like to work in, so that's when I choose to find it through exploratory drawing (much like the sketches from earlier in this study guide), where I experiment with each drawing until I find something I feel works. I chose a red color pencil for this session on white smooth printer paper, so that I could work at a smaller scale to finish or attempt to finish each figure as quickly as possible and to help control staying on model. The Tone of each drawing is a lighthearted, comical one, to counter the negative connotations of absinthe and to underline what the Green Fairy represents (I think of drunken mishaps and general tomfoolery). I multiplied that tone by each of my drawing steps from my Breakdown: the lines of action, the shapes, and the forms have been thought out each time to remain consistent and on model as much as possible. The resulting Style is a simplified, cartoony one, and the character is ultimately depicted as spunky and perhaps slightly mischievous.

The second set of drawings is from a session with Toni in which I had previously thought of the theme for the evening. This was completed around Valentine's Day one year, so the theme was Dark Valentine, since I wanted to avoid anything too sappy but still thought it would be fun to draw something seasonal. Toni interpreted the theme freely, and the resulting drawings from the session are intended to fit the theme. So, once again, thinking of the formula from before, I took into account the Theme + Tone to decide on a stylistic direction and thought of an approach from there. Part of my approach was to use a medium that I felt was best suited for the occasion and to evoke a scratchy, almost silverpoint feel. I wanted the character to feel wraithlike but still appealing. Therefore, most of the exaggeration directly affects the proportions of the figure and the shapes, including the silhouette. My volumetric forms have been downplayed but are still there in order to show some cast shadows and to understand what the skirt is doing. This is an example of implying form, not explicitly stating it, and using it to develop a flat drawing. Because three-dimensional forms have been downplayed, there is notably much less squash and stretch present in the final drawings (it is used extremely sparingly here) and, because of the style I chose for the session and the way I physically put down marks, the arcs that are normally present in my figures have also been downplayed and appear stiffer, as do my shapes.

Exercises

The following exercises are intended to aid the reader in experimenting with shape and volumetric three-dimensional forms.

Assignment: Master Copy

1. Find an artist whose Shape and Forms are designed with care and intent. This can be any artist whose work speaks to you.
2. In a sketchbook, copy as much as you can from that artist. Keep your drawings varied in terms of subject matter, and do as many as you can find. Oftentimes, when assigning this as homework to my gesture-drawing students, a number of them gravitate toward entertainment design artists, such as for videogames and animation, since all of their work must function within the scope of either a videogame or animation. Simply put, those artists' work must be relatable to the world that is being created, so intent becomes easily visible to those of us using their work to study. When completing this assignment for myself, I often choose animators, visual development artists, or cartoonists for this assignment, but any artist can be chosen.
3. Execute a drawing session in which you attempt to draw in that chosen master's style from life, attempting to see and interpret Shape and Form as they would. This means that you must (a) attend an Uninstructed Life-Drawing session; (b) hire your own model; (c) ask someone to model for you; (d) work from a photo or Internet reference. This is now working as Pastiche.

Experimental Exercise: *The Taste Game*

One important aspect of how I view Shape and Form is as an opportunity to develop *flavor* in a drawing. I will often play with my shapes and forms during a single session to develop as many flavors as possible, equating the thesis statement, or the sum of all my choices and actions, to a dish or meal. This approach further helps when developing a painting or larger, more finished project, especially one that is heavily stylized. It is experimental in nature and offered as a fun, "right brain" respite from the more academic analyzation of three-dimensional Form. This is most fun within a group setting, especially if time and space is allotted for class critique, in which every participant talks about their work. If a group dynamic is unavailable to the reader, it can still be performed individually on an exploratory basis or if one finds themselves drawing the same forms over and over and would like a break.

Preparation

Find some small snack items that are suitable for the participants. If playing with a group, it is a good idea to ask if anyone has allergies before starting and to make a note of which snacks contain known allergens. One may choose three to four different snack items. For example, I might choose sour gummy worms, dark chocolate–covered nuts, chili-covered mango, corn nuts, and peanut butter–filled pretzels. Ideally, one is aiming for a good variety of tastes—sweet, sour, bitter, salty, and umami—or combination of tastes; and textures—crunchy, soft, chewy, airy, etc. Each snack will have its own specific flavor and texture profile.

Exercise

Ideally, this exercise will be performed during a drawing session with a live model, but any other scenario will work, such as working from photos.

1. Each participant takes three to five pieces from each snack sample and takes them back to their drawing horse.
2. Each participant will execute approximately three 4-minute drawings from the model for each snack sample.
3. Before drawing, all participants will have 1 minute to taste their first sample and brainstorm key words that come to mind. Write all of the brainstorming on the same sheet of paper that the drawings for that sample will be on. Typically, I will write the name of the snack at the top left of the page, followed by my key words.
4. The model will then perform three 4-minute poses, and each participant will attempt to draw the model using the flavors and texture of that snack sample. If the snack was sweet and crunchy, the drawing should read and feel as *sweet* and *crunchy*. We are using the taste and texture of each snack as the Theme for each set of drawings, and the brainstormed key words allow us to develop an attitude toward that Theme (in lieu of the subject). How will the characteristics of each snack affect the *lines of action*, Shapes, and Forms of our subject? What is the resulting flavor of the drawing? It is not only the Forms that are affected by this experiment; we must think of the relationships between Line(s) of Action, Shapes, and Forms and what happens when we begin to alter different variables such as our Attitude.
5. Repeat with each sample.
6. When finished, if working in a group environment, it is ideal to conduct a class critique at this time. Ask questions such as the following:
   a. *What ideas were you thinking of when drawing?*
   b. *What characteristics of each snack were most prominent to you?*
   c. *How did you attempt to capture those characteristics?*

This is the base version of this game. There are a number of ways to alter, change, add to, or otherwise develop to suit different needs.

Study Questions

How might you change this game to suit your particular needs? What other kinds of exercises can you think of in order to experiment with Form?

Additional Homework

If the readers find that their drawings lack solid communication of three-dimensional Forms and volume, it may be necessary to take a small step back and reassess foundation. If this is the case, the readers are encouraged to regularly practice still life and object drawing. Anything the readers can do to develop solid drawing is strongly advised.

If the readers have not yet taken *instructed* Perspective and introductory Visual Communication classes, it is imperative to do so, as they will aid in the development of Solid Drawing.

Additionally, if the readers have not yet taken an *instructed* introductory Figure-Drawing class and they find their drawings lacking too greatly in structure, it is

Figure 5.19

A character study featuring cartooned forms and volumes.

Figure 5.20

Quick-sketch drawing using simple shapes and forms and exaggeration to clearly communicate the action.

5. Working with Forms and Volume

necessary to do so. It is recommended to begin with classes with titles such as Figure Drawing 1, Intro to Figure Drawing, or Analytical Figure Drawing. Different institutions and studios offer different names for the same or similar courses, so research into each class should be completed. long-pose Figure Drawing should be practiced hand-in-hand with Short-Pose or Quick-Sketch Figure Drawing or gesture drawing, as it will provide the time necessary to understand the relationships between structure, gesture, rhythm, and harmony, in addition to principles such as staging. Again, an instructed introduction to both long-pose Figure Drawing and gesture drawing is ideal as it provides life reference as to how other artists might approach each subject, and provides peers the reader may influence and be influenced by, in addition to offering a teacher present for critiques/class critiques. There is no such thing as too much practice, especially when it comes to developing draftsmanship and solid drawing.

Figures 5.19 and 5.20 show two instances of focusing on volumes during life drawing.

6

Using the Silhouette

We will now revisit the silhouette with the intention of refining ideas, defining plane changes, and reestablishing both visual clarity and clarity of our thesis statement if necessary. The silhouette is one of the most important tools of communication we have, as its graphic nature can make it visually comprehensible in an almost universal way. We can take this opportunity to ensure the clarity of the Action of our subject, and the Acting used while performing the Action; we can also reassess that we have successfully communicated our intended ideas. Again, we can choose the appropriate level of finish for our drawing depending on the application and intention of the artist. We will also see how we can develop a quick sketch using predominantly the silhouette for the linear and shape lay-ins, which has been mentioned before; we will also see how we can bring a drawing to a level of finish using silhouette, shape, and form in conjunction, to give an idea of how interrelated they are. This will further lay the groundwork for the following chapters, in which we will see how we may *re-mix* this general Basic Technique and Breakdown in order to practice flexible problem-solving during quick-sketch gesture studies and drawings, using and reprioritizing the elements that make up the basic architecture of an observational drawing so that we may practice drawing with both speed and accuracy in communication (see Figure 6.1).

We may use the following concepts at this step:

- S curves, C curves, and Straight lines
- Exaggeration
- Acting and Action

Figure 6.1

A study of silhouette.

And we can use the following Principles to aid us in the refinement of our drawing:

- Squash and Stretch
- Arcs
- Exaggeration
- Solid Drawing
- Appeal
- Staging (if working with Composition)

Basic Technique: Step 5

Now that I have all of my *internal* construction completed, I can refine my silhouette, taking into account a more accurately observed sense of Positive and Negative space, and defining as many plane changes as necessary or desired to reflect whatever internal information the drawing contains—such as the forms that make up the anatomy of the figure—depending on my desired effect. If the drawing is meant to be based more in realism or naturalism, I will take time to reflect plane changes that define the three-dimensional structures and anatomy more accurately. I can now further refine the head and face, taking note of any plane changes that are necessary to define, based on the shapes and forms I have previously placed. If drawing utilizing a strong, primary light source (for form lighting, or chiaroscuro effects), I can squint my eyes down to see the shapes of the shadows that define plane changes and show the forms of the anatomical structure, aiding me in the refinement of my ideas. If the drawing is meant to be stylized, one can step away from realism to varying degrees, opting instead for any effect within the *range of naturalistic to extreme exaggeration*, or to any degree of cartooning. As the drawing approaches the more extreme end of the spectrum, the less crucial the plane changes become. They are still important, but may not always be as critical as other aspects of a drawing during quick sketch. However, if lighting is involved, plane changes must still be addressed, as their presence in the drawing makes understanding the way light falls on form simpler, and they can be further organized and utilized to control edges in the work—especially if working on a drawing with an intended high degree of finish.

If desired, upon completion of this step, one may finish the drawing, utilizing finishing tactics—in this case, *finishing tactics* here means making marks on the page that add to the finish of the drawing, so that the drawing has a finished quality to it rather than a *sketchy* or unfinished quality (see Figure 6.2). If the drawing is meant to incorporate lighting and rendering, we can move on to the next step, or Key Topic, of our Breakdown.

I would like to point out at this time, my *autopilot* methodology of drawing—that is, every time I draw or sketch for myself, for personal work or fun, or begin any kind of lay-in for a work that is intended to be finished in some way—I *predominantly* draw using the silhouette. I will use whatever Key Topics from our Breakdown in *whatever order* I deem necessary to achieve my goal for each particular drawing, while working toward a silhouette. This is why not every procedural step is seen in a life drawing; as artists, we economize our efforts to get the drawing done as efficiently as possible. This is why the Key Topics have been presented

Figure 6.2

A stylized study utilizing the silhouette and action.

in an organized, procedural manner, so that the readers may now choose to utilize those Key Topics in any order they please, whether in the order presented, or remixed so as to facilitate efficiency of problem-solving, and to develop ideas during drawing that have purpose. Being aware of each of those Topics helps us define and enrich as many facets of our drawings as possible. The flexibility of the general Breakdown cannot be stressed enough, and again, the reader is invited to experiment with the reorganization of ideas and the idea of stressing individual Key Topics over others during academic life drawing periodically, so that each individual Topic may be studied and the effects of manipulation of each Topic observed. For example, should the readers find themselves struggling to find a solid, forceful, and confident line of action, they may choose to spend an entire drawing session focused on just that one idea. The same holds true for any of the other elements of figure/observational drawing we look at within this study guide: practice each element both individually and in conjunction with other elements (see Figure 6.3). This approach to practicing drawing is systematic and lends itself to self-study and self-critique, and is especially suited to those who do not often have access to instructed or otherwise pedagogically structured life-drawing classes. Simply put: it's up to the individual to keep the axe sharp.

The following demo continues the long pose started in Chapter 5. We will continue to see the development of this long-form figure to see the relationships between concepts and to further demonstrate the importance of practicing both Long Pose and Quick Sketch for the maximization of drawing and gesture comprehension.

Figure 6.3

Shape and form + clear silhouette read; short pose.

Demonstration: Silhouette Construction for Long Pose

This portion of the long-pose demo is fairly simple: my goal at this stage in the development of a longer drawing is to make sure that my silhouette *before lighting/rendering* reflects the gestural *lines of action* of each part of the figure (both the primary and supporting *lines of action* (L.O.A)) as well as the volumetric forms that I have developed (see Figure 6.4). Using the *internal* construction of Steps 1–4 presented in the Breakdown as process, I refine the silhouette by clarifying the positive and negative space present in the pose, especially if I have made changes to it. I further refine the silhouette by indicating plane changes more accurately on the outside contours of the figure. Essentially, the silhouette represents the external information, which, when combined with lighting/rendering, will ultimately be the only aspects of the drawing seen by an audience. My goal with a long-pose drawing that is Realistic/Naturalistic in Tone is for the audience to *feel* the internal construction and anatomy of the figure, regardless of whether they can see it. This concept is what we will use to develop clothed or costumed figures, in which the goal is to feel the anatomy and gestures of the body *beneath* the clothing.

In developing any silhouette regardless of whether drawn during a short-pose or long-pose silhouette, *my main concern is the consistency of ideas*. This particular silhouette demonstrates the degree of refinement we may want to complete during a long-pose drawing session, before our shadow shapes and value have been laid in. For long pose, my goal is not only to keep consistency in ideas but also to make sure that the silhouette is not too tired or stiff. As with most representational artists, I want to maintain a certain freshness to all of my drawings regardless of how long I may have spent on them. Practicing gesture in long pose allows us to take our time to see the relationships between *lines of action*, Shapes, and Forms and how the silhouette helps tie all of our information together. In essence, I develop the *lines of action* and rhythmic/harmonic properties so that the silhouette may reflect those ideas; the clearer my silhouette reflects those properties, the faster my viewer will be able to read what I have just drawn, no matter what my stylistic choices are. Furthermore, spending a little extra time and care with my silhouette allows me to check my rhythms and make sure they

Figure 6.4

Silhouette comparison.

are harmonized; the same holds true for the harmony of my shapes and forms. I will be able to see quickly whether or not something is working by checking the silhouette and the positive/negative space on the page. Taking time to conscientiously develop a silhouette will further allow us to see what areas in our figure are weak and strong. For example, if I never practice long-pose drawing or drawings of long enough duration, I run the risk of not studying plane changes and the geometric aspect of the forms of the body enough to ensure solid drawing. One simply needs an adequate amount of time to do so, and any aspect of drawing that will provide more solidity and strength to one's draftsmanship should be given enough time and patience for development. Drawing cannot be rushed, even during quick sketch. The more I practice defining my silhouette during long pose, the easier it will be for me to develop one during quick sketch or to use the model's silhouette to develop its gesture—reverse engineering. As was mentioned before, I like to begin and end with the silhouette, and I tend to keep it in mind while drawing, as it allows me to be more aware of composition and staging. The importance of visual clarity in the silhouette cannot be stressed enough, simply because it is such an effective communication tool.

Demo Silhouette Construction for Heads, Hands, and Feet

Much like the long-pose figure seen before, I approach the silhouette refinement of the head, hands, and feet in a similar manner, refining the positive and negative space present and refining plane changes (see Figure 6.5). Included in the silhouette refinement of these subjects, I have opted to design and lay in the shadow shapes present. This can be done when working with one's volumetric three-dimensional forms, as it is necessary to squint the eyes in order to see the volumetric forms present in the figure to begin with. We use light to define volume and plane changes, so it is appropriate to lay in the shadow shapes present as early as step 4 when dealing with form. The shadow shapes themselves will help us immensely with understanding the forms we are looking at. If working a bit slower for Long Pose, we can take our time with our internal construction and lay in the shadow shapes after we have developed

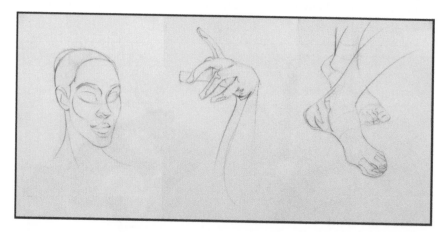

Figure 6.5

Head, hand, and feet silhouette + shadow shapes.

our volumetric structures, as seen here. Note the level of simplification in the head, hands, and feet: I am more concerned with the gestural qualities of each and the individual nature of the forms present, so that I may develop a drawing that reflects Ashli's head, hands, and feet and not just a generic model of what I think they should look like. My goal is to identify what makes Ashli's expressions unique and how her personality motivates how she chooses to hold her head, hands, and feet. This study will be crucial for when we develop drawings based predominantly on acting, expression, characterization, and story. My goal for any kind of long-pose study is always Gesture first, Structure second, as gesture provides me with context, subtext, personality, and life qualities; without these ideas, the subjects will merely be inactive, stiff shapes existing on paper.

Concerning Drawing Multiple Subjects from Life and Applying the Drawing Elements from the Breakdown

Every so often, we have opportunities to conduct life-drawing sessions that include multiple models posing together in a controlled setting. As luxurious as it is to draw multiple figure models at once, drawing multiple subjects offers its own set of challenges. We must now take into account the following: Proportions, Scale, Perspective, Staging/Composition, Lighting (if applicable), and Costuming (if applicable). We will now explore the first four of the listed concepts, and we will come back to lighting and costuming in the chapters dedicated to those Topics, since lighting and costuming an individual versus multiple figures follows essentially the same strategy. We can approach a multisubject drawing using procedural analysis. When it comes to multifigure quick sketch from life, I no longer use the Breakdown in order as I did the long-pose demonstration before. I now consider this type of drawing an *application* of my Breakdown and the elements of drawing that it represents. As always, we must first define our Big Idea or thesis statement of our drawings as early as possible. This may be done before the first mark is placed on the paper or while we lay in our primary line of action. We must keep in mind that every one of our subjects has its own individual primary line of action and supporting ideas in addition to whatever compositional visual flow we intend for our entire picture—that is, if time permits for such opportunity (such as in long pose, or the lay-in of a long pose). Furthermore, each subject has its own *individual silhouette*, full of information, which we may push and pull depending on the narrative we are constructing or the relationships we are developing between the figures (if any; sometimes it's difficult to develop any kind of narrative and/or relationship, and therein lies the challenge of multifigure life-drawing sessions). If we are lucky, the models will act, interact, and react to and with each other; if not, we will have to develop the characterization of each figure more fully. Typically, such a session is not fully supported by a short-pose session format, unless in class or if short poses are being used for warm-ups; it is common for multifigure life-drawing sessions to strategically feature longer poses, most commonly ranging from 5-minute warm-ups to 10–25-minute poses. However, every session is different and as such we must reprioritize our process based on the given lengths of time and what our goals for each pose are.

*Two Variations of a Basic Technique Breakdown
for Multifigure Life-drawing Sessions*

*Basic Technique 1 for Quick Sketch (Short Poses,
Lasting between 1 and 5 Minutes)*

Since I know that I don't have enough time to develop staging, I will put more focus on the first few Key Topics of the Breakdown: thesis statement, Line(s) of Action, Exaggeration, *rhythm*, and harmony, and if I have time, two-dimensional ideas and possibly rudimentary three-dimensional Ideas (such as cylinders or cubes/boxes, or trapezoids if time allows) (see Figure 6.6). Since this is now an application of the Breakdown, we do not need to follow the Key Topics in the sequence presented: we can now re-mix the sequence of ideas to more precisely construct our story. In the case of Quick Sketch, my story may be simple and/ or abstract in concept. It could simply be about the relative Proportions of the two figures; or it might be about the difference in the style of movement between the two models. Whatever it may be, I know that time constraints will limit my thesis statement to a simple one, rather than a complex one that a longer time length may allow me to explore. I will start by looking at the silhouettes of both figures and roughly lay in the graphic two-dimensional space they take up on my paper, controlling the scale and placement. Even though I don't have enough time to necessarily develop Staging to its fullest, I can at least practice control over composition, placing my grouped figures on the page in such a way as to avoid strange cropping or other compositionally bad choices, at least as much as is possible under time constraints. I will then quickly sketch the silhouette of

Figure 6.6

Quick-sketch two-figure study.

6. Using the Silhouette

each figure within that graphic space, beginning with my *lines of action*, then moving on to my Tube shapes. I tend to stay predominantly graphic with quick-sketch–style short poses, designing silhouettes with intent and energy rather than spending too much time with internal construction. Usually, I will opt for laying in very simplified and economized facial features and hands and feet, since this will allow me to explore at least a small amount of acting and characterization in a short amount of time. If I need to check proportions, I will opt for quickly studying and checking alignments on my *X*- and *Y*-Axes, rather than taking full-head measurements.

Basic Technique 2 for the Gestural Lay-in of a Pose of Longer Duration (Whether Single Figure or Multifigure)

In the event that I have a longer pose to work with, such as a 10-minute Pose, or anywhere between 15 and 25 minutes, I can incorporate a higher degree of staging and composition into my drawing, taking care to emphasize the gesture, movement, and life quality of every element of my composition, whether it be just the figures themselves, or costuming and props, or set pieces (see Figure 6.7). In this case, I will more or less use the Breakdown in the sequence presented, since now I have to think about a whole picture, rather than only one figure. I will begin by defining the graphic space my primary subjects take up on the paper; this is a very abstract shape and may be organic, geometric, or completely abstract. This helps me define *where* the action is taking place and lets me be more mindful about composition or, if a specific narrative is involved, staging.

Figure 6.7

A "medium-length" study; medium length can be anywhere between 10 and 20 minutes.

I will also roughly lay in or block in a rough, exaggerated silhouette of any other objects that will be in the picture (costuming, props, etc.). When I block in a silhouette, I am merely using my *lines of action* (even if they are not drawn/laid in beforehand, they are still present and I am aware of their nature) to roughly define the two-dimensional space that silhouette will utilize, using alignments where necessary to understand relative proportions, scale, and depth. If I have time to use head measurements, I will, but I will most likely combine them with alignments to save time and to allow myself enough flexibility for exaggeration. I will then place as many marks as necessary as landmarks, though these landmarks may not necessarily be anatomy based; instead they can be any fixed point in the composition to be used for spatial reference. In the event my figures are costumed, I cannot necessarily rely on anatomical landmarks; thus any other fixed point I can find will fulfill that role. In cases such as this, I will opt for vertices/corners and occlusion shadows as fixed points, since these things don't move around too much unless the model breaks, and even then it is fairly simple to aid the model in repositioning. I then typically choose one figure (if multiple subjects are posing) to start blocking out with more definition and refinement, developing the silhouette using predominantly one- and two-dimensional ideas that have been imbued with whatever exaggeration of my choosing, whether that means exaggerating the action, the acting, the shapes, the proportions, or even (roughly) the facial, hand, and feet expressions. I am holding off on defining three-dimensional ideas for the time being, and any simple 3D ideas that I have incorporated at this stage are few and not heavily defined. I will construct each subject in my composition in this procedural way, working predominantly with 1D and 2D ideas, before incorporating more defined Perspective and Volumetric 3D ideas. This will help me be aware of the graphic nature of the entire composition and make it easier to fix and change things; my goal for a drawing like this is to make the interaction of the figures as clear as possible, since typically this type of drawing aids us in the study of characterization, acting, and expressions, all elements of story. Even if I do not light or render this multifigure life-drawing study, I will have at least practiced each of the Key Topics of the Breakdown and applied them to a pictorial composition with the intent to communicate a more visually literal story, presenting ideas of characterization; acting; costuming; props; and staging/composition (see Figure 6.8).

Regarding Animal Sketching from Life

Drawing animals from life is one of the most challenging and fun exercises one can participate in (see Figure 6.9). While we will only superficially discuss this practice, since this Study Guide concerns itself primarily with capturing the Human Figure and developing the story potential of a drawing, it is *highly* recommended to practice animal drawing from life. Many art schools have one or possibly more dedicated Zoological Drawing courses, and there are also instructional books on the practice as well as on the subject of Animal Anatomy. This particular practice comes with its own specialized set of challenges, most notably capturing the myriad movements different animals are capable of. This makes them excellent subjects for quick-sketch–style drawings and studies in movement, rhythm, and harmony, as well as shape design and proportion. To draw animals from life, we can approach the practice in a way similar to that which we employ for drawing a human figure: we can still utilize the Key Topics from our Breakdown, and all

Figure 6.8

Playing around with staging during a medium-length pose.

Figure 6.9

Short-pose watercolor study of my cat. Quick-sketch techniques are useful when drawing animals from life.

of the story-derived concepts and Principles of Animation can still be applied; we will now have to very quickly prioritize which Key Topics are most directly applicable to each individual situation the artist encounters upon observation. In this way, we can use Animal Life Drawing to practice organization of ideas and creative problem-solving.

Basic Technique

This image shows gestural quick sketches drawn during a recent trip to an equestrian center (see Figure 6.10). Note as well the amount of notes I take while sketching. It is not enough to merely observe an animal; ideally, one will find oneself in a situation in which the handler will be present as well to field questions regarding anatomy and behavior as well as personality and character notes. These are some of the types of notes found in the pages from that particular session. If no handler or trainer is present, opt to take notes regarding character/personality traits or how the animal behaves. Even if we project onto our studies, we will at least have practiced defining character/personality qualities that will aid us in developing Acting. Typically, I will approach an animal subject from life much as I approach a live human: I will quickly analyze the silhouette and decide what Idea (or Primary Idea with Supporting Ideas) feel most important at the moment, and use that Idea as the base for what Key Topics I feel will most contribute to the successful communication of that Idea. This will inevitably depend on the pose the animal takes at any given moment; if the animal is at rest or engaging in an activity that allows it to stay relatively still, I can dedicate more time to developing more complex ideas, such as Shape and Form, plane changes, or even lighting and rendering if at all possible. If, however, the animal is active and a deep study is not possible, I will opt instead to utilize a quick-sketch–style of drawing, focusing on the first few Key Topics: Energy, Line(s) of Action, *rhythm*, harmony, plus Style of movement. If possible, I will also attempt to identify and study any observable instances of the Principles of Animation,

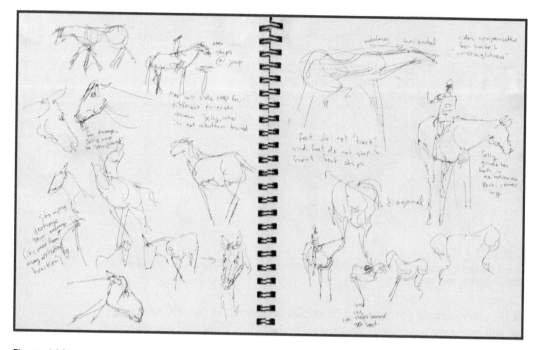

Figure 6.10

A page of horse studies from life.

6. Using the Silhouette

most notably those most concerned with the Mechanics of Motion, Arcs, and Appeal. This Basic Technique is in no way the only method of approaching animal life drawing, or *Zoological Drawing* as it may also be referred to; the reader is advised to study this practice in more depth with instructors who specialize in it if they mean to take animal drawing to more refined levels, or if any kind of Creature Design is an intended specialty. It is recommended that all visual artists practice live animal drawing with some regularity, as animal movement can provide endless inspiration for other works, and the applications are vast and useful. If live animal subjects are not readily available, one can also study from photos, though the sketches produced from them will focus more heavily on silhouette design, Anatomical Study, Shape and Form, and Proportions than on Motion and Energy. For those who are interested in being able to draw different animals, both real and imagined, study from both life and photo reference is ideal, as spending longer developing an understanding of different animals' anatomy is quite useful for a number of creative and illustrative reasons.

Concerning the Development of Gestural Concepts in Inorganic Objects and Stationary Subjects

We can also utilize the silhouette to aid us in developing Gesture-based ideas and ultimately stylization in both Inorganic Objects (such as a light post, fire hydrant, or car) and Stationary Subjects (such as a tree, rock, or mountain). We see stylization and characterization developed in nonliving, inorganic objects all the time, whether it be in books, movies, advertisements, cartoons, etc. These characterizations and anthropomorphic objects still retain appeal and relatability through the use of stylistic design choices and providing a spark of life in their being. Furthermore, stylizing objects and props within an environment contributes to World Building and history. We see this approach in the beautiful, gestural stylized shape/form design of props and environments throughout entertainment, particularly in video games and animation, design that is completed with intent and clear ideas. Although we primarily use concepts from Visual Communication and Perspective to successfully describe the structure of these types of subjects, it is not until we infuse them with Gesture, or Energy, that we can tap into their story potential. While the level of exaggeration employed while describing these subjects is entirely relative and dependent on both the artist and the application, we can still utilize our Key Topics to maximize the ultimate Statement we make when drawing them. This will affect Style, Tone, and Mood in our work, and if these Inorganic Objects and/or Stationary Subjects are drawn in the same composition as a Human Figure, we can play *rhythms* and movement Styles off each other, creating an intriguing *song*. This is how we can approach Costuming, Drapery, Props, and other Set pieces present during our Figure-Drawing session, most notably if working with long pose, or in an illustrative style.

Experimenting with Story-Driven Ideas

Now that we've looked at the Basic Technique of developing a clear silhouette from life, let's look at some of the ways we might now use that concept to develop narrative, acting, and character/personality in our drawings. It has been previously mentioned that my own autopilot method of drawing from life predominantly uses the silhouette. This is because the silhouette allows me to be aware of the bigger picture at all times and the relationships between my figure or figures and any other objects or environment within the composition; it keeps me from getting bogged down in details that, while may be ultimately important, are not necessarily useful for developing a picture with a very clear Big Idea or thesis statement, nor one in which more literal narrative context and subtext is present, such as in an Illustration completed from life. Keeping in mind the silhouette further allows me to practice Staging and what possible changes may need to be made to the pose or model within my drawing in order to make the picture read clearly. We shall see varying examples now of how one may utilize the idea of the silhouette to explore Narrative and Acting during a life-drawing session. The following drawings have different degrees of stylization and exaggeration applied to one or more of my drawing elements as presented in the Breakdown. These drawings have been completed in accordance with my autopilot methodology; that is, using the Key Topics from the Breakdown in whatever order necessary to communicate my intended thesis statement. That means, when drawing for myself, I can prioritize communication concepts in such a way as to work more efficiently.

Using the Silhouette for Quick-sketch Studies of Acting and Body Expressions on a Single Subject

In this particular acting/expression study, we see an example of quick-sketch–style gesture drawings completed with predominantly the silhouette in mind (see Figure 6.11). The forms are implied by the silhouette, overlaps of shape, shape design, and gesture lines that indicate the contortion of facial muscles. The primary objective for this study was to focus on acting/expression of specifically the heads and hands (that is why the model remained clothed for this set of exercises); this is also why the clothes themselves are indicated with shape and gestural indications of folds: they are simply not my main concern for this study. Each pose lasted between 1 and 3 minutes, depending on the intensity of the pose itself—some of the more intense poses were broken early, which is why developing a quick-sketch style of gesture drawing is useful. If one has a go-to process for quick-sketch style sketches and studies, it will be easier for one to study intense expressions that are difficult for the average person or

Figure 6.11

Acting studies.

model to hold for an extended amount of time. The exercise we used in class to develop these sketches was as follows: We each took turns shouting out random emotions or story scenarios for the model to work with. We began with emotions/moods focusing on the head and hands and then progressed to full body expressions and more emotionally complex narrative scenarios; each sketch had the scenario written next to it so that we could keep track of the possibilities of expressions. Note the "clumsy murderer" figure in the third panel of the image: this is an example of the concept of staging when utilized in conjunction with acting (Acting + Staging). The scenario given was Clumsy Murderer, so our model Rick chose to stage himself in such a way as to heighten the *comedic tone* of the expression. The Action feels funny because he chose to stage himself with his back turned toward the audience, his head and upper torso twisted to face us with his shoulders shrugged. Had he not chosen to stage himself in this way the expression would not feel as funny. His body language reads as confused and unconfident, his facial expression slightly befuddled, his hands open with palms facing up in a "I dunno" kind of gesture: the sum of these choices develop the tone of the body expression, which, when combined with the prompt, results in a drawing full of humor due to the amount of visual irony present. We don't typically associate the concept of *murder* with *clumsiness*, which helps to develop the visual irony of the drawing, and when combined with Rick's superb acting, which is normally very humorous in tone and a clear silhouette, we end up with a study that can be used as reference when developing our own personal work. We can use these types of studies to create a visual reference library and to explore how differently individuals express themselves and use body language.

Using the Silhouette for Quick-sketch Studies of Acting and Body Expressions on Multiple Subjects

This image shows two multiple figure studies with two different tones: the drawing on the left is a study based on an Idealized Realism approach, while the drawing on the right is a quick-sketch study based on a Cartooned approach (see Figure 6.12). While the study on the left is a longer pose, it is included here to show contrast in Tone or attitude and how that influences the approach chosen to develop the study. Let's look at this drawing first and see how the Tone has influenced my choices. The theme for the evening was one based on vintage pin-up girls, so both models came in character with full costume and props. To stay in theme I chose to adopt a Tone of vintage, idealized realism, as is present in pin-up works by artists such as Gil Elvgren. Stylistically, this attitude still falls under Realism, so my exaggeration in my *lines of action*, Shapes, Forms, and resulting silhouettes does not feel unrealistic or cartoony, simply idealized. This drawing is one in which I kept the internal construction to a minimum in order to keep the drawing clean and easy to read. It has been developed using predominantly the silhouette, positive/negative space, and a combination of alignments on both a vertical and horizontal axis and head measurements to check proportions. The rough block-in of the silhouette was laid in with *lines of action* built into it. From a gestural standpoint, my lines of action have been subdued and are more about subtlety rather than over-the-top exaggeration. Furthermore, I made sure to include accuracy in the description of the actions of the hands and feet and the subtle expressions in the models' faces.

Figure 6.12

Contrasts in Tone and style.

The drawing next to it shows a two-figure composition executed in a quick-sketch gesture-drawing manner: I worried more about the Action + Acting to lay in the silhouette of each figure. Because this was such a short pose I chose to switch to a medium that would allow for spontaneous decision-making without allowing myself to second-guess my instincts (brush pen). During the session in which this sketch was created, our models came as Sherlock Holmes and Dr. Watson. Our Sherlock was portrayed as a bit of a big-headed, larger-than-life, and extremely extroverted Detective who gets a little too enthusiastic about things, while our Watson was his perfect foil: calm, reserved, studious, and observant. In this particular sketch we see our Watson on the left taking notes in an annoyed manner, while our Sherlock is overjoyed with sharing his cheese with his rodent friends. Because these models are also professional actors and entertainers, they bring full costumes and props so that we may see the effects of Narrative on Acting more clearly. When enacted during class, our Sherlock had merely one plastic rat toy balanced precariously on his lap, while miming the cheese feeding action; our Watson had a real notebook and pen. The narrative was embellished and the acting exaggerated to show the foil between characters. Because I only had a few minutes to capture this, I quickly gauged what my thesis statement for this picture would be (which wasn't too difficult because the models provided it for me) and laid in each character as quickly as possible, keeping in mind that I planned to exaggerate the concept of the rat; this meant that I had to find places within my negative space to place the multiplied rat friends around the silhouette of Sherlock's body and be aware of the resulting addition of mass. Obviously, when drawing this fast, we can't always be as exact as we want, so there will most likely be a few compositional errors here and there, such as tangents. It happens; when drawing so quickly our priorities must change fast, and it is impossible to keep absolutely everything in mind. When sketching like this, do not worry about good or bad, just keep sketching. This sketch further provides an example of exaggeration in concept or story: the rat has been multiplied and the initial concept elaborated so as to heighten the comedic tone of the story present. In this case, the

6. Using the Silhouette

story lies within the individual Action + Acting + Expressions of the two models in relation to each other; the contrast is what is humorous and important and what drives the emotional resonance of the sketch. I was not concerned too much with staging nor even with placing the chairs they are sitting on, due to time constraints, and simply because with this kind of sketch, my priorities lie elsewhere.

Using Quick-sketch Animal Gesture Drawings
for Ideation in Story and Character

These quick ideation studies explore ideas from the previously mentioned Horse Drawing workshop that the horse gestures and notes shown earlier in this chapter come from (see Figure 6.13). During that drawing workshop at the equestrian center, we were introduced to a particular horse named Nox, who happens to belong to a colleague from one of the schools I teach at. Nox has a very outspoken personality, and he's not afraid to let one know how he feels about things. He also has particular notes to his body language, and when speaking to the trainers and handlers present we learned many things about his personality and how he compares and contrasts with the other horses at the center. These sketches were completed upon returning home from the first day of drawing; I didn't want to lose any notes about the animals we were introduced to, so I explored Nox's personality type in a sketchbook while everything was still fresh in my mind. On the far left of the series, we see Nox based on how he appeared when we fed him an apple, his forelegs resting on an imaginary post. This is a blend of reality (Nox's messiness when munching an apple) and imagination (he was standing up normally when we fed him). The next sketch shows him with a bit of an attitude as he rests on the ground in the arena of the equestrian center, which has been loosely sketched for context; and the final sketch on the right shows different character/body expressions that a horse with Nox's personality may perform. This is another example of combining Action and Acting and infusing the acting with a specific personality type. We can explore acting in animals just as much as in human subjects and exaggerate to varying degrees: the actions themselves are exaggerated in concept as well as in gesture and silhouette construction. While I am concerned with maintaining more or less believable horse anatomy, I am

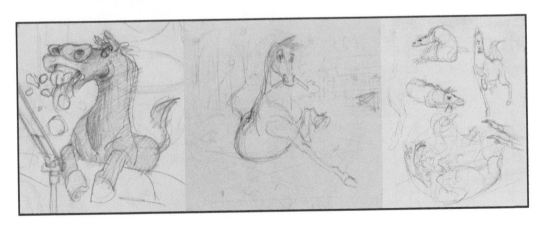

Figure 6.13

Character doodles based on preliminary life studies.

also concerned with the exaggeration of the facial expressions and how far I can exaggerate my horse before the point of absurdity (which is shown in the bottom sketch). Note as well when studying animals, they have more opportunities for finding secondary actions and imagining possible overlapping actions (if thinking of sequential possibilities) than their nude human counterparts, due to their increased number of appendages, as well as fur and tails. Because a lot of animals also have greater mobility in their ears, we can play with that part of anatomy as well and use ear expressions to support our facial expressions and body language. When studying animals and drawing them from either direct observation or photos, it always pays to do at least a minimal amount of research regarding that animal's behavioral tendencies and species-specific body expressions in order to carry out visual investigations of greater depth.

Another way we can carry our animal investigations even further is to create imaginative character or story drawings to which we can *apply* our findings (see Figure 6.14). Studying different subjects via gesture drawing is absolutely necessary for mileage and the development of the mind's eye; we can solidify what we have just learned from our studies through the application of ideas, which should also be practiced often. We will be introducing this idea here and continuing in Chapter 9.

This sketchbook drawing of a nymph and centaur was completed on the second night of the horse gesture-drawing workshop. After collecting gesture notes and sketches from life for the previous two afternoons, I decided to use my more developed understanding of horses to create an illustration with the intent of drawing something that I had either never drawn before or don't draw on a regular basis. For me, I know that I do not draw traditionally appealing, sweet characters or illustrations as often as I should, so I decided to use this opportunity to do so. This is an example of another exploratory sketch based on gesture drawings from live reference. This is something I do quite often as a means to apply concepts that have just been studied, much as homework is meant to do when in school. Once out of school many artists forget how useful homework is as a tool

Figure 6.14

Character drawing utilizing notes from live animal studies.

of comprehension; therefore, in order to keep the axe sharp, I will often assign myself some kind of homework to complete after a particularly educational experience. Usually, because most of my observation sketches are gestural in nature (I always think gesture first, as opposed to structure), I find that it is helpful for me to complete a more *finished* exploration of concepts studied during that initial gestural exploration. This is how we can use gesture drawings to preliminarily explore ideas and to find emotional resonance in concepts. By sketching horses from life for 6 hours over the course of a weekend, I was able to further my understanding of the following: a four-legged animal versus a two-legged animal; personality and its correlation to facial/body expressions; and the general anatomy of a horse (horses are not the easiest subjects to draw). These ideas came together in a fun exploratory sketch created with the intention to incorporate the animation concepts of appeal and staging, both of which happen to be of central importance to the nature of work that I typically create or gravitate to. Because this sketch was exploratory, there was no initial study or thumbnail; it was spontaneously thought of while drawing. The challenge therefore lay in balancing appealing design in the *lines of action* of both figures and their respective shapes and forms, while maintaining harmony in each of those elements. When completing this sketch, the silhouette was indispensable for creating the actions of each character and to place them on the page. The silhouettes were further utilized for staging purposes: because I had no initial thumbnail or study, I carefully considered the placement of the camera before committing to any one particular idea too greatly. To do so, I roughly blocked out the general gesture of the positive space on the page, which can be lightly seen as a semicircle or arc; this was enough information for me to see the drawing and stage it, knowing the limitations of the scale and size of the sketchbook page. This type of sketch can potentially be used to develop a story idea even further, and each character may be further developed to practice character design, expression/model sheets, or even for a set of sequential drawings that explore visual storytelling further.

Using the Silhouette to Develop Sequential or Story-Driven Gesture Drawings

An imaginative gesture-drawing exercise I like to do often for both myself and my students is one in which we work with exclusively 5-minute poses for the entire session (see Figure 6.15). Typically speaking, I consider 5 minutes to be on the longer side of quick-sketch or short-pose drawing, but the narrative and acting challenges presented in this exercise make those 5 minutes pass by fairly quickly. To give students some kind of direction or starting point, I assign them two objectives from which they can choose:

1. Every 5 minutes, draw a new story scenario complete with acting/expressions based on the model.
2. Develop a longer narrative, drawing a new sketch every 5 minutes that pushes a plot or story forward, complete with acting/expressions based on the model in some way.

The first objective allows complete creative freedom, tests the students' limits in imagination and visual communication, and forces them to complete ideas predominantly with gestural sketches with the intent of drawing something new every 5 minutes. They have complete freedom in the interpretation

Figure 6.15

Narrative sketches from a live model.

of the model, and quality is not necessarily an issue with this exercise; the goal is mileage in both gesture drawing, and visual storytelling and communication. The second objective pushes the imagination further, by now requiring an element of sequence to the work. With this objective, one must keep in mind plot and story, as well as the varying interpretations and angles of each of the model's poses and expressions. The students are allowed to stage, crop, or change their subject in any way necessary to produce a drawing that communicates a visual story. This means that if they want to add environments, additional characters, props, animals, etc., they can do so to their heart's content. They are not, however, allowed to use any other reference material (such as a phone), simply because this exercise is meant to test the scope and limits of the imagination.

The sketches of the soldier were completed during such a drawing session. My goals for these studies were as follows: to develop a simplified model of my subject that would allow me to reproduce her for a variety of sketches without veering off-model; to develop individual story scenarios that allow me to place the model's actions within context; and to develop a characterization or personality in my character if possible. Sketching like this forces me to be very aware of staging and composition; possible sequence (which means I may need to think of anticipation so that I understand the nature of the action being performed); exaggeration; secondary action; and solid drawing (which here would be felt in shape and perspective). While I also try to keep in mind appeal, I may or may not be able to control it the fullest extent possible in terms of shape/form design, so I limit my appeal to developing a protagonist who fulfills the role of an action hero. The primary concern for this type of exercise is to practice *Staging*. For this session my model came in full costume and props, and before starting our exercise we completed a partial turnaround to become accustomed to the main costuming; that way even if the model put a jacket on we would still understand what the bulk of the costume looked like. While this is not necessary, it does help when it comes to reproducing a specific character for multiple drawings, even if gestural in nature.

Exercises

The goals with the exercises for this chapter are concerned with developing comprehension of the silhouette, for both long pose and quick sketch/short-pose styles of drawing. It is recommended to use both hand in hand so as to support each practice to a fuller extent.

Before completing each individual exercise, be sure to give yourself a warm-up set that adequately loosens up the shoulder and forces you to practice your spontaneous problem-solving. To do so, warm up with sketches that last anywhere from 30 seconds to 3 minutes. The shorter the pose, the less time for structure and proportions; the longer the pose, the more available time to think through choices and decisions.

Exercise 1—Master Copy Assignment, Long Pose

Working from a master artist who appeals to you, find a work of theirs that showcases strong silhouettes. When assigning this in class as homework, I specifically ask for students to copy artist Charles Bargue, whose *Drawing Course* provides plates of strong silhouette and form studies. It is not necessary for the reader to do so here; simply find different artists and study how they each utilize the concept. When copying the work chosen, note how the artist has developed or used the silhouette. It is easiest to copy drawings rather than paintings, but paintings may be copied as well.

Exercise 2—Long-Pose Studies

Because master copies are not enough to attain full comprehension of drawing concepts, it is recommended to follow up a long-form master copy with a long-form figure drawing, if possible. This means you can complete both in one day or choose to complete the master copy the day before. Ideally, this long-form drawing is completed from life, though if time or money are restrictive, it is adequate to use photo reference for this particular assignment. Now the goal is to create a silhouette that captures one's initial gut instinct in relation to the gestural qualities seen in the subject, as well as weight and stretch or compression of volumes (squash and stretch depending on the level of exaggeration and tone or style of the drawing) where possible.

Exercise 3—Still-Life Studies

Stationary, inorganic, or otherwise nonliving subjects may also be studied in order to more fully broaden visualization capabilities. Because we oftentimes draw characters/subjects with props, costume, or environments, it is necessary to attain mileage in nonhuman subjects as well. To do so, and to further the principle of solid drawing, still-life drawings are recommended. One may choose to draw single objects at a time, or arrange multiple objects together in a composition. Whichever one chooses to draw, the concern here is with the silhouette and positive/negative space. Ask yourself: does the refined silhouette of each object adequately reflect any internal structure or information? Does the refined silhouette of each object read? If so, is it an instant read or slow read? Is there any ambiguity as to what the silhouette drawn represents?

The following images are meant to be used as references for exploratory gesture drawings (see Figures 6.16 and 6.17).

Use these images to create sketches that explore Character, Personality, Narrative, and Possible Sequence. Use the silhouette to construct these ideas, thinking in terms of Line(s) of Action, and Shape and Form to aid in constructing the silhouette. If it helps, one can think in terms of Tone (Line of

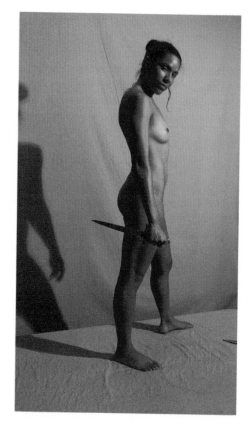

Figure 6.16
Reference photo of Ashli.

Figure 6.17
Reference photo of Ashli.

6. Using the Silhouette

Figure 6.18

Quick sketch of a motorcycle and rider.

Figure 6.19

Character sketch using exaggeration at every level of construction.

Action + Shape + Form) to aid in defining an approach. That is, what Tone or attitude might you have toward the subject in each picture? How would you multiply it by the *lines of action*, Shapes, and Forms? What is the resulting nature of the silhouette? Has it been greatly exaggerated? What stylistic choices were made while developing it?

Study Questions

How often do you use gesture drawing for creating reference notes? Do you ever keep your gesture drawings from when in class or uninstructed workshops/drawing sessions?

Figures 6.18 and 6.19 both utilize positive and negative space analysis plus observation of the silhouette as a graphic shape for their construction during quick-sketch.

7

Working with Value

Now that we have addressed both the internal and external architecture of our drawings, we can begin to study and design the shadow shapes we see on the figure. Our intention regarding lighting within the scope of this Study Guide is not to teach the reader how to render, but rather to introduce lighting as something we can control (to a certain extent) and design to heighten the story elements of our drawings. We will primarily utilize a *two-value system*—that is, high contrast, or black and white—and a *three-value system*—black, white, and a third grey value in between. We can graphically describe all of our information with Two Values and use a third to embellish if and when possible and/or appropriate. (During long-pose studies or paintings, we can keep breaking down value structure until we have a value range we are content with. For quick sketch, we don't have enough time to deal with complex plane changes or subtle value changes; therefore we won't stray into long-pose territory.) We will first look at how we may design our lighting, and then we will look at different ways to incorporate lighting during short-pose drawing, so that we may maximize both the *gestural* elements of the subject itself as well as heighten different aspects of the drawing (see Figure 7.1). This Chapter will concern itself with lighting as applied to both a *nude subject* (as when drawing academically) and afterward a mix of nude and costumed, when altering our approach for story studying purposes.

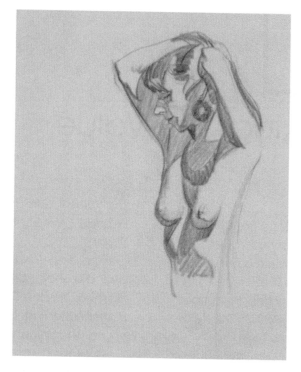

Figure 7.1

Short-pose study with organized shadow shapes.

We may use the following concepts at this step:

- S curves, C curves, and Straight Lines
- Acting and Action

And we can use the following Principles to aid us in the development of lighting in our drawing:

- Squash and Stretch
- Arcs
- Exaggeration
- Solid Drawing
- Appeal
- Staging

We typically utilize a strong, primary, directional key light source during a standard Figure-Drawing Session. This allows us to study and describe the following:

1. The *direction*, *strength*, and *distance* of a light source, and we can change these variables to further study more specific characteristics of different lighting setups and styles
2. *Plane changes* and *forms of the structures* of the Figure
3. *Texture*
4. *The effect of lighting on story*

7. Working with Value

Figure 7.2

Silhouette constructed first, followed by drawing out shadow shapes and filling with value. Gesture always comes first.

We can take cues from Photography and Cinematography to aid us in the design and even stylization of lighting on the figure for maximizing the story potential of our drawings. The following text and demonstrations will utilize this traditional lighting setup: one strong directional light source. That is not to say that one won't find other lighting configurations in different figure-drawing sessions. Indeed, one may find oneself in situations in which there are no single, strong directional light sources, effectively allowing the artist to work with only ambient or ambiguous light; other places utilize soft boxes for diffusion and both cool and warm light sources to mimic daylight; others prefer North Light, or natural light, to light their subjects; others use multilight configurations to produce a more complex or dramatic effect, complete with gels to influence the color and temperature (and ultimately tone and mood) of the scene. There is an abundance of different light configurations, and if the readers have the means to create and control their own dedicated space for figure drawing, it is recommended to experiment with light sources, configurations, and color/temperature, for both academic and creative purposes (see Figure 7.2).

We will first look at designing our *shadow shapes* (see Figure 7.3) in such a way as to infuse them with movement and energy (and thus complement the *energy* within the figure), rhythm and *harmony*, and logic based on observation; then we will look at stylizing our lighting during life drawing to experiment with story-based concepts.

After we are content with the visual information communicated by our silhouette, we may move on to incorporating lighting.

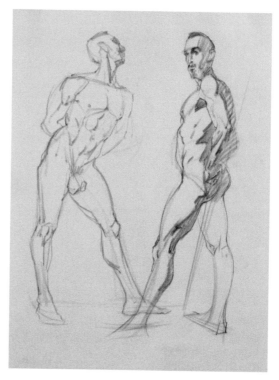

Figure 7.3

Gestural silhouette on the left, figure with rhythmic shadow shapes on the right.

Basic Technique

When drawing, squint your eyes and separate the light and shadow you see on the subject (see Figure 7.4). The goal is to see in only two values: black and white. Can you group the lights together? Can you group the shadows and any other inherently dark-valued shapes (such as dark hair) together? We are striving for logical, and clear organization of lighting. Once we have grouped the values, we can begin to design and draw the shadow shapes we see on the subject, using it to describe not only the shapes and forms of the subject but also textures. If time allows, one can further embellish the drawing by establishing any of the four types of edges: Soft, Firm, Hard, and Lost. If developing a long-pose drawing, it is advisable to design and draw the shadow shapes with a semifirm edge and a relatively soft touch—that is, soft enough to not cause indents in the paper that will affect the rendering of the drawing, but strong enough to be visible enough to use as a guide. In a long-pose drawing, the placement of the four edges becomes part of the rendering, as they are used to describe plane changes and their subsequent value shifts. During quick sketch we want to make these decisions quicker, so if we have to sacrifice edge control a little bit for the sake of visual communication, so be it. In other words, prioritize as is necessary; have a clear goal in mind as to what will be explored and experimented with in each drawing/pose. That is not to say that artists shouldn't challenge themselves: it's never a bad idea to attempt the organization and communication of different edges during short pose, as it will require speedy critical thinking (see Figure 7.5). For those artists who still

Figure 7.4

A lot can be said with black and white.

Figure 7.5

Value indicated during short-pose drawing.

struggle with understanding, organizing, placing, or communicating edges in a drawing, long pose is recommended as a means to practice that concept.

Demo: Long Pose Rendering with Limited Values

When dealing with developing lighting for Long Pose, we have more time to think our way through our value breakdowns and grouping (see Figures 7.6 and 7.7). Typically speaking, I will strive to build a strong sense of lines of action into both the internal and external construction of the figure, regardless of duration of the pose. Therefore, we see the steps taken leading up to the long-form study of our model Ashli. This study was laid in first with a primary line of action, giving me the sense of weight and tension in Ashli's head, neck, and upper back; without this dominant directional force, we wouldn't feel as much weight in our forms, nor would it be as simple to harmonize the actions and rhythms of the rest of the limbs. After the primary line of action is laid in, my supporting actions—or secondary actions, if you will—are laid in as supporting lines of action, each minor in relation to the primary line of action (L.O.A). I usually combine this preliminary step with two-dimensional tube shapes or cylinders, balancing straights with curves for visual interest and to better control my initial volumes. Note, at this stage, my drawing feels like a rough silhouette, with arcs laid in to denote geography/landmarks. My next pass consists of developing volumes to a greater degree, building the structures of the body with three-dimensional forms over the cylindrical forms of the body (again, they are simply my initial tube shapes but with volume denoted). I also chose to lay in cross contours where necessary to denote direction. This pass concludes with the mapping of the shadow shapes. Note that the shadow mapping occurred here before the refinement of the silhouette, as I needed to squint my eyes to use the shadows to denote form; because I was already using a *two-value system* to understand the three-dimensional forms of the musculature, I thought it more efficient to map out the shadow shapes

Figure 7.6

Long-form demo.

Figure 7.7

Previous analyses of the long-form demo.

more or less at the same time. In this case, I combined my form development stage with my *value grouping*. One has the option to decide whether shadows should be mapped while dealing with form or a step after, while dealing with the refinement of the silhouette. Simply put, it depends on the pose, and it depends on the individual artist to make such a decision regarding the prioritization of ideas and sequence of information laid in. Because I took advantage of using the shadow shapes to help me understand the three-dimensional forms of the body, I was able to consolidate two different steps of my drawing process. I then refined the silhouette as necessary to achieve the plane changes I wanted and to further refine the positive and negative space. Once my silhouette reflected the amount of information I wanted it to, I moved on to rendering. In this case, this is only a long-form study rather than a finished rendering. I focused predominantly on the parts I found either most interesting or most useful for me to practice. I found the head, torso, and front leg to be the most intriguing parts of the figure. I proceeded by filling in the shadow shapes with a flat dark value (approximately 80% grey), before laying in any other values or gradients. I then laid in black for the cores of the shadows and any other areas that needed to be pushed to a darker value, before laying in an approximately 25%–30% grey to break down the lights. My key values for the initial value pass are only four: white, black, 25% grey, and 80% grey. From there, I developed my edges around my forms with further value breakdowns—the values in between the four initially laid in. Because the background was not rendered, there are no edges lost around the perimeter of the figure, but I have practiced edge control to some degree within. Again, this type of long-form study is necessary in order to practice breaking down and grouping values and edges in a timely, nonrushed manner. If we only ever practiced short-pose gesture drawing, we would never give ourselves enough time to understand what we are looking at. We must let the eye develop as much as the hand.

Demo: Value Lay-In Head, Hands, Feet

Our head, hands, and feet were developed in the same manner as the long-form study (see Figure 7.8). After laying in shadow shapes, I blocked in my values, keeping them limited. These sketches are on vellum rather than newsprint or white paper, so the hand feel when applying charcoal is much different than for the previous demo. Note the texture present. When producing long-form sketches, it's fun to experiment with different drawing surfaces to see what resulting textures we may end up with. These sketches are not necessarily long-form, since they were

Figure 7.8

Head, hand, and feet silhouettes with value.

built sequentially for each chapter to demonstrate each stage in the development of a drawing. As a result, the manner in which they are drawn is much looser and quicker than the long-form study and the values even more limited. Each of these studies is predominantly two values—black and white—and there are more gradations present to quickly lay in additional values. *Regarding the directionality of strokes:* there are a variety of ways to lay strokes onto paper. Sometimes I will lay down strokes in a uniform direction; sometimes they move lengthwise up and down the form; sometimes they move across; sometimes they move with each individual form. It is entirely up to the artist to decide the manner in which to lay down strokes, especially when laying down fields of value. These sketches show a few possibilities for quickly laying fields of value (note the more informal, looser quality when compared to the long-form drawing presented earlier).

Simplified Rendering for Quick-Sketch/Short-Pose Drawing

When approaching lighting and rendering during short-pose gesture drawing (see Figure 7.9), we must prioritize and restructure our typical drawing process in order to be able to communicate the ideas we find most important. In this quick-sketch, I moved the light around the room while the students drew 3-minute poses using the *silhouette, shadow mapping,* and *gradations.* The objective was to develop a silhouette with a clear action, plus *lines of action*: essentially, to draw a silhouette that has gestural qualities built into it. To do so, I found it useful to draw a bounding box around my initial lay in, before breaking apart the positive and negative space. Within the silhouette can be found the concepts of *simple versus complex,* as well as rhythmic properties such as S curves and arcs. The hand on the ground has been left as a simple geometric shape that represents the grouping of the fingers in perspective. From there, I mapped out the shadow shapes by laying in the core shadows and cast shadows, as well as areas of occlusion. The strokes used are firm, dark, and bold due to the quick-sketch nature of this drawing. To contrast these firm bold lines, thinner, sharper marks were used

Figure 7.9

Quick-sketch gesture + value study.

as well in certain areas. Lastly, gradations were laid in to indicate turn of form and drop off of light; edges have also been indicated to some degree. I have the Firm, bold edges of the core and cast shadows; the Hard, finer lines that denote the contours of the body; the Soft edges that indicate turn of form in the upper back and the recession from the light of the upper leg; and Lost edges where shadow on the gluteus blends into the cast shadow beside it and behind the figure to keep the negative space open and serve as value contrast against the cast shadow from the arm. The medium used to achieve this was a jumbo-sized stick of charcoal in softness 4B, on smooth newsprint. If any value block-ins or rendering are desired for quick sketch, it is recommended to experiment with different combinations of mediums and surfaces. The final texture on a drawing or sketch can add to the level of finish desired and can help to describe tone, mood, and style in the event that such topics become the focus of a gesture drawing.

Ideas for Lighting Studies during Quick-Sketch/Short-Pose Gesture Drawing

Sometimes artists can get a little bored or burnt-out during quick-sketch/short-pose or gesture-drawing sessions; to help break the tedium one can choose to slightly change the focus of one's sketching per drawing (see Figure 7.10). This page shows how I might change focuses during class or an uninstructed workshop. Instead of drawing every single pose, I may opt to deal with individual parts of the body in conjunction with other miniature composition exercises. In this case, we see a leg study to the left of the page, with the objective of describing the action + gesture of the leg (seen in the line of action or arc describing the position and orientation of the leg); cleaning up the silhouette to reflect the anatomy; and drawing in the shadow shapes with core shadows prominent

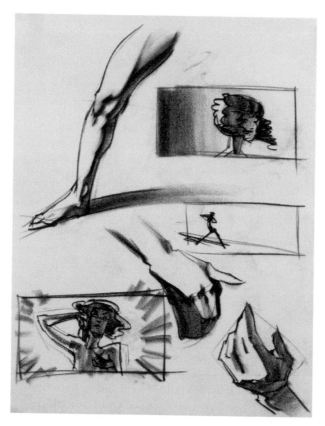

Figure 7.10

A page of gesture, value, and composition/staging studies.

and simplified reflected light. I could affect edges only slightly in the time allotted, so instead of laying in additional values, I opted to use my finger to smudge certain areas. The same technique is visible in the hand studies on the same page. The other smaller composition studies allowed me to play with positive–negative space relationships and direction of light. If you find yourself feeling slightly burnt-out during gesture drawing—quick sketch can get a bit tiring depending on the duration of the session—you can choose to shake things up a little bit by choosing your subject matter or by alternating whole figure sketches with isolated studies. This will further allow you to see the relationships between each of the Key Topics we have mentioned up until this point and to create harmony between them. The shadow shapes present on your figures must complement the rest of the drawing in some way; we can do so with design and harmonizing the gestural and rhythmic qualities in our drawing. Even when shading our drawings, we must do so with intent and clear ideas. This means that we must edit what we see and decide what information is absolutely crucial to each individual thesis statement (or Big Idea, if you prefer) and what information can be disregarded or changed to suit our purposes. We are dealing now with designing what we see for the sake of visual clarity and communication, rather than simply copying what is there.

A Strategy for Ambiguous Light

If we are working in an environment lacking a strong directional light source, the work method used for the previous studies may be challenging in that we may not have a strong sense of the volumes and forms present in the subject (see Figure 7.11). We will have more freedom in what we do with the lighting and may invent it if we so choose, but let us look at a strategy for drawing a subject under either multiple light sources or ambiguous light sources.

When dealing with ambient light such as is present in this drawing, it is often best to develop the silhouette first, by whatever means necessary. This drawing was completed by triangulating the highest, lowest, and widest points of the action and using that smaller graphic shape to develop the rough positive–negative space of the figure. The silhouette was then blocked in, refined, and values laid in. The figure is exaggerated lightly, focused more on capturing the model's flexibility, volumes, and contours, with the rhythmic qualities pulled from the shapes present in the anatomy. That is, most of the gesture we feel in this medium-length pose comes from the contours of the anatomy. Oftentimes I will refer to this idea as *inherent gesture*, or the natural flow and subsequent rhythms of the shapes that create the anatomy. There is still a strong primary line of action within this figure.

Figure 7.11

Ambiguous light study. The silhouette becomes very useful when the lighting is unclear or all over the place.

We can also stylize the light in many ways:

1. We can design the shadow shapes as we see fit, utilizing shape language that will help strengthen our thesis statement.
2. We can reestablish the light source in our drawing, helping us tell the story we see in our subject.
3. We can physically move or otherwise manipulate the light source itself to control the shapes and forms we see and, more importantly, *how* we see them.

The first two stylizations utilize the preexisting lighting of the room, while the last is dependent on the artists' ability to control the room itself.

Once we are comfortable with the basic technique, we can then stylize the lighting so as to emphasize story-derived elements in our drawings. Lighting can be used to describe our five *w*'s (and *h*): *who, what, where, when, why,* and *how*; most specifically being useful for the *where* and *when*. When drawing from a place of story rather than for academic reasons, we can change, stylize, and edit the lighting to accommodate our thesis statement, while still using the shape and form information from the actual light source present in the room. We can also use value as a means of showing mass moving through space, implying visual weight and movement to take up space on the page, as opposed to gesture drawings in which we use only line. There are a great many styles and approaches one can use to develop a gesture drawing or work with strong gestural qualities. We will look at a few different possibilities here and how they relate now to the development of Tone and Mood, in addition to Characterization, Expression, and Acting.

Using Value to Create Mass on a Picture Plane

These butler sketches are an example of using value to create a strong sense of mass on the picture plane (see Figure 7.12). Had they been left as drawings expressed simply with line work, the actions would not read as clearly. While the model himself is already very svelte, his thinness has been exaggerated so as to make the idea much more obvious. As a result, when drawing this model, I felt the need to clarify my positive–negative space in order to clearly see the action. I also felt that the type of line quality used for the initial gesture drawing matched too closely in concept to the nature of the character. That is, he is a thin, long character; to contrast this idea, I used energetic lines to lay in the gesture drawing of the figure. The slight variation in line thickness adds to the energy of the drawing; as a line drawing alone the figure lacks visual weight/mass. In order to combat this and to ground the figure further (done in conjunction with balance and exaggerating angles), I opted to lay in a more or less solid field of value. Now the figure pops off the page, and the actions read more clearly. Essentially, it is the body language that is set off by the addition of value as mass.

This drawing of an Adelita also exemplifies this idea, though for slightly different reasons (see Figure 7.13). This gesture drawing combined the block-in of masses of value (shapes of value, if you will) with the gesture drawing. That is, instead of drawing sequentially through the Breakdown as I would for a longer study, I opted to attack *gesture* and *value* simultaneously, while also using my fingers to soften edges. The resulting drawing is one in which I still have a strong sense of action and silhouette, but the mood of the drawing is slightly more romantic due to the diffusion of edges and the softness of forms.

Figure 7.12

Dark values make the actions pop off the page.

Figure 7.13

La Adelita.

Using Value + Gesture to Practice Composition for Staging

I consider staging to be one of the most important concepts of visual communication. In addition to being an important principle of animation, staging helps us understand the best way to show a specific idea to an audience. As such, we must practice as often as possible. This can be done in a great variety of ways, and we have already seen one exercise in which we may work from the model to create narrative context with our gesture drawings. The following are examples of how we might practice composing with value in order to strengthen our sense of staging when working more illustratively from life, or when working from our imagination (see Figure 7.14).

In this page of gesture drawings lasting no more than 3 minutes each, my objective was to create a clear gestural sketch of the model, in addition to placing him in space in some way. The top drawing shows the model on the model stand, backlit, and behind him the row of artists on the other side of the room drawing. This sketch loosely establishes some kind of foreground, middle ground, and background, in addition to establishing a sense of scale and distance. The bottom drawings are much more focused on developing the lighting on the figure, in addition to pushing contrast in the lights and darks. Both of these drawings play with the idea of contrasting loose, lyrical line work in the gesture drawing of each figure, with strong lines of action and sense of light.

Figure 7.14

Value + gesture in composition/positive-/negative-space studies.

Figure 7.15

Value + Gesture.

The drawing on the bottom right-hand side is what I would consider as having accomplished my objective, whilst the other two warmed me up.

Study question

During a regular drawing session, how often do you feel that you have accomplished your objective(s)?

This quick sketch was drawn al fresco in the middle of downtown Burbank during the CTN "Roadshow," regularly held in the spring of each year. Our models were costumed, in the shade, so there was no Key light or other dominant light source; instead we had ambient light to work with (see Figure 7.15). As a result, the drawings from that session deal predominantly with the action of the subject; positive–negative space breakdown to establish a clear silhouette; and the relationship between the content of the picture plane and the edges of the paper. Instead of avoiding tangents, strange crops, etc., I opted to experiment with the idea of the subject stepping into the picture plane, quite possibly while in the middle of a vaudevillian act, dance, or performance. To heighten this idea, the stage the models were standing on has been indicated, as well as a bit of the background. The background is ambiguous and not defined due to time restraints, but without it the resulting feeling of the character bounding into frame would not be as immediate; he would simply be a bit too floaty. The addition of depth aids in the concept of the sketch. Additionally, value has been blocked into the darkest areas of the subject, since shading was not possible due to lack of strong, directional light source. Instead, any inherently dark-valued shape is laid in with ink and brush, the strokes of which echo the lines of action present within the figure.

Experimenting with Lighting during a Short-Pose Gesture-Drawing Session to Practice Staging

When working with light and value, we have a greater opportunity to indulge in Tone and Mood studies, in addition to practicing composition and the idea of staging (see Figure 7.16). As defined as an animation principle, staging is very broad. One way that we can approach the concept of staging is to think of it as composition and camera placement. Essentially, the artists can think of themselves as the cameraman, and whatever they choose to show in frame is the story they are choosing to tell in the moment. Additionally, the artists can then decide on the type of shot necessary for their story in frame. For example, to create tension in a picture, I might choose to depict my subject with a close-up shot with strong diagonals or dramatic lighting. The sample shown depicts a slightly experimental exercise for this concept. Inspired by the wonderful book *Framed Ink* by Marcos Mateu-Mestre, the goal of this composition/staging exercise is to reenvision and stage the model within a bounding box on the paper, playing with the ideas of camera and light placement. The students work from a live model, and the key light source remains stationary to serve as form lighting. In this case, we use the light to give us information regarding the nature of the forms we are looking at. This aids us with staying on-model if we are attempting to maintain consistency (which is another facet of this exercise that increases the level of challenge). The objectives for each pose are to think of *framing; composition*

Figure 7.16

Invented lighting, staging, and composition studies from a live model.

within the bounding box (positive/negative space relations) and cropping; *panel size* (the aspiring storyboard and comic book students tend to enjoy playing with this concept); *imagining different lighting schemes/configurations* (this allows us to also practice visualization and training the mind's eye); and *shot type* and variety (and how that affects tone and mood). Essentially, we can affect tone and mood by the combination of shot type, framing/cropping, and lighting. If we continue to interpret tone as our attitude toward our subject as creators, we can additionally use this idea to establish the type of approach we might take, which further affects our stylistic/ design choices, as well as the type of media most suitable for whatever theme or story we feel is right for each pose. Since these studies are each based on very short poses, ranging from 2 to 3 minutes, I normally do not expect students to experiment heavily with mixed media for this; such experimentation would be more suitable if this exercise were extended to approximately 5 minutes each. We will see variations on this exercise and possible ideas in the exercise portion so that the readers may experiment with staging for themselves. This exercise further serves to practice the concepts of exaggeration and solid drawing, as both are necessary for visual clarity and understanding how to place imaginary light on forms, respectively.

Working with Value + Gesture + Tone and Mood

To further see how Tone and Mood can be affected by exaggeration, appeal, solid drawing, and how to use gestural ideas in hand with value/lighting, we will look at two samples that show contrast in both Tone and Mood (see see Figure 7.17).

The first image shows two medium-length sketches side by side, each different in Tone. These are not quick sketch in nature, but they do show how one might approach a longer study while maintaining gestural qualities. These sketches are from the same session with the same model. The study on the left is stylistically based in Realism, my stylistic approach affected by my attitude. The tone I attempted to create with this sketch was an academic one; as such, the gestural qualities of the study have been created to match that idea. My resulting thesis statement reads as

Figure 7.17

Contrast in tone.

Figure 7.18

Contrast in attitude and mood.

calmness or tranquility, and I approached each line of action present within the figure with delicacy and sophistication; note the arcs that make up the *lines of action* of the limbs. While they are there, they are downplayed, and the architecture of the body is more present within the shapes and forms used to describe the anatomy and the resulting silhouette. The objective was accuracy within the time allotted. For me, the expression of the face and the subtle rhythm of the braid were my focus, and most time was spent there. The legs and delineation of features such as the hands and feet have been sacrificed in order to practice organizing values under an ambiguous, multilight configuration. What happens when I alter my attitude toward my subject and subsequently change the Tone of the drawing? A possible solution to this question is the sketch next to it: the tone of this sketch is a much less formal study, with more appeal in the design choices made throughout. Stylistically, it veers away from Realism, toward the cartoonier side of the spectrum (though it is still not a true cartoon). What choices were made to alter the resulting Tone of the drawing? Firstly, there is a greater amount of exaggeration present at every stage of this drawing: all lines of action including the primary and supporting lines have been exaggerated using arcs; proportions of the figure and resulting positive/negative space relationships have been exaggerated; the shapes and forms present have also been affected, in both nature and scale, which means the perspective has been altered to be more apparent; the resulting silhouette is one that takes up more space on the paper, and as such feels more dynamic when compared to the sketch next to it; the value organization has also been addressed and has been simplified and exaggerated in order to read in a less tedious manner than would have resulted from so many conflicting light sources. Additionally, the hair has been used as an opportunity for secondary action, albeit loosely interpreted: rather than giving it some grand action, it deals more with contrasting a dynamic, twisting, and relatively more complex rhythm against the simpler rhythmic arcs of the figure. The change in one's attitude toward one's subject can make either a notable, obvious difference, or it can result in minor changes. It is recommended to experiment with this change in Tone and the resulting changes in approach and stylistic choices during a single drawing session, as doing so will result in seeing immediate differences.

These sketches deal with experimenting with mood during quick-sketch, and how we might approach it with tight time constraints so as to incorporate strong gestural qualities into each facet of our drawing (see Figure 7.18).

Much as with the previously mentioned lighting exercise, the objective during class with this set of poses was to practice constructing a strong silhouette with which to read body language/expression clearly, value organization, shadow mapping, and the relationships between these ideas and staging. Instead of controlling the staging, the intention was to see how each of the aforementioned concepts directly affects the ultimate thesis statement of each picture (these were also developed with bounding boxes so as to control composition and cropping) and the resulting Mood of each. In nature, they are exploratory drawings meant to allow the artist to explore how mood and staging relate to one another. When sketching these studies with the students, I found it extremely helpful to lay in a bounding box for each miniature composition, simply so that I would have an idea of where the action is taking place. Doing so while drawing from life allows me to practice the type of compositional challenges that arise when working with sequential art, such as with comic pages or even a comic strip. After building the bounding box, I proceed to lay in the silhouette of the figure, exaggerating as is necessary to make the Action as clear as possible. This helps me feel an appropriate mood for each sketch. Because the lighting was not changed between poses, the study of mood comes into play by observing when lighting thematically harmonizes with the intended thesis statement as dictated by the body expression of the model and when it strikes slight discord. This contrast is seen within these two studies: the study on the left depicts harmony between the thesis statement of the figure and the Mood created by the lighting and staging; while the study on the right depicts an instance when the Mood created by the lighting does not necessarily match the Mood expressed by the subject's body language. The study on the left is able to match in theme (which I read as *anguish*) in both the position and action of the figure (which is a component of staging) and the dramatic lighting. The study next to it has conflicting themes and moods: the body language reads as confident, playful, perhaps even sexy, while the lighting does not thematically relate to those ideas. When developing studies with value, we can experiment to our heart's content with the element of Mood and utilize our findings in the development of story-based works.

Exercises and Study Questions

How often during drawing do you practice the concepts of Tone and Mood, however loosely interpreted? How might you keep reinterpreting these ideas? How literally or abstractly can these concepts be utilized?

The following exercise ideas can be played with in order to practice as few or as many different aspects of draftsmanship and storytelling as is desired, and a couple of variations have been included. How might you change each exercise? What are your goals or objectives while drawing either short-form or long form with value and lighting?

Warm-Up Drills

It is always a good idea to incorporate some kind of warm-up into your regular drawing routine; a good warm-up sets the tone for the work day and allows you to loosen up, which is necessary for the maintenance of gesture and gestural properties within work that may require a higher level of finish, or if working with long-form studies at all.

Thirty-Second Mass + Movement Drills

Although these have been previously mentioned, they are being brought up again here because of the idea of infusing mass—that is, the positive space that your subject takes up on the picture plane—with movement and gesture, and the varying degrees of exaggeration that one can apply to either concept. These are best completed with a large, blunt stick of charcoal, preferably ranging from 4B to 6B.

Two-Minute Silhouette Contour Line Drawing

This drill aids in developing observation skills and hand–eye coordination, both of which are necessary to control the intended statement made with a silhouette. The goal is to avoid breaking contact between the drawing tool and the drawing surface, working slowly with great concentration. How accurately can you reflect a refined silhouette in 2 minutes using contour line drawing technique? This is meant to be sighted—that is, one may look back and forth between the model and the drawing surface.

Variation: 4-Minute Contour Line Drawing with Shadow Shapes - This drill is the same as the one above, with the addition of mapping the shadow shapes that are present within the figure. Note the time length is much longer so as to provide a concentrated study in accuracy. It is OK if the gesture in the figure is overlooked, as it is not the objective here. To complete this drill, approach the figure much as you would a regular silhouette contour line drawing, starting from whichever point makes the most sense at the moment, given the pose. From there, work back and forth between the outside contour of the silhouette and moving *across* the forms to map the shadow shapes present in the figure. This means that you may also map out shapes of the hair or features, since they will most likely be affected by lighting on the subject. While it is recommended to attempt this drill without lifting the drawing tool, it is quite the challenge to do so, and it is acceptable to break contact with the drawing surface whenever necessary to reposition the hand, to make shapes work, or if you get lost on the figure.

Lighting Exercise 1: Using Light to Develop Staging and Composition

This exercise is meant for a drawing studio in which one might be able to move around to view the model from different positions, though it is not necessary to do and may still be completed while the artist remains in a fixed position.

1. Work with 3-minute poses.
2. Leave the key or dominant light source in a fixed position on the model; this provides the reference for the forms present and to understand the information of the subject.
3. For each 3-minute pose, develop a new composition study. This means, on your drawing surface, create bounding boxes to frame each drawing. Use any aspect ratio desired, and if you are interested in experimenting with framing for comics/graphic novels, choose any type of panel design, varying widths and heights to see the relationship between the subject and the frame. Additionally, experiment with shot type, and, if feeling

ambitious, eye level. If experimenting with eye level, keep in mind what effects that will have on the perspective of the scene, and applied perspective on the subject. Think about cropping the figure in different ways and how that subtly changes or alters the mood of the drawing.

4. As soon as the composition has been laid in, reimagine the lighting in the scene. Because the model has been lit with a key light the whole time, we have some understanding of what forms make up their anatomy. There is essentially no right nor wrong way to do this, and you may approach the reimagining of the lighting within the scene by designing and drawing the shadow shapes on the subject first, thinking graphically with only white and black (two values) before filling in the shadow shapes with value. If there is enough time and it is desired by the artist, gradations to indicate turn of form or light drop-off, or a third value (such as a 50% grey) may be added. Keep in mind that the shadow shapes should reflect the forms of the figure and as such can be used as both a descriptor of information and as a tool for storytelling.

Ask yourself the following questions: *What mood is created with different light choices? Can you develop the lighting of the scene to match an intended mood, or is the mood dependent on the imagined lighting? What is the nature of the relationship between staging, lighting, and mood within each composition? Can you still retain gestural properties of the figure, such as rhythm, lines of action, etc.?*

Lighting Exercise 2

Much like the previous one, this lighting exercise is meant for a drawing space that allows the artist freedom in moving around the room and, more importantly, affecting the light source. For this exercise, we want to be able to move the light around the model and change its position however possible. If working with color, we can experiment with tone and mood further with the addition of gels, and instead of utilizing only short-pose gestures we can extend our studies into medium-length poses, such as 5s, 7s, and 10s. As always, the main objective is to create composition/staging studies that contain gestural properties.

1. Work with 3-minute poses.
2. Let the model work in 9-minute sets of 3-minute poses, total of three poses per lighting scenario. Move or otherwise affect the key light source every 9 minutes. Instead of imagining the light, we are using what information and ideas we are presented with and recording the resulting combinations of body language/expressions, actions, and lighting to understand the possibilities regarding Tone (our attitude toward the subject, which is ultimately expressed in how we develop the silhouette of the figure) and Mood (the resulting atmosphere created by the sum of our choices).
3. Much like the previous exercise, experiment with bounding boxes and panels, shot variety, cropping, and framing. The only thing not directly imagined in this exercise is the lighting on the model; we want to draw the light as we see it.

What is the difference between the two sets of drawings in regards to the story moments created within each composition?

To get acquainted with the basic technique of each exercise, the following reference photos of our model Ashli have been provided (see Figures 7.19 and 7.20). How might you approach each exercise using this reference?

Figure 7.19

Reference photo of Ashli.

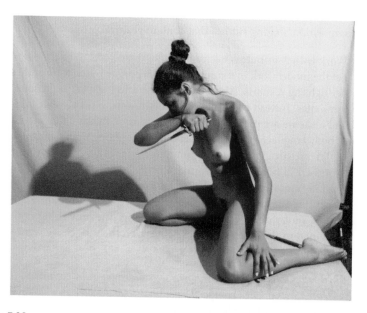

Figure 7.20

Reference photo of Ashli.

7. Working with Value

Figure 7.21

Mixed media to create subtle tone/mood in a character drawing.

Figure 7.22

Playing with value.

Variations

Possible variations for each exercise include the following ideas. The reader is invited to manipulate, change, reimagine, etc., both of the previous exercises to continue conducting investigations into drawing, gesture, and visual communication and storytelling.

1. Use multilight configurations in lieu of a single light source.
2. Extend pose length to venture into either medium or long-form studies.
3. Experiment with mixed media.
4. Practice with the addition of color.
5. Work with nude and costumed figures and if desired include props and set pieces.

This is the type of exercise that can be reinvented as often as is desired, for different drawing or visual communication objectives. *What are other exercises you can think of, invent, or develop to aid you in your comprehension of gesture, staging, tone, and mood?*

Figures 7.21 and 7.22 utilize different media to create different Tones and Moods during life drawing.

8

Using Gesture in Clothing and Costume

Now that we have seen how to break down the architectural aspects of the nude figure and how to begin to manipulate and combine them with story-derived concepts, we will now look at draping and costuming (see Figure 8.1) and how we may simplify it for capturing ideas quickly with life and energy.

Instead of attempting to laboriously capture every single fold and detail of drapery and costume, it is imperative that we edit. During quick-sketch style gesture drawing, we have a limited amount of time available to us to capture the most important ideas in both the figure beneath the costume, as well as the costume itself.

While long pose affords us more time to observe and make decisions, it is for the sake of visual clarity and communication that we must edit: too much detail and the drawing may lose impact. Therefore, we will look at the most common behaviors and ideas present in drapery and costuming as seen in life drawing; we can then combine these ideas with each other to achieve more interesting (or accurate) effects if necessary. We will be looking at the following ideas: (1) *tension points*; (2) *cowls*; (3) *pulls*; (4) *gathers*; (5) *cascades*; (6) *puddles*; (7) *trains*; (8) *spiral folds*; (9) *zig-zag folds*; (10) *half-lock folds*; (11) *ease*; and (12) *fit*.

Take note that sometimes the nomenclature for these concepts varies, and different artists and/or instructors will have different names for these ideas or will have combined multiple ideas under a different name. These concepts are gathered from different experiences and resources, such as from drawing in class with my

Figure 8.1

A fashion sketch.

Otis Fashion students, during which I learned a great deal about drawing, designing, and constructing garments and why clothed life drawing is so crucial for fashion students to maintain in order to anticipate what their designs may look like on a living, breathing, moving human being. This sentiment is true for the nonfashion artist or drawing student as well: the more we observe and draw a variety of subjects, the easier it is to visualize what our designs may look like in our mind's eye, which allows us to anticipate how those designs would work in space and motion.

While there is more to costumed life drawing than indicating movement in drapery and garments, these ideas are enough to visually communicate what the costuming/drapery is, and they are simple enough to identify so as to be able to manipulate them in accordance to any story-driven context. We can combine these ideas with the Key Topics from our architectural breakdown as well as with story elements and any applicable Principles of Animation.

Ideas That Occur Regularly during Observable Costumed Figure Drawing

Tension Points

Tension describes stress or strain in materials. A tension point is a point in a garment or drapery from which lines of tension originate due to stress or strain (see Figure 8.2). In garments, it is often the seams that create points of tension. Other points of tension may be caused by buttons, accessories, zippers, grommets, etc. We can often see folds and other properties of drapery seem to originate or flow from these points. When a garment is worn on a person, we will often see multiple points of tension due to the additional strain caused by that person's movements, and indeed our folds will be affected by them.

Cowls

Cowls are created when two or more tension points are close enough together for fabric to collapse (see Figure 8.3). The folds they create are cuplike in nature and will hug or *spoon* each other. The further from the tension points, the looser the folds appear, until disappearing entirely if the fabric is long enough. This fold may sometimes be called a *diaper fold*, and when named as such is sometimes seen with accompanying cascades. The accompanying image shows cowls drawn gesturally on the model, focusing on capturing the body weight and only implying ideas of the garments being worn. During class, we work with fairly short poses so that the students may learn to indicate and *imply* rather than spend too much valuable time rendering or otherwise trying to build the volumes of the fabric.

Pulls

One can think of a pull as the opposite of a cowl. In drapery, *pulls* can be interpreted literally: the fabric appears taught between tension points. This is worth

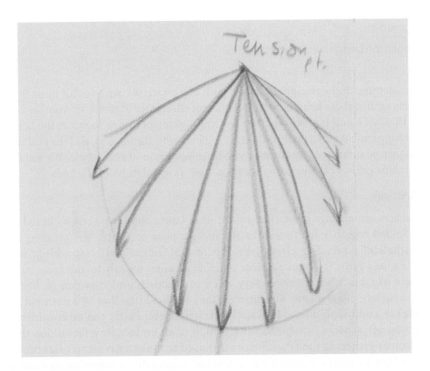

Figure 8.2

Tension points tend to radiate in curvilinear lines rather than straight ones, as they must wrap around the volumes of the figure.

Figure 8.3

Cowls can be seen in this model's top.

mentioning for the straight lines that pulls can create; we can contrast more fluid ideas against these straight lines for different effects (see Figure 8.4). Another way to think of a pull is when a person wearing a garment begins to move; the fabric of that garment will usually pull in accordance with the motion, and the pull will further be influenced by the material or composition of that fabric. We usually combine pulls with other draping ideas, such as spiral or half-lock folds.

Gathers

Gathers are exactly what they sound like: fabric that has been gathered or collected together for functionality and purpose or simply for creating an aesthetically pleasing effect (see Figure 8.5). Functionally speaking, one often uses gathers to make a piece of fabric smaller, usually to join to another piece of fabric. We see them very often in clothing, and they can be found in a variety of garments. Oftentimes, they are held together in a garment by a seam, commonly found in waistbands, cuffs, etc. Pleats can be considered a type of gather, as can smocking, which is an embroidery technique that involves gathering the fabric before it is used to make a garment; oftentimes, it is best to indicate smocking as texture, especially if meaning to convey the idea within a quick-sketch gesture drawing. It is advisable to edit this particular property, due to the amount of information gathers and pleats usually convey.

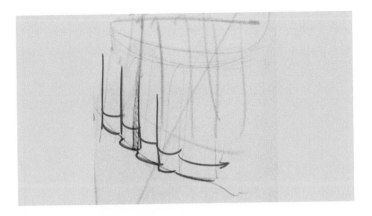

Figure 8.4

The straight line in red color pencil from which this pipe fold falls is a pull. In this loose sketch the drapery turned into pipe folds as the tension from the pull fell away. The pipe fold itself is highlighted in bright red. Note this sketch is a very exaggerated demonstration of the concept.

Figure 8.5

Loose, quick sketches of gathers.

Cascades

These occur when fabric drapes over something unevenly, or in a garment with enough loose fabric to hang and collapse (see Figure 8.6). We can see this in both women's and men's garments, such as in an asymmetrical skirt, wrap, or sarong; we can also see this property in drapery when setting up a still life that includes fabrics, or during life drawing with drapery. The *cascade*

Figure 8.6

Cascade seen in drapery versus how it looks on a clothed figure.

refers to not only how the material falls but also the lyrical, fluid *edges* of the material. Note that when a skirt or dress does not have an uneven base, instead of cascading, folds will appear more vertical and pipelike—hence the name *pipe folds* that is given to folds that occur in dresses/skirts/draping with an even base. These pipe folds tend to occur at a regular interval unless in motion. A common place to see pipe folds occur is in curtains, which happen to be swaths of fabric that are suspended with an even, flat base.

Puddle

Again, a *puddle* is often what it sounds like—anytime drapery or costuming falls and collects onto the ground (see Figure 8.7). The successful communication of a puddle is dependent on maintaining consistency in perspective of the ground plane that the subject is on; if the ground plane of the puddle is skewed in relation to the ground plane of the subject, the puddle will not look as intended. This is another concept that may need editing depending on the body of the material/fabric and the complexity of the puddle itself. We can see puddles in very long dresses, curtains, or when the life-drawing model poses with drapery.

Trains

Most of us are familiar with bridal trains in wedding dresses, but we can find them in other garments and costuming as well (see Figure 8.8). Trains are fun for the opportunities they provide in embellishing ideas and in the application of physics-related ideas, such as drag and inertia. We commonly see trains when

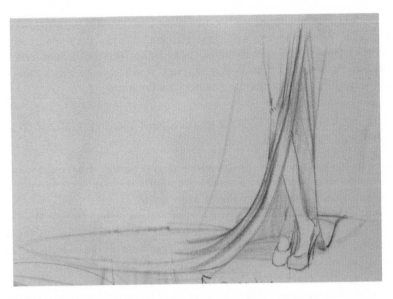

Figure 8.7

Garments that are long and extend past the feet generally puddle on the ground when the wearer is at rest.

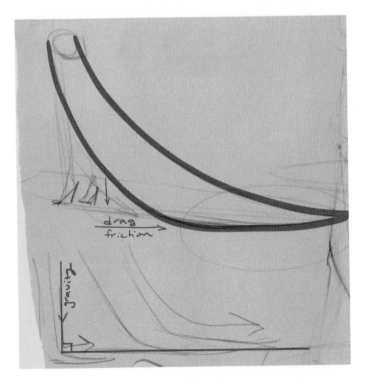

Figure 8.8

Sometimes garments are long enough to train behind the wearer.

our models wear costuming with garments or fabric long enough to collect on the ground. When standing still, these garments will puddle; when in motion, they will train. We can further embellish our trains with the ideas of secondary action, overlapping action, and follow-through, if we choose to utilize those concepts during life drawing, picture making, or animation.

Folds That Regularly Occur in All Street Wear/Sportswear Garments and Costumes

They may be combined with the previous ideas regarding drapery/garments in different combinations so as to allow for simplicity in implying and indicating during short-form drawing (see Figure 8.9).

Spiral Folds Spiral folds are a type of compression seen in fabrics. Most commonly seen on garments, spiral folds occur when the fabric is pulled by the body in motion. The folds spiral *around* the cylindrical forms of the human figure and may be interrupted by seams or other points of tension.

Zig-Zag Folds Zig-zag folds are a type of compression seen in fabrics. In garments, we often see them occur in joints or when fabric collapses and compresses. The folds created may be indicated by the *Z* gesture that runs through them. The volumetric shapes and forms created by zig-zag folds often look like *X*'s and *Y*'s and may also be given structure by drawing them as triangles. Keep in mind, if using only triangles or *X*'s and *Y*'s, we must wrap them around the volume of the

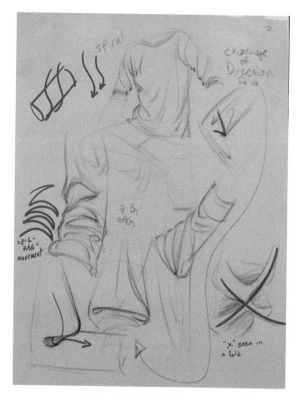

Figure 8.9

Spiral, zig-zag (or "X" and "Y" folds), and half-lock (or turn-of-direction folds).

8. Using Gesture in Clothing and Costume

figure in accordance to both perspective and the action undertaken by the model. If we neglect their inherent gestural properties, we run the risk of not feeling the human figure beneath the garments/clothing. We use a zig-zag motion to infer them in quick-sketch gesture drawing simply because attempting to draw their actual volumes requires time and organization, and it is much easier to infuse such a motion with rhythmic gesture, which we can harmonize with the rest of the model.

Half-Lock Folds Another type of compression, these folds typically occur when the fabric has become so compressed that it folds in on itself, due to a sudden *change in direction*, such as when we bend our arms at the elbow. We see them occur in the joints, and we can often see them occur in conjunction with Zig-Zag and Spiral Folds.

Ideas That Come from Garment Construction and Fashion Design

The concepts of *Ease* and *Fit* are dealt with more regularly in a fashion-based figure drawing class (see Figure 8.10). However, I have found that these ideas aid the regular, nonfashion draftsperson just as well, and for those who are interested in character design and costume design for characters, these ideas are worth investigating further, with a variety of different garments and materials.

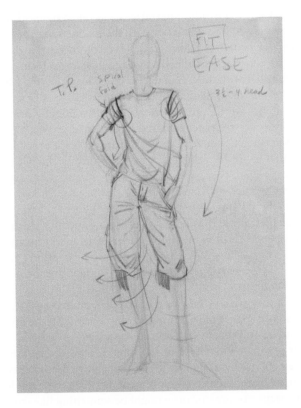

Figure 8.10

Showing the body beneath the garments.

Ease: A concept from fashion, sewing, and garment construction, *ease* refers to the space between the body and the garment. It is related to the Fit of a garment. While this concept is used typically in sewing and garment construction, we will use it as something to be aware of while drawing a costumed figure, as it may be used to inform decisions made during the drawing process. Understanding the ease in a garment will help us understand any effects on movement—and thus effects on our gestural analysis of the figure—the garment will or may incur.

Fit: This term describes how close to the body the garment is meant to wrap or drape around. A *tight fit* or a garment that is *form-fitting* means there is little to no space between the garment and the body, and the garment is meant instead to hug the wearer's contours and make them apparent. An *over-size fit* indicates that there is meant to be quite some distance between the garment and the body. Understanding how a particular garment or garments fit our subject will impact the choices we make while drawing them. Depending upon the intended function, different garments are meant to fit the body differently. For example, a tailored fit, such as in a full-tailored suit or a blazer, is neither too tight nor oversized; instead, the garment tends to skim or lightly hug the contours of the wearer and provide structure to different areas, such as in the shoulders.

Props

Props are a great way to introduce narrative ideas into a figure-drawing session, and help to provide additional practice with the interaction of organic and non-organic shapes and forms (see Figure 8.11). It is recommended to draw with props as often as possible to practice different types of creative problem-solving, as well as to become familiar with different but common ideas, such as "a figure holding and aiming a pistol," or "a figure riding a broomstick," etc. Essentially, it helps create a mental encyclopedia of experiences we can literally draw from in the future and helps make reference material more relatable. When planning out a figure drawing or quick-sketch drawing, it helps to place props fairly early on, during the initial lay-in for a longer drawing or during the placing of lines of action.

The inherent gesture, movement, or use of the prop should be taken into account. If heavily stylizing and/or exaggerating, the artist has much freedom in the shape language utilized throughout the drawing and thus the gesture of those shapes or movements. If drawing more academically, and thus more grounded in realism, or naturalism—that is, with limited exaggeration—we can choose instead to look at proportions and scale and juxtaposing or contrasting the organic shapes and gestures of the figure with the inorganic shape and gesture of a mechanical or inorganic prop. When utilizing organic props (I don't consider animals props, as it makes more sense to group them with the model and treat them as secondary subjects or additional characters), we can still compare and contrast their gestures with those of the subject, and we may find it easier to create complementary ideas; that is, it will probably be less challenging to harmonize linear, or one-dimensional movement, between the organic subject and those organic props. An organic prop might be something like fruit or a plant—anything that is reminiscent of life. An inorganic prop will feel deader in contrast to the living subject, and the use of straight lines helps with this association.

Figure 8.11

Using props in a composition.

Indeed, we can utilize the idea of arcs versus straight lines to define the contrast between our organic subject and any inorganic or mechanical props or objects: we can exaggerate these two ideas in different combinations to achieve different stylistic effects and thus affect the ultimate thesis statement or story we tell with a single drawing.

Costumes

When drawing a fully costumed figure, it helps to have a procedural mindset. Feeling out the best way to go about constructing each drawing, having a clear idea in mind with the intended story while still maintaining visual clarity (the function of the thesis statement): these are habits that help greatly when examining a costumed figure. Technically speaking, I usually make sure my class gets a solid round of warm-up drawings before the real work is done; depending on the complexity of the costume, I may assign a turn-around or set of drawings that serve as schematics to plan out the editing that the costume may need if our focus is predominantly short pose. If the reader is in a position to administer their own private life-drawing session, it helps to include warm-ups that are so short as to force one to edit information. The reader may also choose to give themselves the benefit of drawing a turn-around of the figure with the intent of understanding the different aspects of the costume or the fit and silhouette. They don't have to be very long drawings; simple, rough sketches are enough of an aid. From there, it is helpful to carefully observe the silhouette, the large shape ideas or language present, and the inherent gesture of each piece or portion of the costume.

Troubleshooting Exercises for Common Challenges During Costumed Life Drawing

Depending on the amount of costuming present, different challenges will arise. The most common issues we see in a costumed or clothed figure-drawing session are the following:

A. Lack of structure of the human body beneath the clothes
B. Lack of editing
C. Lack of comprehension of shape and form fundamentals

These issues ultimately lead to the disruption of visual clarity, which may in turn affect the artist's intended statement or story.

Let's tackle each of these issues one at a time:

Issues A and C: Lack of structure typically comes from a few different places. Oftentimes, it will happen if the student or artist is lacking in the drawing mileage necessary for solid drawing and either more life drawing is needed or more experience with essential ideas from Visual Communication is needed (such as primitive form drawing, perspective, etc.). The more nude life drawing done, the easier it is to understand how clothing or costuming would wrap, drape, and fit around a human figure. Sometimes lack of structure results from the lack of comprehension of basic shapes and forms and *understanding their presence in the construction* of a human or otherwise organic (such as an animal) figure. Here are a few tips to help with fitting clothing/costuming around the body so as to address underlying structure.

Tip 1: Identify the Shoulder Line and Hip Line

These are the most pronounced horizontal architectural ideas in the figure. We tend to drape our clothes off of these lines, so it makes sense to locate them and place them *before* drawing any portion of the garments. If necessary, one may also choose to observe and place the center-front line, that is, the front y-axis/vertical center line of the torso. Alternatively, if looking at a back pose, the center back may be laid in.

Tip 2: Using Tracing Paper to Practice Fit

If fitting clothing is still an issue, it may be necessary to do tissue paper studies, essentially paper dolls but with drawing (see Figure 8.12). This technique was taught to me by fashion illustrator and instructor Miguel Angel Reyes to utilize in our clothed figure-drawing classes for Otis Fashion, and it's a fun and efficient way to study fitting different garments on the figure. It can also be reinterpreted and manipulated so as to create different exercises. The basic technique is to draw a nude or bikini-clad figure on bright white drawing paper first, then have the same model put clothes on and repeat the same pose. The artist then overlays a sheet of tracing paper onto the initial drawing and draws the clothes on top. This will both train the eye to be aware of the body beneath the clothing or costuming and will provide further practice in

Figure 8.12

Tracing paper exercise; nude or bikini figure on white paper, garments on tracing paper on top.

the comprehension of silhouette, shape, fit, and scale. If this is not possible to do from life in the life-drawing sessions available to the reader, the next best thing would be to do the same exercise utilizing drawing reference from either books or the Internet. Again, start the initial nude or seminude drawing on white paper. You can then either invent the garments on tracing paper or utilize garments from magazines, shopping sites, etc., essentially figuring out the fit of the garment on the drawing, resulting in more of an exploratory-type creative exercise rather than an overtly academic one. This can also be done in the digital medium, using multiple layers. When doing this without the availability of a life model, the same basic technique becomes trickier; it is nevertheless encouraged to try it at least once. Alternatively, you may also go to a clothing shop or store, try on different garments yourself in the fitting room, and take notes or reference photos showing the type of garment, its intended use, the materials the garment has been made from, how the garment actually fits on your body, and the correlation between the fit and the space between the body and the garment. This is a simple errand/task that many of us do when we are interested in investing in or purchasing clothing and provides quite some insight into how clothes fit and move on a person. Be aware that this suggestion requires artists to be aware of their body type, measurements, and silhouette.

Tip 3: Practice fundamentals of Visual Communication, Such as Shape and Form

If lack of structure stems not from the comprehension of clothing on the figure but rather from lack of experience or mileage with perspective and geometric shapes and forms, then more practice is needed with those essentials. Furthermore, an analytical figure-drawing class or learning resource will also aid the artist in relating those geometric ideas to the human figure, which will in turn aid in providing the structure necessary for garments to be placed upon. This same comprehension of the geometric shape and form configurations of the human figure will further aid in the drawing of garments themselves, which are usually constructed with basic shapes. Clothing patterns can be typically characterized as simple, geometric shapes; it is not until they have been sewn together that they result in volumetric, three-dimensional forms, which still retain properties of form, such as when lit or when seen in space with perspective applied.

> *Issue B:* The most common issue I see with costumed quick-sketch style gesture drawings is the lack of editing. We have all heard our instructors tell us time and time again to edit, but sometimes we see a costume that is so arresting or visually stimulating that we are tempted to draw every detail or idea present. While it's always fun to get lost in a drawing, it's a good idea to practice the editing of information so as to avoid sacrificing the integrity of our visual clarity and thesis statement. This is why mileage is so critical: with mileage and experience comes the ability to edit out superfluous or otherwise unimportant information, allowing us to improve our choices and practice the simplification—and implication—of ideas.

When drawing costumed characters from life, we can change our priorities and choose to focus more on storytelling, narrative, and characterization rather than practicing fundamentals as we typically do with traditional academic figure drawing. We have the opportunity to practice conveying different personalities, attitudes, and character types; acting and facial/body expressions; tone and mood; and exaggeration and visual clarity. The primary drawing and visual communication objective when sketching costumed figures becomes one focused on feeling the body beneath the garments and showing that structure as much as possible. That is why most of the draping and fold samples shown previously are *gestural* in nature: we do not want to sacrifice the gestural integrity of the figure for the sake of drawing the clothing. We are using the clothing and costuming to elaborate on contextual narrative ideas, such as history, profession/occupation, age, period of time, technology, genre, etc. Let us look at a few ways we might explore these ideas through the use of costuming and clothing when approached during a quick-sketch gesture-drawing session, what kinds of drawing issues may arise, and how to deal with them. As is always recommended, costumed long-pose or painting sketches are always an excellent idea to balance out short-form life-drawing studies, as long-form studies will allow for more intense and intimate investigations into fabrics, materials, garment types, and garment history.

Infusing Gestural Qualities into the Implication of Folds and Other Draping/Garment Properties

These drawings of model Barry concern themselves with the implication of the following ideas: *fit*; *ease*; *silhouette* and *shape relationships*; *proportions*; *simplified but naturalistic anatomy*; and making sure the *lines of action* present within the figure are followed through the garments themselves (see Figures 8.13 and 8.14). Simply speaking, the garments should harmoniously echo all of the information we feel in the action of the figure. This is the basis for exaggeration later on. It is recommended to the drawing student to begin with costumed figure sketches with an academic approach and Tone before moving on to any kind of stylization, change in Tone, or change in approach. Solid drawing must be accomplished in academic costumed drawing before moving onto more creative or imaginative investigations. Both of these sketches of Barry have been completed by looking at the silhouette of the pose first, such as in the first image, which has been laid in with a graphic triangular shape before attacking the breakdown of positive and negative space. Take note of the prominent shoulder line and the angle present; in order to distribute the weight correctly in the upper torso, it was necessary to slightly exaggerate its subtle angle. This gave me the basis for the *pull* in the shirt. The ripples and folds present in the tank top have been both edited—any confusing or inconsistent ideas have been simply disregarded—and idealized in order to match the movement of the model. Because the *fit* of the shirt is not very tight, ripples have been indicated. The shorts were approached in much the same manner, though structurally speaking, it was necessary to use the box of the pelvic area to understand the perspective on the garment. From there, the garment is laid in a shape that is consistent with the figure's anatomy and lines of action of the legs. The folds present are a combination of spiral folds that wrap around the cylindrical volume of the leg and pulls from the tension line created by the pull in the other leg. These are activewear-style sweat pants that allow for range in mobility and are therefore stretchy in nature. As a result, they may be pulled beyond their original shape.

Figure 8.13

Quick sketch of a clothed figure.

Figure 8.14

Quick sketch of a clothed figure.

The second gesture drawing of Barry shows a standing figure, with a strong primary line of action and minor supporting lines of action in the limbs, as well as a combination of contrapposto and a lean in the upper torso. In a case such as this, a good solution would be to use the Breakdown as procedure so as to allow all of our gestural information to be mirrored within the garments. In addition to using this procedural analysis to work through the figure, the silhouette must be considered in order to establish the *fit* and *ease* of the clothing. When drawing using my autopilot mode—that is, naturally working my way through a drawing without being too concerned about procedure or even thinking too much for the sake of enjoying the act of drawing—I do not make fit or ease a literal concern of mine. Instead, I look to the silhouette and the shape relationships to understand what it is I am looking at. Because I have been trained to see the figure before the clothing, my natural tendency is to find my gestural information regarding the *action* and *acting* first, before laying in any garment ideas. Note the information that has been included, as it shows an example of what kinds of garment details one may include. Both drawings are concerned with the *shape* of the garment and stylistic ideas present, such as the type of garment; the style of the sleeves or arm holes; length of the garment; and waistbands (seen in the shorts and indicated quickly with textural strokes, while the gathers connecting the body of the shorts to the waistband have been implied with little zig-zaggy motions), hems, and edges. We will see other costumed figure drawings that include more detail in construction so that the reader has some idea of further important garment details that embellish a drawing and, if added to quick-sketch gesture drawing, help provide narrative context when dealing with storytelling, characterization, and acting.

Approaching Short-pose Gesture Drawing with
a Costumed Figure, 1 Minute and Below

This page of 1-minute sketches shows an example of the implication of costume during a session focused predominantly on 30-second and 1-minute poses (see Figure 8.15). It is recommended that the artist employ different strategies for different possible scenarios of sketching. Shown here is a possible solution for strategizing a fully costumed character while dealing with spontaneous gut reactions. One of the advantages to hiring one's own models—students, you may not have a chance yet, but for those artists who have the resources and space, this is a tip to think about—is that one may strategically request costumes or garment types that fulfill certain functions; in this case, I requested that Mather, the model, come in a costume that would enable the drawing group to clearly see the actions, contours, and silhouette of the body, without

Figure 8.15

One-minute costumed model sketches.

having to guess as to the structures beneath. The more minimal or form-fitting the costume or clothing, the easier it is to practice ultrashort poses. Note as well the strategy in changing scale of the figure across the page; while the scale of the figure has been altered to fit the negative spaces created in the picture plane, at no point has the consistency in proportions been broken or missed too egregiously. The proportions of both the figure and the shape relationships of the garments and accessories have been kept fairly consistent. In this case, for quick-sketch gestural investigations ranging from 30 seconds to a minute, the costuming is *secondary* to the integrity of the figure. At no point should the Action, *lines of action*, or *rhythms* of the figure be sacrificed for the sake of the costume.

Useful Ideas from Fashion Sketching

Because most of the techniques and ideas I employ while dealing with garments, clothing, and costumed figures come from having taught figure drawing for fashion applications, we will look at a drawing from Otis Fashion and see how gesture, solid drawing, Tone, and approach have been dealt with (see Figure 8.16). Fashion sketching has its own set of criteria and range of styles; this sketch is a very straightforward, classic fashion sketch. Many of the aforementioned exercise techniques and ideas concerning garment properties and

Figure 8.16

A fashion sketch.

8. Using Gesture in Clothing and Costume

concepts come from previous fashion students, from both working directly with them in class and solving problems relating to visual communication for their illustrations and garment design concepts. In short, our drawing problem-solving skills were used to solve visualization problems in the students' garment sketches that would ultimately be constructed into real-life, wearable, and functional garments. Different observation and drawing strategies were taught to me during a training period with my colleague Miguel Angel Reyes, and my resulting approach to a costumed figure is one that encompasses both previous drawing experience and such training. At no point should the artist feel that they are so good or adequate enough in their problem-solving skills as to no longer be open to instruction and wisdom, regardless of the source. Sometimes it comes from an older, wiser, and more experienced artist, and sometimes it comes from students or even younger, more fledgling artists. In short, there is always something more than can be learned, and part of being an artist is to foster one's own curiosity for investigation into the craft of drawing throughout one's lifetime. The following ideas have been used in the completion of this fashion sketch: a strong, clear *silhouette* that reflects both the action of the pose and a *primary + supporting lines of action*; clear indication of the expressions of the *head, hands, and feet*; a concern for *shape relationships* between the figure and the individual garments; *fit and ease*, so that the garments are depicted with some accuracy; *editing* of information and detail, in both the draping and folds of all garments, and judicious inclusion of garment details. All of these ideas are what I use to aid me in exaggerated, more stylistic gesture sketches based in developing narrative, story, and character. The attitude or Tone of a fashion drawing tends to deal more with effortless *cool, sexy,* or *confident* qualities, and the same attitude can often be seen in runway shows or fashion advertising. We are all familiar with the expressionless fashion model who seems to effortlessly exude cool and confidence while being nonchalant. In fashion sketching from life, we will often try to match the body language and expression of the model to the style or types of garments we are sketching, and either the model will use his or her abilities to convey that to us or we have to incorporate it ourselves (this is why modeling is a craft that requires development, and why our life-drawing models are so important and integral to the further study of drawing). This is an example of dealing with Tone for this type of drawing. Gesture is absolutely the first and foremost drawing principle considered, as it is what will allow us to convey the attitude of the model within the drawing, which allows us to capture Tone and Mood. Oftentimes, in a fashion sketch, we feel both elements. We can also begin to see how principles from animation may overlap into this type of sketch: This drawing of Daniella contains a large amount of Exaggeration and Appeal (in addition to Solid Drawing), in both the anatomy of the figure and stylistic idealization. Essentially, we are dealing with Idealized Realism or Naturalism when working with this type of sketch, and the appeal here is directly influenced by aesthetics from fashion.

Study Questions

Have you ever tried your hand at a fashion sketch? If so, how did it go? Can you think of ways to incorporate some drawing ideas from fashion into your everyday drawing of costumed figures or characters? Is fashion sketching something that you would like to experiment with?

Short-Pose Gesture Drawing with a Costumed Figure to Imply Narrative Context, Acting, and to Explore Character Archetype and Story Possibilities

Let us take a look now at how we may start combining different ideas from costumed gesture drawing with story-based ideas. The following set of sketches are short-pose to medium-pose length character investigations, with the objective of harmonizing stylistic choices based on Gesture + Action + Acting + Theme, which ultimately conveys Tone and, if extrapolated further, may form the basis of Mood (which may not be as evident or obvious within a line drawing but can be seen in the shape choices employed, as part of world building). If we can maintain consistent flavor throughout the design of a character and extend that flavor through to the costumes, props, or additional set pieces, we will have a *flavor base* (which we can think of as Theme + Tone + Mood) for which to envision/imagine the type of world the character inhabits. We can then use these investigations to aid us in our own personal, creative work. For those artists who are interested in illustration, visual development for different projects, and sequential storytelling such as comics, these types of explorations not only aid us in creating a visual library or reference encyclopedia but allow us to also take risks that we may not otherwise be able to take. Now we are using gesture drawing from life to practice ideation, brainstorming, consistency in visual language/communication, and different aspects of Visual Storytelling. For now, we will look at practicing these ideas in single character drawings, before looking at more thorough investigations, explorations, and applications of multimedia gesture work.

The first sketch we see is a quick sketch of model Gabby in a costume with a great deal of drapery (see Figure 8.17). This was one of those sessions in which the major challenge was to feel the gesture of the figure beneath a multilayered costume, which included a full skirt, cape with accordion pleats, dress, wrap/toga, and jewelry. As a result of so much costume, much of the information within the garments had to be edited. What we see here is a drawing concerned primarily with the action and attitude of the character, and the body has been stylized using shape and form that is generally regarded as appealing and feminine. The soft, delicate arcs of the arms are echoed throughout the drape lines of the shoulder wrap and skirt, and due to the large shape of the skirt, it has been allowed to run off the page (which is an idea borrowed from fashion sketching when dealing with long, flowing gowns). The gestural relationship of the hair and long lines of the skirt show the idea of *simple versus complex* and contrast in *rhythm*. The model's hair was full and voluminous, and the shapes used are meant to echo shapes in the face and muscular contours of the outstretched arm. The shapes employed are harmonized with intent, in both nature and lines of action present. The thesis statement or Big Idea that I was explicitly interested in pursuing and conveying is a culmination of *kind and sweet* and *soft and feminine*, and each major choice in the construction of the drawing has been made with that intent. This is ultimately a study in appealing feminine characterization, and whether I feel this approach to such an idea would be appropriate for different Story/Plot roles, such as a Protagonist, or Mentor. Thinking in terms of possible story/plot roles and character archetypes allows us to practice another tool of storytelling. In this case, our investigations are made with the goal of seeing how we might approach a character and design our way through it with not only a Theme in

Figure 8.17

A short-pose character sketch from life.

mind but now also a specific function that character can or may potentially fill if they were placed in a plot with emotional resonance. Costume helps provide the narrative basis for these explorations.

The following short-pose gesture drawing of Sebastian (see Figure 8.18) shows a character who would not feel out of place in the Wasteland that is the central environment of the *Mad Max* cinematic universe.

For this class session focused on capturing Acting, Expression, and having freedom in stylistic design choices, our model came dressed in full costume, complete with an abundance of textures and props. The entirety of the session was based in exploring this character as fully as possible, and we included slight costume changes as well to slightly alter the flavor of the character. My objective for this set of character explorations was to capture Sebastian's furious, exaggerated intensity for each action and push that energy through each aspect of the construction of the drawing. It is most notably felt in the exaggeration of the *lines of action*, in both the *primary line of action* running through the length of the body and the *supporting lines of action* running through each limb. To make the drawing humorous and feel slightly ridiculous/goofy, the shapes have been developed with varying exaggeration in scale, and details such as the teeth, tongue, and water spilling from the canteen have each been designed with intent, with rounded shapes. Nearly every component of this drawing has been built from arcs of varying degrees. The reason for including the idea of the tongue hanging out of the mouth and the bushy foxtail hanging from the belt (it is obscured,

Figure 8.18

A short-pose character sketch from life.

behind the figure's right leg) stems from imagining what this character might potentially look like in motion, and, if animated, those parts of the character would be an opportunity to play with the ideas of follow-through and overlapping action. It is typical during this type of character drawing for me to imagine what the character would look like in sequence for each pose, much as we saw in earlier chapters dealing with exploratory sketches. Thinking in this manner allows me to feel the character more intimately and further challenges me to consider the imagined character's emotional impetus for each action. This in turn aids me in discovering possible mind-sets for different types of characters and where in a plot or storyline that mind-set would be most appropriate, especially for developing the type of character who can propel a story or plot forward. While we all have different approaches to story, storytelling, and plot structure, we all appreciate strongly developed characters who feel real and emotionally relatable. My personal preference for storytelling involves plot to be driven by the characters rather than just spontaneously happening, and when I develop a story I tend to begin with the following: Theme (or sometimes Genre) as an emotional idea; Tone, which is necessary for me to understand *my* attitude as creator toward the Theme and will provide logic and continuity to my design choices; and the intended overall Mood (atmosphere) of the story (if it's a short story, I will have limited changes in Mood depending on the plot structure developed), or the intended Mood for different scenes, which will give the audience emotional context with which to feel the story and characters. These concepts allow for me to

8. Using Gesture in Clothing and Costume

feel my way through character possibilities and roles. This is why my studies are character/figure heavy and why my body of work may look different than a colleague's or a friend's: we all have different tastes, approaches, and objectives in regard to developing story and visual storytelling skills.

Study Questions

How do you approach story development? What kinds of stories do you gravitate toward? Are there any Themes in particular you find compelling? Have you ever completed your own story, whether it be a collection of Visual Development work for a particular story, Concept Art for building a world with believability and consistency/harmony, a set of story boards for either a scene or sequence, etc.? Do you ever write short stories? Is writing used as a tool in any part of your creative process? How might dealing with plot and story structure aid you in your drawings?

The following sketch (see Figure 8.19) is from a *medium*-length pose (ranging from 5 to 25 minutes each) from a themed costumed drawing session featuring multiple models. The theme of the night was "Pirates."

This drawing of Jonnathen as a pirate reflects the Tone with which I regarded him: because of his age in comparison to the younger models present and his style of acting during the session, his character felt more appropriate as a mentor-type character, rather than a villain. That attitude is reflected in the stylistic choices regarding the *lines of action* and *shape* design. While this drawing does

Figure 8.19

A "medium"-length character study.

not contain a great deal of exaggeration in the *lines of action* present, the shapes throughout the figure—including the costuming, accessories, and props—have all been exaggerated and harmonized; that is, my objective is to design with a consistent flow of energy throughout each piece of the character and costume. Although the *lines of action* are not overtly exaggerated, there is still a great deal of *rhythm* present throughout: there are S curves and C curves everywhere. This type of slower, more methodical character drawing helps us with maintaining consistency of ideas and energy flow throughout a figure. It also allows for us to develop the head, hands, and feet with a greater degree of information. Much as Long Pose is recommended for the academic comprehension and observation of gesture in a realistic figure, so too are Medium and Long Pose recommended for stylized character drawings. The last sketch (see Figure 8.20) for this section deals with greater degrees of cartoon in relation to costumed/clothed character drawing and exploration.

This sketch shows the difference between approaching a character sketch with semicartoon inclinations versus a fully cartooned character. Though similar in construction—they both contain a similar use of arcs and *rhythm*—both characters belong to entirely different worlds, regardless of having been drawn consecutively from the same model. They were used in class to show possibilities regarding change in attitude toward the subject and completed as demos for a fashion-drawing class. When compared to the previously shown fashion sketches, the difference in attitude toward the subject becomes apparent and strikingly different.

Figure 8.20

Contrasts in style during the same session.

8. Using Gesture in Clothing and Costume

Costume as Secondary to Action and Acting

The following two pages of sketches are included as an example of how the costume should be treated as secondary to the Main Action + Supporting Actions and the Acting of the model (see Figures 8.21 and 8.22). To develop a character, we do not necessarily need to see the costume in order to feel our way through their personality or why they choose to move the way they do. We can accomplish the same emotional investigations with a nude model. The costume allows for us to kick-start character and story possibilities a bit quicker, as we have immediate contextual information at our disposal.

Both pages of short-pose gesture drawings have each been completed with the explicit intention of developing the action, acting, and personality of the character and leaving the costume implied, exaggerated, and edited. They further serve the function of showing how I might use key ideas from fashion sketching in conjunction with traditional gesture drawing. Not only is the figure exaggerated but the costume as well to maintain visual clarity. For example, the dress on Rachel as Alice in Wonderland has been simplified and developed as a shape, keeping in mind where the bottom edge of the skirt is in relation to Rachel's knee. This type of analysis is quick and allows me to maintain consistency in costume, which allows for practice in the concept of staying on model. The second page shows how I may exaggerate the fit or ease of garments so as to make the nature of the costume obvious and quick reading. For this session

Figure 8.21

Actions, acting, and costume.

Figure 8.22

Actions, acting, and costume.

based on Bollywood expressions, dancer and model Sara wore tight-fitting garments to allow for range of mobility. As a result, the garments were drawn as closely to Sara's silhouette as possible so as to read as skintight. In both pages, effort was conscientiously placed in developing the individual expressions of every head/face, hand, and foot.

Exercises for Dealing with Clothed or Costumed Models

Warm-Ups

- 1–2 minute gesture drawings of a fully clothed figure
- 2–4 minute contour line drawings of a fully clothed figure

Exercises for Practicing Garment/Figure Relationships: Paper Dolls

The following exercise is meant as a fun way to understand the relationship between shape, garment, fit, ease, and the silhouette of the figure (see Figure 8.23). It was first introduced to me by Miguel while teaching fashion figure drawing at Otis. Not only did the students have fun, it caused them to slow down their observations into shape relationships greatly. It is presented here in the event the readers do not slow down their observations enough, or in case the readers would like to practice this particular exercise as a way to create pictures. The readers are invited to play with this exercise in whatever way they desire.

8. Using Gesture in Clothing and Costume

Figure 8.23

Paper doll exercise.

To complete this exercise from life, you will need the following: a live model, whether professional or not is up to you; a set of garments; construction paper; scissors or a blade such as an X-ACTO knife; glue; drawing paper.

1. Dress your model in a set of garments, complete with shoes.
2. Looking at the silhouette, Positive/Negative Space present, and the Shapes of the garments, cut the whole shape made by the garments, or, if necessary, each individual garment, out of construction paper, freehand if possible. If freehand presents too much difficulty, because of motor functions or cutting tool issues, you may sketch the garment before cutting.
3. Glue the construction paper garment to your drawing paper. My sample includes tiny tick marks that tick off the proportions of a fashion figure, rather than the exact proportions of the model. You may choose to utilize whatever method of gauging and recording proportions you may like. If this ruler is not necessary, skip it.
4. After the garments have been glued to the drawing paper, draw out the rest of the silhouette of the figure, including the shoes.

The last two sketches incorporate many previously mentioned ideas in their execution and focus primarily as stylized character studies (see Figures 8.24 and 8.25).

Figure 8.24

A costumed character sketch.

Figure 8.25

Two different styles of the same character.

9

Explorations within Gesture Drawing

Collaborative Character
Explorations in Mixed Media
to Develop Tone and Mood
during Life Drawing

Gesture Drawings and Quick
Sketches Exploring Acting
and Staging from Life
Using Our Gesture Drawings
to Develop and Practice
Our Craft

Let's look at different ways to use and apply skills developed from gesture drawing to explore characterizations, staging, and storytelling from life, via drawing from costumed character models. This is a common practice in and around Los Angeles, and we as artists are lucky to have such talent in the model pool. Most if not all of the models in Los Angeles are some kind of practicing artists as well; many are skilled in acting, visual arts, performing arts, dance, etc., and are all able to provide great insight into many facets of the humanities that make drawing them so enriching. Working with such professionals allows us to develop the distinct crafts of drawing and visual storytelling. The remainder of this study guide concerns itself with different ways to approach and use gesture drawing to create and develop ideas from life, as well as ideas for using one's own gesture studies to carry out further investigations into illustration, world building, and story development.

The first section deals with approaching character studies via *mixed media* to reflect Tone and Mood within a theme and creating harmony between that theme and the creator's attitude. The atmosphere created by the artist for the audience may in part be influenced by choices in approach and media; that is, when drawing, the artist should be concerned with not only the theoretical approaches to any drawing or investigation but also the physical, mechanical means of showing that idea on a picture plane. An appropriate tool must be chosen for each idea expressed in order to maximize the intended emotional impact or resonance of a drawing. When drawing for sheer mileage and experience—as one does when developing solid drawing or when learning new ideas—the medium chosen should lend itself to the ease of drawing lines from the shoulder and making broad, sweeping strokes that glide on the page. Usually students and artists will opt for a traditional drawing medium such as charcoal or Conté on newsprint paper for mileage studies, as those materials are usually the simplest to learn and become accustomed to, as well as being erasable. Once enough mileage is attained to be able to incorporate character and story-based investigations into their normal drawing regimens, it is advisable to explore different media as well.

We shall be looking at sets of drawings from the same group of models, so that the reader may see the range of collaborative investigations possible when working with character and story models.

Collaborative Character Explorations in Mixed Media to Develop Tone and Mood during Life Drawing

Our first character sketch is a 3-minute gesture drawing of model Mather as La Catrina, executed in pastel on newsprint (see Figure 9.1). This initial investigation was completed during the warm-up set of a drawing workshop I held one

Figure 9.1

Study of La Catrina.

9. Explorations within Gesture Drawing

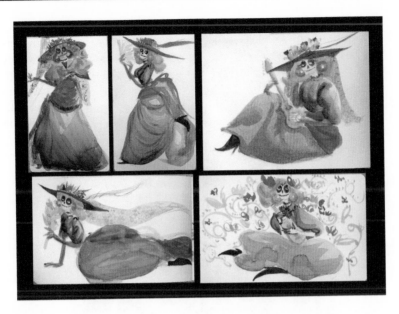

Figure 9.2
Study of La Catrina.

Figure 9.3
Character studies; finding the character's attitude, as well as my own toward the subject.

Figure 9.4

A study in mood to fit the theme of the subject.

autumn. The Theme was La Catrina, and our model came in full makeup and costume. Because Mather's costumes and characters are usually multilayered and very detailed, I utilized the warm-up set to edit details and ideas present in the drapery and costume to make the rest of the session more approachable. I had decided beforehand to use watercolor to sketch Mather, but instead of doing small watercolor studies during the warm-up, I opted for pastel, as it is a more direct media and a more suitable choice for quick sketch, without having to sacrifice color; using these initial notes I utilized watercolor for the remainder of the session (see Figure 9.2). A full color sketch such as this tends to be executed with minimal blending and instead is made up of strokes layered on strokes. Pastel lends itself to edge-finishing techniques and, if blending or smudging is needed, presents ease of usage. *Mixed media* warm-up sketches such as these allow me to investigate my attitude toward the character or theme; in this case, the Tone I developed for the evening was a festive, sweet, and sensitive one, since the subject matter does have a sense of gravitas to it. It is literally a physical representation of death, albeit a satirical and clever one. Instead of developing a dark and brooding set of drawings, I opted for an air of homage, sensitivity, and respect toward the tradition of La Catrina.

9. Explorations within Gesture Drawing

Study Question: How Do You Utilize Your Warm-up Sets
Before Drawing a Costumed Figure or Character?
What Are Your Major Objectives (if any)?

The next two studies of Mather contrast in both Tone and Mood (see Figures 9.3 and 9.4):

The first image is a set of quick sketches of Mather as a saloon girl, and the character has been developed as a capricious lady. Though Mather herself was not portraying this character with that particular quality, this particular set of studies went down that path based on some of the poses/actions chosen. Furthermore, the style has been exaggerated to read as cartooned, which means that in terms of technique, I was focused on harmonizing exaggerated rhythms present throughout the character's body with stylized shape and form information present in the costuming and anatomy. The resulting stylistic choices are all made with the intention of communicating a humorous and slightly juvenile Tone.

The following image marks a high contrast in Mood and approach between it and the previous studies of Mather. This particular sketch was developed with a "sepulchral"—as a friend put it—mood in mind. The paper was first covered in India ink with a paper towel before the figure was quickly and loosely laid in using soft black charcoal and positive/negative space + gesture to complete. Much of the drawing was not in fact laid in to the extent that a painting or other finished work would be; because this was still executed during a predominantly quick-sketch format gesture-drawing class, I did not have the time or luxury to plan extensively, and as a result, most of the drawing was laid in quickly focusing mostly on the Action of the model and the *gestural* information of the robe. There is very little actual figure present in the drawing, but the body is felt beneath the clothing, thus implying volume and visual weight. This type of brooding Mood is one I stylistically gravitate toward, but it is far from the only mood that may be developed during life drawing. Keep in mind mood is harder to accomplish during short pose, but it can be approached and the beginnings brainstormed for possible applications or development in the future.

The next image shows how one may utilize mixed media to embellish movement and character moments (see Figure 9.5).

Figure 9.5

Mixed media character studies.

Figure 9.6

Daniella as a punk rocker.

This double-page spread in a toned paper notebook was developed during a drawing session with multiple costumed models with props. Because most of the poses were 25 minutes in length for the entirety of the session, I opted to draw each character multiple times, collaging their actions across both pages, using the Actions provided by the models and embellishing or adjusting them for the action–comedy type Tone I had in mind. The expressions have either been drawn as given by the models or embellished by myself to explore the individual characters. For example, our lady soldier is a tough gal, while our sharpshooter is a stoic warrior. It is not necessary to draw exactly what one sees or even finish a single figure on page while exploring stylistic possibilities and characterizations/personalities. Furthermore, if the reader finds themselves in a situation where the poses provided are much longer than they would like, there is absolutely nothing wrong with changing one's typical approach to life drawing, and it is a good idea to embellish or experiment to get the most out of such a situation.

The next set of gesture-drawing/character studies are of model Daniella, and once again the Tone of each study is a result of Theme + (Approach and Style), and the drawing concerns present are Lines of Action + Shape Stylization. Each drawing concerns itself first with showing *what* the action is and *how* it is presented to the viewer. Note that these do not necessarily indicate staging choices or narrative context (see Figures 9.6 through 9.9).

Figure 9.7

Daniella as a punk rocker.

Figure 9.8

Daniella as a saloon girl.

Figure 9.9

Daniella in a fashion-inspired sketch.

Gesture Drawings and Quick Sketches Exploring Acting and Staging from Life

The following sets of sketches concern themselves with embellishing and exaggerating Gestures (including all *lines of action* and Rhythmic ideas), Acting, and Staging, in addition to stylistic experimentation (see Figures 9.10 and 9.11).

These two acting studies of Jonnathen concern themselves with a clear silhouette and exaggeration in all ideas present, from the lines of action that make up the gestures of both the whole body and its pieces through to the concept (the action of the pose) and acting. Jonnathen has a very explosive modeling and acting style, and these studies are an attempt to capture that dynamic energy. Note as well the detail present in the development of the face, hands, and feet: not only are they designed with intent, but they have been drawn to capture either the acting expression present within them or some character element, such as the type of shoes our madman is wearing. Once more we see Jonnathen's rodent friends make an appearance. Though it may be but one small prop, it may be embellished to the point of creating secondary characters who amplify the scenario with their presence. Jonnathen is an excellent actor and model, and he may sometimes be seen in action with model Toni, who foils and complements his style with her own sensitivity and approach to portraying a character and visual storytelling. Often the figure models themselves think of little narratives or ideas as context, and we as artists seek to push those ideas just a bit further and further. This approach to drawing and capturing narrative moments in time can be seen in the following studies of Jonnathen and Toni (see Figures 9.12 and 9.13).

Figure 9.10
Study of Jonnathen in a "Sweeney Todd" themed costume/character.

Figure 9.11
Study of Jonnathen.

Figure 9.12

Jonnathen and Toni as Mad Scientists.

Figure 9.13

Jonnathen and Toni.

9. Explorations within Gesture Drawing

These two moments in time portray two wacky scientists out of their league; stylistically, I altered my approach to feel their erratic behavior a bit more: I completed nearly all drawing from that particular set with my nondominant hand, resulting in a nervous looking scribble, which I hoped would reflect the concept of "mad scientists." In addition to such studies, I took advantage of the models' superb acting and storytelling skills to develop small sequences of ideas, thinking of the principles of anticipation, staging, and, as always, exaggeration. In the following set of quick sketches, Jonnathen provides a beautiful sequence of actions that imply narrative (see Figures 9.14 through 9.17).

The first sketch was a pose from earlier in the session, in which one of our scientists decides to test his sample on himself, in lieu of his lab rat. The larger sketch is the action Jonnathen undertook, while the smaller inset panel is how I might explore an anticipatory moment to pursue or establish some small narrative context. I will often do something like this during life drawing as it allows me to annotate the drawings as I go, much how one annotates a book while reading. The next three sketches are the whole sequence as completed in a later set from the session, where our model once more explored the initial concept of the reckless mad scientist and completed the narrative. Sound effects and onomatopoeia are great ways to further enliven a gesture drawing, and sometimes I will include both sound effects and imaginary dialog as a means of engaging the viewer just a bit more.

When it comes to practicing and studying staging and choices related to it and composition, it is often easiest to work with longer poses, ideally with lighting,

Figure 9.14

Narrative sequence of Jonnathen as a mad scientist.

Figure 9.15

Second pose of a narrative sequence of Jonnathen.

Figure 9.16

Third pose of a narrative sequence of Jonnathen.

9. Explorations within Gesture Drawing

Figure 9.17

Fourth pose of a narrative sequence of Jonnathen.

costuming, and stage sets/pieces. Unfortunately, we do not always have access to such facilities, or we may find ourselves in a particular situation where we have a stripped-down set, simple costuming, and basic lighting (or sometimes inadequate light or ambient daylight). We must always be prepared to work within the time frame given and strategize accordingly. This brings us to the next set of sketches focused entirely on composing and staging a scene, given the staging limitations of the models on the model stand and time limits (see Figures 9.18 through 9.20).

They were all drawn within 15–20 minutes (which I consider the long side of gesture drawing, and instead categorize it as a medium-length pose), so size and medium informed my approach and decision to investigate Narrative, Character, Personality, and Acting, rather than a simple character sketch. My concerns were as follows: staging the action within a story-driven scenario while retaining strong and descriptive *lines of action* in all characters + Solid Drawing to imply space and volumes. The compositional concept of Foreground, Middle Ground, and Background was utilized to make each picture, and each picture features development of at least two of those three grounds. Each picture utilized the whole of an 18" × 24" sheet of newsprint, completed with brush marker to keep myself from second-guessing any decision. Indeed, permanent medium is a great way to practice and achieve discipline in decision-making and confidence.

In each I took into consideration the relationships between the characters and added any kind of environmental context to each scenario, as well as minor secondary characters to populate the same world as our principal duo. This is an example of staging around a fixed point of observation of our subjects: during drawing, I could not change viewing angles, so instead I dealt with the angle

Figure 9.18

Daniella and John as a Cowboy and Saloon Girl.

Figure 9.19

Utilizing Acting and Staging to improvise a narrative.

given during each pose, placed the principle figures and scenario first, and then built some kind of environment around them to place the action of the scene. The level of exaggeration present has been more or less harmonized within each item drawn within frame. That is, nothing sticks out too greatly or breaks continuity within the scene.

Figure 9.20

Staging + Acting.

In addition to developing characters, personalities, narratives, and acting from life, we can also use our sketches to practice different kinds of assignments at home. I find using my sketches developed from life as a great way to practice creating and exploring different kinds of characters, character archetypes, worlds, and stories, and it is useful to keep gesture drawings that are rife with narrative and acting as reference for future possible use. The following section concerns itself with such a practice.

Using Our Gesture Drawings to Develop and Practice Our Craft

The following set of studies demonstrates how I might utilize gestural studies from a life-drawing session to begin the development of a character (see Figures 9.21 through 9.24). This set concerns itself with visual investigations into a sci-fi–action genre character, inspired by classics such as *Aliens*; exploring genres one enjoys is an entertaining way to complete self-assignments. This is the type of homework one may give oneself after any particularly enjoyable drawing session, or if one finds oneself feeling burnt out—which does happen from time to time and affects all artists of different disciplines. This is one type of solution offered for such an occurrence.

The first image shows a collection of quick sketches drawn from model Catherine, who excels in character acting and infusing narrative within her poses, including sequence and reactions, so as to aid the artist in sequential visualization. The following study continues with the study of the same character; this time the objective of the short-pose session was to develop a different story scenario for each 5 minute pose. While drawing, the narrative premise of a network sitcom-style relationship between our Space Soldier and Xenomorph

Figure 9.21

Space soldier sketches from life.

Figure 9.22

Narrative space soldier scenarios.

(inspired directly—though drawn from memory—from the *Alien* franchise, a staple of the sci-fi–action genre) suddenly appeared. This relationship seemed to offer many humorous story moments between the two characters, so I pursued it for the remainder of the session. This humorous tone led me to develop a study of a hyperstylized character, one who might serve as some particular character archetype in a story, seen here executed in the digital medium. It is followed by a small sampling of expressions. Further development of the concept could include the following: environment studies and layouts, other characters, story and plot design, prop and vehicle design, mood boards (developed with staging, lighting composition, and color), etc. When self-assigning homework and studies to oneself, there is no limit to the type of work or quantity to be completed. This is the artist and creator's opportunity to use their gestural studies to develop worlds, ideas, and characters who have a basis in emotional reality, as the groundwork

Figure 9.23

Character developed from life studies.

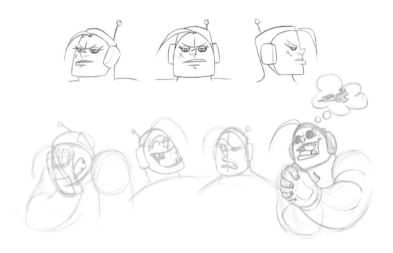

Figure 9.24

Expressions of our space soldier.

has been laid down via direct human observation. There is no substitute for the emotional impact one can capture during a life-drawing session. Instead of merely letting one's life drawings sit around collecting dust, why not begin using life studies twofold: firstly as a means of attaining mileage and understanding of visual communication, and secondly as a means of understanding the human condition and how best to portray such an infinitely complex and varied range of emotional possibilities?

This type of imaginative investigations into visual storytelling can be developed further with the continued use and development of Tone and Mood. The next step in the development of those concepts would be to move in an illustrative direction, completing images with Staging, Lighting Composition, and Color. The readers are strongly encouraged to study illustration, picture making, and painting as part of their continued training.

This concludes the final chapter of this study guide. The readers are encouraged to continue pursuing and developing their life drawing and observation studies as often as possible, by whatever means necessary. Quick sketch, short pose, long pose, whatever the time constraints present, remember that it is the artists' prerogative to *see* and *pull as much gesture as is necessary and possible at all times*, regardless of the subject. This gesture will become the emotional driving force that will influence all of one's narrative choices, and the lines and marks put down on paper are the result of this emotional and narrative context. There's no such thing as too much life drawing.

Remember to take your time when observing and thinking, and always draw with intent and purpose. Your choices always matter: whether big or small, simple or complex, your choices made during observing and interpreting your subject will always unfold some narrative truth to your audience, so be mindful and use that opportunity to *say something*.

Afterword

I sincerely wish the best of luck to the readers in their drawing and storytelling studies. As previously stated, there is no such thing as too much life drawing, and it should be practiced on a regular basis. It doesn't matter if they are informal studies, or drawings created in class under the tutelage of an instructor. Gesture drawing is a study that allows one to draw from a variety of sources, and a traveling sketchbook is highly recommended to the reader. Keep a small sketchbook with you constantly: there's no telling what you might encounter or observe that will inspire you to capture that moment in time. Draw with friends, take turns modeling, or go out for a drink or snack and keep sketchbooks in tow. There are quite a few ways to go about getting more drawing in. If the means and facilities are available, think about hiring your own models and putting together your own sessions, complete with drawing objectives so that you may practice mileage and solid drawing. These are but a few suggestions to inspire the reader to get as much scribbling, sketching, doodling, and mark-making as possible.

I would like to thank the wonderful model Ashli Gonzales-Griffin, an intelligent and inspiring woman, for providing her likeness for study. This study guide would not have been possible without her.

The following people are artists whom I always find to be in my corner and who continue to generously offer and provide feedback, insight, and inspiration to myself and other artists: Peter Kim, who taught me invaluable knowledge concerning *perspective, visual communication*, and *visual and sequential storytelling*; Miguel Angel Reyes, who sharpened my drawing skills and mentored me in Fashion Sketching; Daniella Traub, who provides exciting and challenging collaborations in story and character; Bob Kato, who knows a thing or two about the crafts of Teaching, Illustration, and Picture Making and has been a source of advice and insight to me for years; Amy Yung and Charles Hu at 3Kicks Studio, for the years of friendship and putting up with my strange humor; and Andrea Adams at Gnomon School of Visual Effects, who continuously allows me to develop drawing exercises and pedagogy freely and supports my sometimes unorthodox approach to problem-solving.

A huge thank you and round of applause to all of my drawing students, who provided valuable feedback and encouragement during development.

Thank you to James Morioka for providing equipment.

And, lastly, to my mother Rocio, who has always been a fan of my silly doodles.

Recommended Reading

The following resources and books are recommended to the reader:

- Thomas, F. and Johnston, O. 1984. *Disney Animation: The Illusion of Life*. New York: Abbeville Press.
- Huston, S. 2016. *Figure Drawing for Artists: Making Every Mark Count*. Beverly, MA: Rockport Publishers.
- Kato, B. 2014. *The Drawing Club: Master the Art of Drawing Characters from Life*. Beverly, MA: Quarry Books.
- Williams, R. 2001. *The Animator's Survival Kit*. New York: Faber and Faber Limited.
- Mateu-Mestre, M. 2010. *Framed Ink: Drawing and Composition for Visual Storytellers*. Culver City, CA: Design Studio Press.
- Mateu-Mestre, M. 2016. *Framed Perspective*, Volumes 1 and 2. Culver City, CA: Design Studio Press.
- Silver, S. 2009. *Passion for Life*. Simi Valley, CA: Silvertoons Inc.

For those readers and artists interested in uninstructed life and character drawing in the LA area:

- While there are a great many classes, workshops, and spaces/sessions to choose from, I highly recommend the reader to consider the Drawing Club drawing workshop, hosted and run by Art Center instructor and artist Bob Kato, who is generous with his time and instruction. As of this writing, it is located within the Gallery and Bookstore Nucleus, in Alhambra, CA, and runs Thursday nights.

The following books are recommended for further studies:

- Mattesi, M.D. 2006–2011. *The Force Drawing Series*. Boca Raton, FL: CRC Press.
- Husband, R. 2013. *Quick Sketching with Ron Husband*. Burlington, MA: Focal Press.
- Pastrana, R. 2014. *Simplifying Perspective: A Step-by-Step Guide for Visual Artists*. Burlington, MA: Focal Press.
- Bancroft, T. 2012. *Character Mentor*. Waltham, MA: Focal Press.

Glossary

action and acting: *action* refers to the deed or pose performed by the subject. *Acting* refers to the emotional, character, or narrative context/subtext of any action, sequence, or scene performed by the subject.

breakdown: the building blocks of drawing presented in an organized manner to the reader.

center front and center back: ideas borrowed from fashion. The Center Front Line is the imaginary vertical centerline running down the torso of a human subject. The Center Back is the back view equivalent.

exaggeration: presenting any idea in a more spectacular or dynamic way. Nearly every aspect of a drawing may be exaggerated to any level chosen by the artist.

flow: how we feel the movement of energy or life force within an organic subject. It is a concept directly associated with the movements present in water.

geography: the spatial distances and relationships between structures (such as features, details, or anatomical landmarks) and their relative placement or location.

lay-in or block-in: largely interchangeable, though *lay-in* usually refers to the initial marks put down on paper from which a drawing will be built. Block-In usually refers to a similar idea but typically refers to block of value/color or large visual ideas.

line of action: directional force line; refers to the directional energy or life force of any particular action.

microgestures: small Rhythmic ideas that embellish or heighten the overall Rhythm and musicality of a drawing. They are small flourishes that add another layer of depth and individuality to a gesture study.

mood (as we use it within this study guide, and as defined by the editors of LiteraryDevices.net): the emotional atmosphere felt within a work by the audience. The Literary usage of Mood is very much similar to its Visual counterpart, and the visual equivalent can be explored further by choices in composition, mark making, lighting, staging, and color design.

rhythm and harmony: rhythm is often used in visual works to imply tempo, movement, or flow of ideas or energy. *Harmony* refers to the unity created when rhythms are varied but complementary.

S curves (and B curves), C curves, and straights: rhythmic ideas that help create the visual flow present in organic anatomical organization. They help create and establish Rhythm and are simple to harmonize with each other. The B Curve is extrapolated from the S Curve and is typically seen in a standing straight, front-view leg.

shoulder line/hip line: the imaginary lines created by the upper torso/arm structures and the imaginary line across the iliac crests, respectively.

silhouette: the Positive space created by the subject.

tone (as we use it within this study guide, and as defined by the editors of LiteraryDevices.net): the creator's attitude towards a subject or audience.

Index

Printed and bound by CPI Group (UK) Ltd, Croydon, CR0 4YY

18/10/2024

01776218-0001